The
EVERYTHING®
Grilling Cookbook

Dear Reader,

For years my wife, Eve, has lovingly referred to me as "The Grillmaster," probably as a result of my indefatigable devotion to the art, be it in the luxurious heat of summer or the icy chill of winter. Somehow this name caught on and as a result we have hosted more than our share of neighborhood cookouts. One of our greatest moments was watching the delighted faces of a visiting French family as they experienced their first barbecued chicken dinner.

This little hobby got a big boost when a high-powered friend decided our burgers were something special. He brought a television camera crew to the house and made us look good on TV.

No doubt about it, most of our meals are homespun and simple. There are bigger and fancier outdoor cooking layouts out there, and you'll read about some of them in this book. Grill cooking is for everyone—not just the master chef, but the beginner, too. Even the "kitchen impaired" can make a dinner that will rock the house.

Rick Marx

The EVERYTHING® Series

Editorial

Publishing Director	Gary M. Krebs
Managing Editor	Kate McBride
Copy Chief	Laura MacLaughlin
Acquisitions Editor	Kate Burgo
Development Editor	Karen Johnson Jacot
Production Editors	Jamie Wielgus
	Bridget Brace

Production

Production Director	Susan Beale
Production Manager	Michelle Roy Kelly
Series Designers	Daria Perreault
	Colleen Cunningham
Cover Design	Paul Beatrice
	Matt LeBlanc
Layout and Graphics	Colleen Cunningham
	Rachael Eiben
	Michelle Roy Kelly
	John Paulhus
	Daria Perreault
	Erin Ring
Series Cover Artist	Barry Littmann

Visit the entire Everything® Series at www.everything.com

THE
EVERYTHING®
GRILLING COOKBOOK

From Vegetable Skewers to Tuna Burgers—
300 healthy recipes for any grill

Rick Marx

Adams Media
Avon, Massachusetts

*To my wife, Eve, who invented "The Grillmaster." You're the
best in the kitchen—thanks for leaving the outdoors to me!*

An Everything® Series Book.
Everything® and everything.com® are registered trademarks of F+W Publications, Inc.

Published by Adams Media, an F+W Publications Company
57 Littlefield Street, Avon, MA 02322 U.S.A.
www.adamsmedia.com

ISBN: 1-59337-149-7
Printed in the United States of America.

J I H G F E D C B A

Library of Congress Cataloging-in-Publication Data
Marx, Rick.
The everything grilling cookbook / Rick Marx.
        p.   cm.
ISBN 1-59337-149-7
1. Barbecue cookery. I. Title. II. Series: Everything series.

TX840.B3M385 2005
641.5'784–dc22

2004009924

This publication is designed to provide accurate and authoritative information with regard to
the subject matter covered. It is sold with the understanding that the publisher is not engaged
in rendering legal, accounting, or other professional advice. If legal advice or other expert
assistance is required, the services of a competent professional person should be sought.
—From a *Declaration of Principles* jointly adopted by a Committee of the
American Bar Association and a Committee of Publishers and Associations

Many of the designations used by manufacturers and sellers to distinguish their products are
claimed as trademarks. Where those designations appear in this book and Adams Media was
aware of a trademark claim, the designations have been printed with initial capital letters.

*This book is available at quantity discounts for bulk purchases.
For information, call 1-800-872-5627.*

Contents

Acknowledgments

I would like to thank my assistant and recipe tester Nancy T. Maar for her invaluable help in compiling this book. She brought originality, inventiveness, an attention to detail, and a long cooking background to help make this book a reality.

My wife, Eve, dubbed me "The Grillmaster" in her weekly column, "The View From the Porch." I'm not sure how much that had to do with me getting this book deal, but it is true that we cook outside year-round, in every kind of weather. Thank you for the title and for sharing the table. My son, Sam, deserves special credit for his humor, appetite, and remembering to close the valve on the propane tank.

Thanks to Tom Dawson of NBC-TV for featuring me in a grilling segment on national TV. That segment sparked superagent June Clark of the Peter Rubie Agency to toss my "chef's hat" in the ring to Bethany Brown at Adams, who was seeking the right author to do *The Everything® Grilling Book*, and who guided the manuscript through its early stages. Editor Kate Burgo was an enthusiastic supporter and a pleasure to work with as we brought the final book to fruition.

To my mother and father, Joe Franklin, and those who generously helped with recipes, cooking tips, expertise, and moral support: Caroline C. Sherwin; Jay and Debbie Chumsky; Josh Katz; Gregg Glaser; Linda Kavanagh and Heather Saunders of Maximum Exposure; Jeff Cleveland of Broilmaster; John Ducate Jr. of Ducane; Randy Bigelow of Tiernan Outdoor Products, who introduced me to intravection; Dave and Jim at Charles Department Store for their expertise on everything grill-related over the years. Fabienne Bizet, of Paris, France, provided an invaluable international perspective on America's homegrown cooking form.

Introduction

▶ GRILLING IS A NOSTALGIC COOKING STYLE. For me, the scents and aromas take me way back to the days when I was a hungry suburban kid living outside of Chicago. When we weren't eating succulent, sauce-dripping barbecued ribs from the take-out place nearby, or grilled hot dogs from the best Chicago dog joint I ever ate at, Stash's, at home, Dad would reach for the briquettes and rattle them from the bag into the shallow no-name grill. The shiny black coals glistened with promise, especially when spattered with lighter fluid, which came squirting ominously out of the metal can in a steady stream. As soon as the first match hit the briquettes, there was the intoxicating whoosh of flame—blue, black, orange, and white, seemingly all at once—sparkling in front of my eyes, and I knew that this was for me. As we waited impatiently for the coals to roast hotter, until they were illuminated with a fiery orange glow, we felt connected to primal urges, primal rituals.

Those were days of grilled chicken, hot dogs, and big fat sirloin steaks that came alive with the smell and flavor that only the grill could impart. In years to come, the palate grew in sophistication, and along with discoveries of such culinary delights as mushrooms, brie, and escargots came encounters with grill masters. These were not just backyard barbecuers, but serious chefs, gourmets, restaurateurs, who wielded their spatulas in ways that were at once more adventurous and more arcane than the ways of all the dads in our town.

A career in dining out taught the delicious exotica of Brazilian barbecue, churrasco, cooked on spits and served on metal skewers, accompanied by toxically delicious caipirinhas; or Thai barbecue, with blazing slices of chicken served with coconut milk or peanut sauces. Indian tandooris, barbecued food slow-cooked in clay pots, was luscious and unparalleled, whether chicken, shrimp, beef, lamb, or even lobster. Then there is the great barbecue of America: roadside stands, slabs of pork ribs slathered in sauces, dripping wet; barbecued beef and big chicken thighs that you grip in your fist. Every country in the world has its own grilled cuisine, its own method of cooking. What is a backyard barbecuer to do?

The answer is, enjoy what you can make at home and have a blast when you go out to eat. Search out the great barbecue places. And hone your skills. You, too, can explore the wonders of barbecue in your own backyard. Whether it is the old, shallow piece of metal that your dad cooked in; whether you are on a ranch spread in Arizona or a 15th-floor terrace in Manhattan, grilling is the great democratizer.

In these pages you will find the methods, the ingredients, and the tastes to get you started on your way to a fun-filled and social dining experience. The *Everything Grilling Book* will open your eyes to not only the barbecue favorites but to new tastes and savory snacks, opening up your senses to a magic that can be found only in cooking outdoors. You are sure to find the same pride and passion in your endeavors that I have—and you, your guests, and your family will be *ooh*ing and *aah*ing all year round.

This book introduces you to the tools of the trade, opens up the world beyond burgers and franks, introduces you to the tricks of the masters, and gets you smoking with the most flavorful cooking this side of paradise.

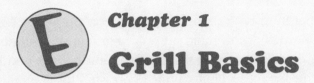

Chapter 1

Grill Basics

Grilling is so simple that you can get started with a kettle and briquettes from the local hardware store or supermarket. In a matter of minutes, you'll be able to start trying out your newfound skills. This chapter will help you choose the right grill for your needs and to suit your budget. It will be your guide to getting started with your outdoor cooking experience.

A History of Grilling

Grilling brings out an elemental feeling in people. Going back to prehistory, people have always loved to hunt, kill, and cook their prey. Today, even though the meat is "caught" at the supermarket, cooking outdoors can be a more direct, more visceral and satisfying experience for the cook.

Grilling is a primal form of cooking. Food was cooked after a fresh kill. The Mongolian hordes would build a fire and grill food on their shields. Prehistoric people, soon after the discovery of fire, learned how to spit-cook meat. The Japanese hibachi has been used for centuries, since the Iron Age. The range in sizes is tremendous. A small hibachi can be only six to eight inches across, holding just enough charcoal to cook rice, heat a wok, and make tea.

In Africa, grilling has been epitomized by the sizzle of the nganga, the iron pots favored by Nigerian Ogun tribes, in which they prepared all their food, creating an outdoor oven rich with savory, pungent flavor. Every culture has its own native form of outdoor cooking.

In the 1950s in America, grilling went from the primal to the mainstream. Barbecue grilling became a stylish accoutrement to the good life, and baby boomers made outdoor grills a fixture of every backyard. Dad was in command and dining outdoors became a family experience. With the swelling pocketbooks of Americans, grills became more complex and more advanced.

FACT

Today, Char-Broil, Coleman, Kenmore, and Weber account for more than 60 percent of gas-grill sales. Three-fourths of all U.S. households own a grill of some sort, and most own both a charcoal and a gas grill. Grilling is big business!

By the 1960s and 1970s, grills were de rigueur at any home or gathering. In the 1980s, it was the California influence that ruled. Chefs like Jeremiah Tower of northern California's Chez Panisse and Spago's Wolfgang Puck played up grilling as essential to the California lifestyle, and made mesquite charcoal a household item. In recent years, the

George Foreman Grill brought outdoor cooking to the city—30 million units were sold in a seven-year period. The former boxer recently sold his company for $138 million. Eateries around the country have adopted grill recipes, from four-star gourmet restaurants to roadside "bbq" joints.

In the 1990s, charcoal gave way to elaborate gas grills with thermometers, temperature controls, and different cooking surfaces. By the end of the millennium, the transformation was complete, with great outdoor grill islands, rotisseries, and smoking chambers, along with accessories like refrigerators, warming drawers, and beer taps. Companies like Weber, Broilmaster, Char-Broil, Jenn-Aire, Great Outdoors, Coleman, Kenmore, and Ducane lead the market.

Equipment You'll Need

It's wise to determine exactly what you need before buying something, since high-tech features can add a lot of expense that may not be worth it if you don't really need or want them. Simple charcoal or gas grills can cost as little as $75 to $125. Realize that the smallest grills will limit the amount of food you will be able to cook, and that they may be made of cheaper materials.

Better gas grills generally have two or more separate burners—not just control knobs—which allows greater control of heat. Most lower-priced grills have only one burner, which is shaped like an H or a bar, some with one control, some with two controls. Grills with one burner don't allow you to control heat as well as grills with multiple burners and you may find hot and cold spots on the cooking surface.

Special Features

When cooking on a gas grill, juices from the food drip down and accumulate near the heat source until they reach a flash point and burn off. The best systems quickly flash the drippings, eliminating flare-ups and creating flavorful smoke. Most manufacturers rely on lava rock or ceramic briquettes to distribute the heat from the burners to the cooking surface. Drippings from the food tend to pool in these systems, causing flare-ups.

The best grills use a steel bar system that funnels the grease away from the burner flames, greatly reducing flare-ups.

For a long-lasting grill, use a grill made of high-grade steel with a baked-on porcelain enamel surface. While cooking grates are commonly made from nickel or chrome-plated aluminum, a thicker, heavier-gauge cooking grate will last longer and distribute heat better. The best grates are made of cast iron, stainless steel, or porcelain-coated aluminum or cast iron.

Outdoor cooks accustomed to charcoal and wood-fire cooking are often reluctant to make the change to gas grills, which they believe offer convenience but little else. They are willing to put up with the inconsistent temperature, flare-ups, and difficult clean-up for the tradeoff of the aroma and flavor unique to wood smoke and pure wood charcoal. However, the ease of use of gas grills is a major advantage, providing higher, consistent temperatures, versatility, and durability. And the same kinds of flavorings and cooking flexibility are now available for the gas griller as well.

QUESTION?

How much should you spend on a grill?
You don't have to spend top dollar for a gas grill that sizzles. While a few cost more than $1,000, *Consumer Reports* top-scoring grills come in at around $600. And one of the *Consumer Reports* "Best Buys" runs just $200.

Size and Power

Consider what you want to grill and for whom. Do you give a lot of big parties? Are you grilling for a small family, a party for two, or a convocation of family and friends? These questions should become your guidelines. Most grills have 340 to 490 square inches of cooking surface—enough to grill eighteen to twenty-four 4"-diameter burgers at once. Choose a grill sized to match your cooking and entertaining needs.

Don't worry too much about the BTU (British thermal unit) rating. This is a measure of the potential heat the barbecue can put out. BTUs are not necessarily a measure of cooking power. They indicate the volume of gas a grill can burn. Tightly engineered grills use fewer BTUs and cook food more efficiently. Sometimes less is more. Too many BTUs can cause damage to burners and reduce the life of the grill. In general, large grills with large cooking surfaces require higher BTU ratings. Get a grill that can produce at least 30,000 BTUs. More may overheat your grill, waste gas, deteriorate components, or make it cumbersome to open and close your grill's lid.

For a gas grill, lava rocks are ideal conduits of heat. The right amount arranged properly is the perfect formula. If too many rocks are distributed unevenly, the heat doesn't reach the food and the grill doesn't get as hot. Too few rocks can cause the heat to escape faster, and again, the heat can be uneven. An added benefit is that lava rocks create smoke, which adds flavor to the food.

When buying a high-quality grill, check the burner warranty. Look for gas burners warranted for at least ten years. Burners are one of the most commonly replaced grill parts. *Consumer Reports* ratings point out which models and materials hold up best.

Special Options

Is there such a thing as "too much grill" for one person? For grilling the occasional burger, a basic grill is fine. But for the past several years, grill chefs have found that "more is more," and that there are lots of ways to enhance the grill experience, with professional-quality features like stainless steel cooking grids, higher-temperature burners, and side burners, among others. A stainless steel–rod cooking surface absorbs heat well but doesn't retain it for long, so it's an ideal choice for gourmet grilling. Another benefit is its durability—you can toss stainless steel racks in the dishwasher for easy cleanup.

A thermometer on the lid tells you the grill's internal air temperature, which indirectly cooks thick meats and fish without charring them. Options for upgrades or conversions can be found by paying a visit to your favorite hardware store or grill outlet. When purchasing, make sure you can add a burner or rotisserie without buying a whole new grill. Upgrade kits may add to the cost, but it is worthwhile for the serious chef.

Drains

Make sure grease can drain. Grills without a grease cup or other device that catches or drains grease from the burners can flare up if the grease catches fire. To prevent flare-ups, make sure the grill has a drain!

Outdoor Design

Many people put their grills on their decks or patios. But if you have more space, you may want to consider landscaping a portion of your property to handle your grill system. A grilling island is a popular way to create an outdoor kitchen, creating a central location that places the grill within cabinetry or masonry. These do double duty as a work surface for preparing the meal and a buffet area for serving it.

Island Cooking

Grilling islands come in two forms: permanently installed custom-built masonry islands and semicustom prefabricated units. Permanent masonry islands are totally customized to meet your needs, and they afford the most flexibility in terms of design and materials. You can use the same stone or brick as your patio or house exterior for the island base, or you can exactly match the island's countertop with your pool tiles.

Custom masonry islands are more expensive and require more legwork in terms of coordination with a contractor or mason and securing building permits, but they may add value to your home. Semicustom prefabricated grilling items offer homeowners a variety of choices, configurations, and exterior finishes. After you've provided dimensions for the grill and other built-in appliances, the island can be manufactured off-site before being delivered ready for installation. Surfaces may be as elaborate as stucco or faux stone finishes with many counter tile colors and sizes. Five- to six-foot rectangular shapes are on the smaller end of configurations, while models with multilevels, L shapes, or rounded table ends to accommodate bar stools for dining can be designed for a more elaborate setup.

Freestanding Carts

If an island, prefab, or custom unit is not in your budget, a grill mounted on a freestanding cart may be your best option. Freestanding carts are easiest for the homeowner in terms of affordability and portability. If you like to be able to wheel your grill and cook poolside, then a freestanding cart is right for you. Freestanding grill carts include high-end options, among them sliding drawers for storing utensils, countertop prep areas, and umbrella attachments that shade the chef. Some units contain a refrigerator in the base of the cart, making it easy to grab a beverage or cooking ingredient without going into the house. Carts can be customized with stainless steel or porcelain enamel finishes to match pool and patio furniture.

The cart is the part beneath the firebox and lid. The best are cast-aluminum carts, which won't rust. Carts made of stainless steel also resist corrosion, but they tend to discolor from heat and weather. Painted-steel carts can eventually scratch and rust. You'll want a cart with four wheels or casters if you move your grill often. Models with just two wheels or casters, including some high-priced models, must be lifted at one end.

Stainless steel grates are best because they resist corrosion. Grates made of porcelain-coated cast iron are also a good choice; they're sturdier than the usual porcelain-coated steel and hold more heat for better searing.

Tools of the Trade

Once you have your grill, you'll want a variety of cookware to enhance your experience. You could probably survive with a good knife and a spatula, along with standard kitchen tools like colanders, can and jar openers, measurement tools, a citrus zester, basters, and tenderizing mallets. You may want to add some of the following items:

A basic set of grill tools should help you to flip burgers, baste ribs, or turn ears of corn. Stainless steel tools are recommended, and may include a spatula, a knife, a basting brush, and locking tongs. Many sets will have loops for hanging the tools on the grill itself. Knives that are useful include a slicing knife, a carving knife, and a paring knife.

Chimney starter. This is a large canister that helps light a charcoal fire easily. A good-quality chimney starter will hold enough briquettes for a 22½" kettle.

Grill cleaning tool. A good grill-cleaning tool combines a brass scrub brush, a stainless steel scraper, and a rugged nylon scouring pad, making it easy to remove burned-on bits of food.

Grill press. A press is the key to preparing many of Italy's traditional grill dishes. The heavy press holds chicken flat against the grill, so it cooks faster and more evenly. The tool is also great for weighting down pork chops and tenderloins.

Food processor. From a "mini-prep" to a 14-cup food processor, these appliances simplify the task of cutting, chopping, slicing, and dicing. Most models feature metal blades, a dough blade, shredding and slicing disks, and a rubber spatula.

Pots and pans. There are many types of cookware that can be placed on the grill, such as a Dutch oven or a rectangular cast-iron fish pan.

Grill baskets. These are indispensable for cooking anything that might not stay in one piece. A nonstick porcelain enamel grill wok is perfect for veggies, shrimp, and scallops; a nonstick rectangular grill basket can hold smaller cuts of meat and fish without pieces falling into the grill. A wooden handle will make flipping easy.

Oven mitts. Don't forget these! It's always important to have a heavy-weight cotton oven mitt, maybe two. The hardware store may have them, or you can find them with comfy terrycloth lining. Grilling gets hot!

Firing up the Grill

Obviously, how you light your grill depends on if it is a gas or charcoal grill. The fire in either is used to control the heat of the grill, so to get the temperature right (and to make sure it cooks evenly), it's important to light up right.

Lighting the Charcoal Grill

The number of briquettes required depends on the size and type of grill and the amount of food to be prepared. Weather conditions also have an effect; strong winds, very cold temperatures, or high humidity increase the number of briquettes needed for a good fire. As a rule, it takes about thirty briquettes to grill one pound of meat (a little less than half a five-pound bag of charcoal).

There are many ways to light briquettes. One of the best is to start with a high-quality charcoal lighter fluid. First, stack briquettes in a pyramid, then pour lighter fluid over the top of the stack. Use 1.6 ounces of fluid per pound of briquettes; another way to determine the amount is that the briquettes should appear glossy.

Light the briquettes with a match. The briquettes are ready for cooking when they're 70 percent ashed over. This usually takes twenty to thirty minutes.

Chimney starters and electric starters also provide safe, efficient methods for lighting briquettes. Be sure to follow the manufacturer's directions when using these devices. Finally, never use gasoline, kerosene, or alcohol to light briquettes.

For direct cooking, food is placed directly over the coals. Make sure there is enough charcoal to extend in a single layer one to two inches beyond the area of the food on the grill. Pour briquettes into the grill to determine the quantity, then stack into a pyramid for lighting. For indirect cooking, food is placed over a drip pan and the briquettes are banked either to one or both sides of the pan. This is recommended for large cuts of meat, like roasts, and for fatty meats, to prevent flare-ups. However, charcoal lighter fluids and coals with accelerants can leave the food with a nasty chemical taste. You can use a metal chimney filled with newspaper and some charcoal to start your fire. The charcoal is ready when you can hold your hand five inches over the coals for only three to five seconds.

Lighting the Gas Grill

Most gas grills come with electronic ignition systems. Some gas grills have simple rotary igniters that produce an electric charge via an internal hammer striking a ceramic element. The electrode wire carries this charge to the electrode tip and a spark occurs across the gap to the burner. Electronic ignition systems automatically ignite the burner and power control-panel indicator lights.

ALERT!

Never use gas-treated briquettes in a gas grill. Smoker grills are used for barbecuing for up to ten hours. Because briquettes need to be added every forty-five minutes, applying Match Light will cause lighter fluid to permeate the meat, and adding to an existing fire may also cause a flare-up. Treated briquettes shouldn't be used in gas grills because the fire may damage the grill.

Once your propane tank is filled and properly hooked up, you are ready to turn on the grill. Open the grill lid, and open the tank valve. Turn the first front burner to high. This will allow the gas to enter the grill to meet the ignition spark. Allow 2 to 3 seconds for gas chamber to fill. Push the igniter button firmly. The burner should light after only one or two pushes of the button. Once the first burner is lit, turn the next burner or burners to high, and repeat until all burners are lit. Close lid. Preheat your grill at high temperatures, up to 550°F. Place food on cooking grate and adjust burners to correct cooking temperatures.

Always keep the bottom tray and grease catch pan of your gas grill clean and free of debris. This not only prevents dangerous grease fires, it also deters visits from unwanted critters. A sprinkle of red pepper is another safe way to discourage animals. If a flare-up should occur, turn all burners to off and move food to another area of the cooking grate.

Any flames will quickly subside. Then, light the grill again. Never use water to extinguish flames on a gas grill. Do not line the funnel-shaped bottom tray with foil. This could prevent the grease from flowing into the grease catch pan. Grease is also likely to catch in the tiny creases of the foil and start a fire.

Always seek adequate and even heat. The grill should reach 600 degrees across the entire cooking surface. If there are cool spots, your cooking will be uneven.

Use high heat to sear your steak, but less intense heat for the rest of the cooking time. If your cooking surface doesn't cool when you turn down the heat, you'll end up with meat that is dry and flavorless. You will want to put most of the coals at one end of the grill, a few in the middle and none on the far side. Thus, you'll have hot, medium, and warm temperatures. With gas grills you need to turn the heat up and down and play with the lid to achieve the zones.

Grill Safety

According to the Insurance Information Institute, Americans enjoy more than 3 billion barbecues each year. The safety experts at Underwriters Laboratories, Inc., and the National Safety Council urge backyard chefs to study and employ safety measures before the hot dogs hit the grill. There are numerous hazards associated with grilling. Here are some rules you should always follow:

- Never use a grill indoors. Use the grill at least ten feet away from your house or any building.
- Do not use the grill in a garage, breezeway, carport, porch, or under an awning or any covering that can catch fire.
- Never leave the grill unattended, especially when small children and pets are present.
- Be cautious of overhead obstructions, including tree branches, while grilling.
- Keep a fire extinguisher handy when grilling and know how to use it.
- Always follow the manufacturer's instructions that accompany the grill.

For gas grills, always observe these special safety measures:

- Check the tubes leading into the burner for any blockage from insects, spiders, or grease. Use a pipe cleaner or wire to clear a blockage and push it through to the main part of the burner.
- Check grill hoses for cracking, brittleness, holes, and leaks. Make sure there are no kinks in the hose or tubing.
- Replace scratched or frayed hose connectors, which can eventually leak gas.
- Check for gas leaks, following the manufacturer's instructions, if you smell gas or when you reconnect the grill to the propane tank.
- Keep lit cigarettes or open flames away from a leaking grill.
- Do not attempt to repair the tank valve or the appliance yourself. Take it to your local home improvement store, hardware store, or a qualified appliance repairperson.
- Use caution when storing propane tanks. Always keep the containers upright. Never store a spare tank under or near the grill, or indoors. Never store or use flammable liquids, like gasoline, near the grill.
- Be sure your propane tank has an overfill prevention device. As of April 2002, by law all tanks sold or refilled are required to have the device to protect against propane leaks that may cause fire or explosions.
- Never keep a filled tank in a hot car or car trunk. Heat will cause the gas pressure to increase, which may open the relief valve and allow gas to escape.
- You should use extreme caution. Always follow the manufacturer's instructions when connecting or disconnecting a propane tank to your grill.
- Certified grills are the exception—not the rule. Many are not manufactured under strict guidelines and may not hold up after regular, rigorous use. Ask to make sure a grill is certified by a national testing service before you buy it.

For charcoal grills, observe these precautions:

- Charcoal should never be used indoors, even if ventilation is provided, because charcoal produces carbon monoxide fumes. Do not store the grill indoors until the charcoal is completely extinguished.
- Never use gasoline or kerosene to light a charcoal fire. Both can explode.
- Never attempt to restart the flame by adding additional lighting fluid to a grill that is already lit; the flame can roll upstream and explode the can in your hand.
- Keep a spray bottle of water nearby to control flare-ups while grilling.
- Place your grill on a flat, level surface so it won't tip over.
- Wait until the coals have completely cooled (which may take a few hours) before disposing of them.
- Remember, coals get hot—up to 1,000°F. Use insulated, flame-retardant mitts when cooking or handling any part of the grill.
- Also use long-handled barbecue tongs and utensils for safe handling of food and coals.

Keeping the Grill Clean

Cleaning the grill is very important, so be sure to scrub it well. Also, thoroughly clean outdoor utensils, coolers, and other containers with hot, soapy water before cooking. Never reuse a platter that has held raw food for serving without washing thoroughly. Marinades, too, should be discarded unless boiled to make sauce. Separate raw from cooked foods to prevent cross-contamination. This holds true for your refrigerator as well—store raw meats on lower shelves to prevent juices from running onto ready-to-eat foods.

The American Dietetic Association's "It's in Your Hands" program advises food preparers to wash hands often; to keep raw meats and ready-to-eat foods separate; to cook to proper temperatures; and when refrigerating, to keep food below 40°F.

When traveling to outdoor events, picnics, and parties, use ice packs to keep foods refrigerated outdoors at temperatures below 40°F. Keep the cooler with food in it in the air-conditioned backseat of your car instead of the hot trunk. Once at your outdoor dining destination, try to keep foods out of direct sunlight. Set up camp in the shade to make sure your food and guests stay cool.

Technique: To Cover or Not to Cover?

When a grill is covered, it is difficult to control the flares. In a charcoal fire, you can keep the grill covered but move the meat or fish away from the hottest part, creating a two-zone cooking surface with many coals on one side of the grill and fewer, or none, on the other. If a piece of meat such as a pork chop or a chicken breast is too raw in the center but beginning to blacken on the outside, move it to the cool side of the grill. This is a technique used by professional grill cooks.

Another popular innovation for connoisseurs is the infrared grill, which can reach temperatures of 1,200°–1,500°F, far hotter than traditional grills.

Superhot, convection principles drive hot air to grill. Most conventional gas grills will reach 750 degrees on the surface of the burner itself. Because infrared is different from conventional gas grills, it actually emits a wavelength of heat that passes straight through air and moisture and goes right to the product directly.

In lieu of an expensive infrared system, you may want to use a combination of open and closed cover: closing the lid when searing, opening the grill for slower cooking, and venting the closed grill for smoking over cooler temperatures.

Healthy Grilling

Grilling is serious stuff for another reason: Grill right, eat right, and you will live a longer, healthier life. But outdoor cooking has raised health concerns, from the smoke that may add to air pollution to the cancer-causing compounds that come from red meat, poultry, and fish when grilled. These concerns need to be considered, and grilling should be placed within the context of a healthy lifestyle and a balanced diet.

When cooking, the higher the heat, the greater the amount of potential carcinogens that may be released. The American Institute for Cancer Research recommends that you marinate your meat before grilling. Research has shown that marinating meat for even a brief length of time prevents the formation of cancer-causing compounds during the grilling process. The ingredients found in many marinades, such as vinegar, citrus juices, spices, and oils, all seem to help with prevention.

The Quaker Oatmeal Company recommends such healthy tips as choosing leaner meats such as skinless turkey, chicken, or fish instead of hamburgers or steaks. Trim off any excess fat from the meat before cooking. Don't soak meat in salt, and grill corn rather than boil it.

Make It a Party!

There's nothing wrong with hanging out while your food slow-cooks, talking and laughing and not being worried that something will incinerate while you are greeting a guest. Adapt the ideas in this book! Have a "kabob" party so your guests can choose what they eat and help with the cooking. Invite ten of your best friends for a prime steak, one that's three inches thick, and cook it with some mesquite. Have your friends bring side dishes and set out a cart with luscious drinks. Cheers!

For the next holiday, try smoking your Thanksgiving turkey. Or make a true Western barbecue for a graduation party. Stuff or grill vegetables for a lunch of fabulous salads and sandwiches, and give the kids a backyard pizza party, made at home on your grill. Or do an Asian holiday with friends who like to eat on the light side. Above all, have fun with your grill and the recipes in this book!

CHAPTER 2

Build a Better Burger

Sirloin, Round, and Chuck Burgers

Serves 4

You can also mix in finely chopped onion, minced fresh garlic or garlic powder, or barbecue sauce, but this recipe starts out with the basics.

½ *pound ground sirloin*
½ *pound ground chuck steak (not overly lean)*
½ *pound ground round*
1 *tablespoon of your favorite steak sauce or Worcestershire sauce*

Salt and freshly ground black pepper to taste
4 *slices tomato and/or sweet onion for garnish*
Catsup, mustard, and pickle relish to taste

1. Mix the three types of ground meat together, tossing lightly with steak sauce, salt, and pepper. Don't be heavy handed here.
2. Preheat grill to medium-high.
3. Form burgers without too much patting and squeezing; this keeps them juicy.
4. Grill burgers over medium heat until they are nicely browned on the outside and pink on the inside, about 5 minutes per side. Timing depends on how thick the burgers are and how done you like them. Don't press the juice out with a spatula while cooking unless you like dry burgers.
5. Serve on hamburger buns, hard rolls, Portuguese rolls, or Tuscan bread with the toppings of your choice. Garnish with tomatoes and sweet onions.

The Birth of the Burger

The concept of hamburger came to the United States in the mid-1800s on an ocean liner called Amerika. *It took passengers from Germany to New York. The cook ground "Hamburg beef," a smoked, salted, and dried beef that traveled well. Thus, the hamburger was born. It's as American as apple pie—almost!*

Beef Burger with Melted Cheese and Smoky Bacon

24 ounces medium-lean chuck
   steak, ground
1 teaspoon salt
Freshly ground black pepper
   to taste
1 tablespoon steak sauce
4 to 6 slices high-quality
   bacon, cut in half across

4 1/4-inch-thick slices of sharp
   cheddar, American, brie, or
   Camembert cheese, enough
   to cover each burger
4 tomato and/or sweet onion
   slices for garnish
Catsup, mustard, and pickle
   relish to taste

> **Serves 4**
>
> These burgers are so
> hearty and wonderful!
> You can also try them
> with Thick Cheddar
> Cheese Sauce
> (page 27) and
> shredded lettuce
> and pickles.
>
>

1. Divide the beef into four patties, mixing in the salt, pepper, and steak sauce.
2. Heat grill to medium.
3. Grill the bacon until brown and set aside on paper towels.
4. Grill the burgers until they reach the desired state of doneness. When the burgers are almost done, add the cheese and close the top of the grill to melt the cheese. Place on your favorite buns, cheese up, and arrange the bacon on top. Garnish and top with your choice of toppings.

Chuck, Round, or Sirloin?

Does chuck really make a tastier burger than round or sirloin? After years of experimentation, we have learned that of the three cuts of beef, round is the least flavorful, with chuck and then sirloin coming in second and first. Many restaurateurs believe that a mixture works best.

Savory Duck Burger with Roasted Apples

1½ pounds skinless, boneless
    duck breast
2 apples
Salt and pepper to taste
1 tablespoon butter
1 tablespoon prepared Dijon-
    style mustard
¼ teaspoon cinnamon

¼ teaspoon nutmeg
¼ teaspoon ground cloves
½ teaspoon garlic powder
2 teaspoons dried sage leaves,
    crumbled
2 slices bacon or pancetta,
    minced

1. Place the duck in a bowl; add salt and pepper. Halve the apples and core them; set aside.
2. In a sauté pan, melt the butter and add the mustard, cinnamon, nutmeg, cloves, garlic, and sage. Sauté over low heat for 4 minutes.
3. Add to the duck meat and mix gently and well.
4. Set grill to medium.
5. Form patties and place the minced bacon or pancetta on a piece of waxed paper. Turn the patties in the minced bacon or pancetta so that a bit sticks to each side. Grill until medium, about 6 minutes per side.
6. While cooking the duck breast, place the apples on the grill cut-side down. Grill for 3 minutes.
7. Serve with cranberry relish, canned pie cherries, or Sweet Caramelized Onions (page 23).

Never a Dull Burger

Next time you go to the supermarket, look at all of the condiments, fresh and dried fruits, and vegetables to get ideas for toppings. Substitute chopped dried prunes for the cranberries or cherries on the duck, or try different salsas.

Burger à la Française

1½ pounds ground sirloin
1 tablespoon steak sauce
Salt and freshly ground black
    pepper to taste
1–2 tablespoons green pepper-
    corns, rinsed, or substitute
    dried cranberries or cherries
1 tablespoon garlic, minced

1 tablespoon herbs de Provence
    or your own mixture of
    dried oregano, thyme, and
    rosemary
4 brioche or high-quality rolls
Sweet Caramelized Onions
    (page 23), for garnish

Serves 4

Garnish this with a
Classic Béarnaise
Sauce (page 241) for
an elegant flair.

1. Mix the ground beef with all of the condiments, spices, and herbs. Gently form into patties.
2. Set grill to medium. Grill burgers until they reach the desired degree of doneness. Serve on toasted brioche or rolls and garnish.

Burger with Sicilian Spices, Pine Nuts, and Raisins

1½ pounds chuck or round
    steak, ground
2–3 cloves garlic, minced
Salt and freshly ground black
    pepper to taste
1 teaspoon dried oregano

1 teaspoon dried red pepper
    flakes, or to taste
¼ cup pine nuts (pignoles)
½ cup raisins, coarsely
    chopped

**Serves 4 as a main
course or 12 as
hors d'oeuvres**

Any good, basic
homemade or com-
mercial marinara
sauce goes great
with this recipe.

1. Mix the beef with the rest of the ingredients, tossing carefully.
2. Set grill to medium.
3. Form patties—either tiny for hors d'oeuvres or larger ones to serve on Italian bread with sauce.
4. Grill until brown and done to preference. Serve the small ones on bread rounds and the large ones on toasted pieces of Italian bread with the sauce on the side.

Lamb Burger à la Grecque

½ cup sour cream
½ cucumber, peeled and chopped
Juice of ½ lemon
Freshly ground black pepper to taste
2 cloves garlic, minced
1 tablespoon dried mint or 2 tablespoons fresh, chopped
1 teaspoon dried rosemary, crumbled, or 1 tablespoon fresh, chopped

⅛ teaspoon freshly ground coriander seeds
Salt and freshly ground black pepper to taste
½ cup extra virgin olive oil
1½ pounds lean shoulder lamb, ground

1. Mix the sour cream, cucumber, lemon juice, and pepper together and store in the refrigerator. (This can be made a day in advance.)
2. Whisk the garlic, herbs, and spices into the olive oil. Mix the infused oil with the lamb, tossing carefully.
3. Set grill to medium.
4. Form into either 4 big patties or 12 appetizer-size patties. Grill patties to medium. The small ones will be done in 2 to 3 minutes per side, the large ones according to your desired level of doneness.
5. Serve with pita bread (large for big burgers and cracker-size for appetizers).

Don't Get Stuck!

Never feel stuck in a rut when creating a burger dinner or picnic. You can use many different meats, fruits, and nuts as well as herbs and spices to prevent ho hums at your table.

Elegant Gorgonzola-Stuffed Burger

1½ pounds lean ground beef
4 ounces blue cheese
1 large red pepper, roasted
*   and peeled*

Freshly ground black pepper to
*   taste*
4 teaspoons fresh or 2 tea-
*   spoons dried oregano*

1. Form the ground beef into 8 thin patties. Chop the roasted pepper and crumble the cheese.
2. Four patties will serve as the bottoms and 4 will be the tops of the stuffed burgers. Divide the cheese among the 4 bottom patties. Put the red peppers on top of the cheese. Sprinkle patties with pepper and oregano. Place a plain patty on top of each of the 4 filled ones. Press to close, making sure that none of the filling is going to leak out.
3. Heat grill to medium and brown burgers. Then turn to low to make sure that the cheese melts and the peppers are hot.

> **Serves 4**
>
> This is as good as it gets! The cheese melts inside the burger to make a delicious treat.
>
>

Sweet Caramelized Onions

3–4 onions, peeled and sliced
½ stick unsalted butter

1 teaspoon sugar
Salt and pepper to taste

Place the onions, butter, and sugar in a large sauté pan over low heat. Sauté gently, stirring frequently. When the onions are brown but not burned, place them in a bowl, add salt and pepper, and serve. These can be made well in advance and stored in a covered jar in the refrigerator.

> **Makes approximately 1 cup**
>
> Caramelized onions are a delicious addition to any burger and to many other dishes. Use large, sweet, white onions such as Vidalias or Bermudas.
>
>

Fresh Tuna Burger

Serves 4 as a main course or 12 as an appetizer

These are delicious as appetizers served on crackers or toasted pita rounds. If you can't get ground tuna, buy fresh and grind it in your food processor.

2 tablespoons fresh lemon juice
2 tablespoons teriyaki sauce
2 cloves garlic, minced
Freshly ground black pepper
    and salt to taste
1½ pounds fresh tuna steak,
    coarsely ground
4 strips bacon

4 toasted rolls or 12 small
    pitas, toasted
4 thin slices sweet red onion
1 cup bean or alfalfa sprouts,
    rinsed
4 leaves lettuce (optional)
4 slices tomato (optional)

1. Mix the lemon juice, teriyaki sauce, garlic, pepper, and salt into the ground tuna and divide it into 4 patties or 12 small ones for appetizers.
2. Set grill to medium. Grill the bacon until crisp and set aside to drain on paper towels.
3. Grill the main-course burgers 4 to 5 minutes per side and the small ones 2 to 3 minutes per side.
4. Stack the rolls or pitas with burgers, bacon, onion, and sprouts, and, if you like, add lettuce and tomato. Serve with steak sauce or teriyaki sauce on the side.

Cook Quickly!

Tuna steak is best cooked quickly. Grill over high heat for best taste; this will seal juices inside and provide the outside with a caramel-colored crust.

Savory Turkey Burger

1½ pounds ground turkey,
 preferably dark meat
1 tablespoon dried sage
 leaves, crumbled
1 tablespoon dried thyme
 leaves, crumbled

2 tablespoons Worcestershire
 sauce
Salt and pepper to taste
2 shallots, finely minced
½ cup dried cranberries
½ cup chopped walnuts, toasted

1. In a large bowl, mix the turkey with the sage, thyme, Worcestershire sauce, salt, and pepper. Make sure to evenly distribute the herbs, sauce, and spices. Sprinkle with cranberries and nuts and toss gently.
2. Set grill to medium.
3. Form 4 patties, then grill until well done, about 8 minutes on each side.
4. Serve with all the fixings for a great dinner! You can put out sides of cranberry relish, plenty of mashed white or sweet potatoes, fresh salad and vegetables, and especially cornbread.

White Meat or Dark?

A mixture of white and dark meat or all dark meat is very good. The dark meat is more flavorful and slightly more fatty, helping the burgers hold together better than if you just use white meat. Also, the dark meat is far less expensive.

Serves 4

The flavoring is very important in these burgers, as they can be bland. Try adding dried cranberries, walnuts, and herbs to give them some zip.

Meaty-Flavored Veggie Burger

½ cup olive oil
1 small yellow onion, chopped fine
1 small green bell pepper, cored, seeded, and chopped fine
2 cloves garlic, peeled and minced
1½ cups brown rice, cooked according to package directions

2 cups black beans
2 tablespoons tomato paste
1 teaspoon ground cumin
½ cup Italian (flat leaf) parsley, chopped fine
Salt and pepper to taste
4 pats unsalted butter (optional)

1. Heat the olive oil in a sauté pan over medium flame. Add the onion, green bell pepper, and garlic and sauté over low flame until soft, about 10 minutes.
2. Scrape the peppers and onions, rice, beans, tomato paste, cumin, parsley, salt, and black pepper into a bowl. Mash the mixture with a potato masher.
3. Set the grill on medium. Form into patties and cook on one side for 4 minutes. Turn the patties.
4. Just after turning, add the optional butter to the patties. Grill 4 more minutes until nice and hot. Serve on toasted whole wheat English muffins with your favorite salsa.

Smashed Garlic

This simple procedure makes garlic easy to peel and chop or mince. Simply take an unpeeled clove of garlic and smash it with the side of a heavy oriental knife or cleaver. The papery skin will split and come off easily. Discard the skin and you have a clove of garlic that is already in pieces. Just chop or mince and use!

Thick Cheddar Cheese Sauce

2 tablespoons unsalted butter
2 tablespoons all-purpose flour
1 shallot, peeled and minced
1 cup warm milk
Pinch ground nutmeg
4 ounces sharp cheddar cheese

Freshly ground black pepper to taste
1 cup shredded iceberg lettuce
½ cup chopped sweet "bread and butter" pickles

1. Make a roux by melting the butter over low heat and stirring in the flour and shallot. Cook, stirring, for three minutes.
2. Add the milk and nutmeg, stirring until thickened. Stir in the cheese and turn off the stove. Add pepper to taste. Add the lettuce and pickle and serve hot on burgers.

Makes 1½ cups

This old-fashioned sauce is now in vogue—absolutely terrific for burgers, grilled chicken, even meatloaf.

Bright Chili Bean Topping

½ cup vegetable oil
2 cloves garlic, peeled and minced
2 red onions, peeled and chopped
2 jalapeno peppers, cored and seeded
1 sweet red pepper, roasted, peeled, and chopped

1 13-ounce can red kidney beans or black beans
1 tablespoon Worcestershire sauce
1 teaspoon Tabasco sauce
1 tablespoon cocoa powder
6 ounces beer

1. Heat the oil in a large pot over medium-low heat. Add the garlic, onions, and peppers. Cook, stirring to soften the vegetables, 5 to 7 minutes.
2. Stir in the rest of the ingredients. Cover and cook for 4 to 5 hours. If it's too soupy, uncover and let the liquid cook out. Use as a topping for burgers.

Makes 2 cups

This delicious topping will keep for a week in the refrigerator. It's also good with hot dogs, ham, pulled pork, and barbecue.

Caponata (Eggplant Relish)

Makes 2 cups

Make a lot and serve on crackers as well as on burgers. This is a favorite for picnics and can be used with chicken, beef, turkey, and veal.

1 large eggplant or two medium ones

4–5 teaspoons salt

¼ cup olive oil

1 large onion, peeled and chopped

4 cloves garlic, peeled and minced

2 stalks celery, tops included, chopped fine

4 ripe tomatoes, seeded and chopped

½ cup small Italian capers

½ cup Sicilian or Greek olives, chopped

1 teaspoon cocoa powder

2 ounces balsamic vinegar

1 tablespoon red pepper flakes

1. Peel the eggplant and slice it horizontally in about ½-inch slices. Salt the eggplant slices on both sides and stack them on a plate. Place a heavy pot on top of the eggplant to press out the brown juice. Give it a half hour.
2. Dice the eggplant and brown it in ¼ cup olive oil. When the eggplant is soft, remove to a bowl and set aside.
3. Add the onion, garlic, and celery and cook over medium heat until soft. If the pan is dry, add more oil.
4. Stir in the rest of the ingredients and put the eggplant back into the pan. Cover and cook for 20 minutes.

A Dish That Improves with Age

This improves with age and is terrific on burgers or good Italian bread. Caponata is a versatile side dish that can be served presented on a bed of lettuce. It is also low in calories.

CHAPTER 3

Hot Dogs, Wursts, and Sausages

Grilled Sweet and Tasty Sausage Slices

Serves 10 as snacks (about 3 per person)

Sausages and small dogs are barroom staples—they are salty enough to make a drinker order more drinks.

8 thickly cut slices salami or bologna

16 slices pumpernickel bread

8 ounces mustard pickles

4 teaspoons honey Dijon mustard

1. Heat the grill to hot.
2. Place the sausage slices on the hot grill and turn after 1 minute.
3. Toast the bread on the side of the grill until lightly crisped on both sides. Cut the toasted bread slices into quarters and place on a serving platter.
4. Remove the sausage slices from the grill and cut into fourths. Arrange the slices of sausage on the pieces of toast. Garnish with mustard pickles or honey dijon.

Beer Sausages

Yields 16 sausages

This basic recipe is especially good with bratwurst, bauernwurst, knockwurst, or kielbasa. Save the cooking liquid for boiling potatoes, beets, or cabbage.

16 of your favorite sausages

1½ bottles or cans of rich beer, not light

1. Prick the sausages with a fork. Open the beer and pour into a large pot. Let the beer defoam for about 10 minutes.
2. Add the sausages, then bring to a simmer and cook for 20 minutes.
3. Turn off the stove and let the sausages cool in the beer. Grill and serve.

A Belgian Tradition

Cooking with beer is a Belgian tradition. Belgium has more Michelin-starred restaurants per capita than France, and part of the reason may be from their highly developed system of "cuisine à la bière."

Bauernwurst with Spicy Red Cabbage

*1 head red or green cabbage,
  rinsed and trimmed*
2 ounces unsweetened butter
½ large, sweet onion, sliced
4 ounces cider vinegar
1 tablespoon brown sugar
*1 green apple, peeled and
  diced*

2 cups water
⅛ teaspoon ground cloves
Salt and pepper to taste
*8 bauernwurst, also known as
  Farmer's sausage*
2 tablespoons butter, melted

Serves 4

These are sturdy, flavorful country sausages. You can use knockwurst or bratwurst also. Make the cabbage recipe below one day in advance.

1. Shred the cabbage in a food processor; then soak cabbage in cold water for 1 hour. Drain.
2. Heat 2 ounces of butter in a large pot. Add the sliced onion. When the onion is soft, add vinegar, brown sugar, green apple, water, and cloves. Cover and cook until the cabbage is soft—about 1 hour. Check every 15 minutes, and if the liquid is dry, add water or red wine.
3. When the cabbage is cooked, taste for salt and pepper, adding as necessary. Cool, store in a refrigerator container, and chill. Warm when ready to serve.
4. Heat the grill to medium.
5. Place the sausages on the grill and brush occasionally with melted butter. Grill and turn until well browned. Serve with crusty rolls and the reheated red cabbage.

What Is Bauernwurst?

Bauernwurst is available at German specialty stores and on the Web. The sausage has a coarse texture, and mustard seeds and marjoram provide a spicy flavor. It is tasty in vegetable, potato, and lentil soups.

Cider Sausages

Makes 16 sausages

When you use this cooking liquid for potatoes, halve new potatoes and either serve them hot and buttered or chilled in potato salad.

1½ cups cider
1 cup cider vinegar

16 flavorful sausages, such as knockwurst or kielbasa

1. Put cider and cider vinegar in a large bowl. Prick the sausages with a fork and place them in the cider-and-vinegar mix.
2. Bring to a simmer and cook on low for 30 minutes.
3. Cool in the cider mixture. Then grill until brown and serve.

Bologna and Salami on the Grill

Makes 4 sandwiches

The kids will go crazy over these sandwiches. Add cheese, pickles, relish, mustard, and salad dressing for a delightful supper or lunch.

4 hamburger rolls
4 thickly cut slices salami or bologna, or other luncheon meat
4 slices Muenster or white American cheese

4 thin slices tomato
4 thin slices sweet onion
4 pieces lettuce
Choice of toppings—mustard, relish, pickles, tartar sauce, and so forth

1. Toast the rolls and keep warm.
2. Grill the sausage slices on one side and turn.
3. Place a piece of cheese on top of each sausage, making sure the cheese fits the meat—if it drips onto the grill, it will be smelly and hard to clean up.
4. When the cheese melts, build your sandwiches with the tomato, onion, lettuce, and toppings.

Homemade Sausages

1 pound ground chuck
½ pound ground pork
*1 teaspoon sage leaves, dry
   and crumbled, or 1 tablespoon fresh, minced*

½ teaspoon ground nutmeg
¼ teaspoon ground cloves
*Salt to taste and plenty of
   freshly ground pepper*

1. Mix all ingredients together; form into patties.
2. Set grill at medium.
3. Brown the sausages on both sides, then turn grill down to low, or if using coals, move the patties to a cooler area. Close the top and make sure the patties are cooked through. Serve warm.

Serves 4

Serve with a fried egg on top of each patty, toast, grilled tomatoes, and apple pie with cheese.

Good Old Dogs

2 rolls per person
*2 dogs per person, your favorite
   "breed"*

*Mustard, relish, catsup, hot
   sauce, barbecue sauce,
   sauerkraut, beans, chopped
   onions, chopped tomatoes,
   cheese, and so forth*

Lay out condiments and fixings. Heat grill to medium. Place the first dog for each person on the hottest part of the grill, placing the rest on the cooler side. Toast rolls, add grilled dogs, and encourage guests to dress their own dogs.

**Yields 2 dogs
per person**

Dogs and baseball are inextricably married in American culture—the Hebrew National all-beef frank and Nathan's are popular on the East Coast; Vienna All-Beef is a Midwestern favorite.

Subtly Flavored Bratwurst

4 bratwurst
1½ bottles or cans of rich
   beer, not light
1 pound sauerkraut, either
   jarred or canned
¼ pound butter

1 teaspoon cider vinegar
½–1 teaspoon caraway seeds,
   bruised in mortar and pestle
1 teaspoon brown sugar
   (optional)
4 whole cloves

1. Prick bratwursts with fork. Open the beer and pour into a large pot. Let the beer defoam for about 10 minutes. Add the sausages, then bring to a simmer and cook for 20 minutes.
2. Prepare the sauerkraut while the sausages are cooking in beer. To make store-bought sauerkraut taste like homemade, drain and rinse the sauerkraut in cold water. Place it in a saucepan with the butter, cider vinegar, caraway seeds, brown sugar, and cloves. Bring to a boil and simmer over very low heat for 10 minutes. Remove cloves before serving.
3. Heat grill to medium.
4. Grill sausages until golden on both sides. Serve with sauerkraut.

Milwaukee's Finest

In Milwaukee, Wisconsin, a great settlement for Germans, Poles, and Scandinavians, the ballpark serves bratwurst instead of franks. Made by the famous Usinger's, a fine old sausage house, the brats are a toast to the roots of Milwaukee's population. The brats are grilled and dipped in a "Sweet Stadium Sauce," then served on a crusty roll with plenty of sauerkraut and brown mustard.

Hot and Sweet Italian Sausages

4 Italian frying peppers (light green skin)
¼ cup olive oil, more if needed
2 sweet onions, thinly sliced
2 Italian hot sausages (about ⅓ to ½ pound each)

2 Italian sweet sausages (about ⅓ to ½ pound each)
1 8-ounce jar marinara sauce
4 split hero rolls or 2 loaves Italian bread, split and cut in half

Serves 4

This is a favorite on any Italian menu. When cooked out-doors over coals, the sausages get an added smoky flavor and are fabulous!

1. Rinse and seed peppers, and cut into chunks.
2. Place olive oil in a pan over medium heat. Add peppers and sauté until they are soft. Add the onions and continue to sauté. (Add more olive oil if needed.) Once peppers and onions are soft, remove from heat and set aside.
3. Place the sausages in boiling water for 10 minutes.
4. Preheat the grill to hot. Place the sauce in a pan to warm. Prepare the hero rolls or bread for toasting.
5. Grill the sausages quickly, browning on each side. Toast bread while the sausages are grilling.
6. Build hero sandwiches on toasted bread: Add sausage and then peppers and onions. Top with marinara sauce, and put out plenty of paper napkins!

Sausage Story

The flavorings vary from region to region and from cook to cook. People in northern areas of the United States make tasty sausages from moose, elk, and reindeer meat. These are smoked and will keep all winter. In some areas, sausages are made with ground fish mixed with shrimp and/or scallops. Actually any seafood that's plentiful and cheap can become sausage. Some gourmet shops add apples and cranberries to sausages made from pork, beef, turkey, or venison.

Cheese and Potato Stuffed Dogs

Makes 4 dogs

This is great comfort food for kids and adults. An excellent way to use up extra dogs or mashed potatoes.

8 heaping tablespoons mashed potatoes
4 dogs (your favorites or leftovers)

4 tablespoons cheddar cheese, shredded

1. Heat grill to medium.
2. Warm up mashed potatoes.
3. Grill the dogs and split lengthwise. Place them on an ovenproof platter. Spoon on the potatoes and sprinkle with cheese. Place on grill and cover. Heat until the cheese melts.

Polish Kielbasa with Spicy Beans and Apples

Serves 4

This is a delicious fall meal. The garlicky sausage will add a great deal to the beans and the flavors will become complex.

1 pound kielbasa cut in 4" pieces
1 quart canned or jarred baked beans
2 tart apples, peeled, cored, and cut into chunks

½ teaspoon ground cloves
½ teaspoon chili powder
2 teaspoons Dijon-style mustard

1. Preheat grill, then place the kielbasa over medium heat for 10 minutes, browning on all sides.
2. Mix the rest of the ingredients together in a large flameproof pan. Add the kielbasa to the bean mixture and cover with foil.
3. Bake over indirect heat on the grill for 25 minutes or until hot and bubbly.

Chili Cheese Stuffed Dogs

2 cups chili
8 dogs
8 rolls or buns
8 ounces Pepper Jack cheese,
   grated

½ cup chopped sweet onion,
   for garnish
Sour cream to taste, for garnish

1. Heat the grill to medium.
2. Place the chili in a saucepan to heat, either on the grill or on the stove.
3. Grill the dogs and toast the rolls. Split the dogs lengthwise, place on buns, and arrange on an ovenproof platter. Spoon on the chili and sprinkle with cheese.
4. Place platter on grill and close lid for a few seconds or until the cheese melts. Garnish with onions and sour cream to taste.

Serves 4

For something different, try eating your dog on rye bread, pita pockets, or kaiser rolls.

Homemade Mustard

⅔ cup yellow mustard seeds
½ teaspoon dill weed, dried
½ teaspoon celery seed
1 teaspoon salt

2 tablespoons dry white wine
2 tablespoons white vinegar
1 tablespoon honey

Using a mortar and pestle, grind the seeds. You can pulverize them to a powder or leave them coarse, whichever you prefer. Place the ground seeds or powder in a bowl. Add the dry spices and the salt. Add the wine, vinegar, and honey, whisking vigorously. Depending on the fineness of the seeds (powder will take more liquid than coarse), you may need to whisk in more liquid. Taste to adjust for seasonings. If too wet, add quick-blending flour (e.g., Wondra).

Makes 1 cup

Mustard seeds are the basis of all prepared mustard. Seeds come from plants that produce black, brown, or yellow seeds.

Homemade Horseradish Sauce

Makes 1½ cups

This is great on any kind of beef, giving a lively and spicy flavor.

½ cup fresh horseradish, cut in small pieces
1 cup sour cream
½ cup mayonnaise
2 tablespoons cider vinegar

1 teaspoon salt
½ teaspoon celery salt
⅛ teaspoon freshly ground white pepper

Place all ingredients in blender and grind until minced. Place in jar or plastic container. Refrigerate for 24 to 48 hours.

Spicy, Tart Applesauce

Makes 2 cups

Spicy, tart applesauce is great with sausages and with many other meats.

6 large, tart apples such as Granny Smith or Macintosh
Juice of 1 lemon and a 1" strip of lemon peel
½ cup water
2 tablespoons brown sugar

1 teaspoon ground cinnamon
¼ teaspoon ground nutmeg
1 teaspoon salt
1 teaspoon Tabasco sauce (optional)

Peel, core, and coarsely chop the apples into chunks. Place the apples in a saucepan with the rest of the ingredients. Bring to a boil and then lower the heat. Simmer for 10 minutes. Serve hot or cold.

Exotic Fruit Chutney

2 ripe mangoes, peeled and
  chopped
3 tart apples, peeled, cored,
  and chopped
1 cup white raisins (sultanas)
1 cup apple cider vinegar

½ cup brown sugar
1 teaspoon salt
2 tablespoons fresh gingerroot,
  minced
1 tablespoon Madras curry
  powder

Mix all ingredients together in a saucepan. Bring to a boil. Simmer for 15 minutes, or until sugar melts. Cool and store in the refrigerator. This will keep for two weeks or more.

Who Was Major Grey?

The original chutney of India was usually a relish made from fresh fruits and spices. During the colonial era, the British took it home. Major Grey's Chutney was the leading British chutney, named for a probably mythical British officer who loved to eat curries and made his own chutney as a result.

Makes 2 cups

Chutney is good with many sausages, especially pork sausages such as bratwurst. It's also fine with cooked, cold poultry and most meats.

CHAPTER 4
Steak-Out

Juicy Filet Mignon

4 6–8-ounce filets mignon
1 tablespoon freshly ground black pepper

1 clove garlic, peeled and cut lengthwise
8 strips bacon

1. Heat grill to medium, or let coals turn white.
2. Let the filets stand until they reach room temperature. Pat them dry with paper towels.
3. Spread the pepper out onto a large piece of waxed paper. Rub the garlic all over the meat. Roll the filets in the ground pepper, pressing it in so that it sticks. Wrap the filets in bacon, making packages. Secure the bacon with thin metal picks.
4. Grill the meat for 6–8 minutes per side. Don't worry if the bacon chars.
5. Remove the filets from the heat; take off the bacon and discard. Let the meat rest on a platter in a warm (150°F) oven for 8 minutes before serving.

A Bacon Wrap

Wrapping steak in bacon will serve two purposes: The bacon will keep the juices in and it will add to the flavor. Do not plan to eat the bacon; let it char. Serve steak with mushroom sauce, red wine sauce, or homemade mustard.

Herb-Crusted Filet Mignon

4 tablespoons unsalted butter,
 at room temperature
4 tablespoons fresh parsley,
 minced
1 tablespoon chopped rosemary (dried is okay)

1 teaspoon dried oregano,
 crumbled
Salt and freshly ground pepper
4 filets mignon, 6–8 ounces
 each
A.1. steak sauce

1. Mix the softened butter, herbs, salt, and pepper in a small bowl and set aside.
2. Sprinkle the filets with A.1. sauce.
3. Preheat the grill or prepare the coals.
4. Let the filets reach room temperature. Pat them dry with a paper towel. Spread the filets with the butter/herb mixture. Grill to the desired degree of doneness. Place on a platter.
5. Let rest for 5 to 8 minutes in a warm place.

Serves 4
This is very delicious. The herbs will char onto the outside of the steak and give it a wonderful flavor. This is extra good with mushroom sauce.

Wood Charcoal Versus Briquettes

Wood charcoal is very different from briquettes. Briquettes are made from compressed charcoal powder, often impregnated with an accelerant to get them started faster. Wood charcoal is natural—it's pieces of actual charred wood. Wood charcoal gives a more woodsy, smoky, flavorful taste.

Succulent Stuffed Filet Mignon

Serves 4

This is an elegant
entrée for a special
dinner. It's easy to
double the recipe to
serve 8. Do everything
but the grilling in
advance.

2 garlic cloves, minced
2 shallots, minced
1 cup chopped mushrooms
½ cup melted butter or olive oil
½ cup soft breadcrumbs
Salt and pepper to taste
2 tablespoons parsley, finely
    chopped

½ teaspoon red pepper flakes
    (optional)
4 very thick filets mignon
4 wooden toothpicks, soaked
    for 1 hour in water

1. Sauté the garlic, shallots, and mushrooms in the butter or oil over low
   heat for 10 minutes.
2. Add the breadcrumbs, salt, pepper, parsley, and red pepper flakes, if
   desired.
3. Cut slits in the side of each filet. Divide the stuffing between the 4
   filets and press into the "pockets." (At this point, you can refrigerate
   for up to 8 hours.)
4. Prepare the grill to medium-high.
5. Grill the filets for 5 minutes per side, then let them rest. Sauce and
   serve with oven fries and grilled asparagus.

Let It Rest

*There are some very good reasons for resting meat after cooking. First
is that the juices do not run out, they stay in the meat. Second, the
cooking continues in a very even way, giving you a piece of meat that
is nicely pink all the way through. Rest meat on a platter in a 150°F
oven for up to 10 minutes, depending on the thickness of the cut.*

London Broil with Italian-Style Marinade

½ cup olive oil
1 cup dry red wine
Juice of ½ lemon (fresh only,
   please)
2 cloves garlic, minced
3 whole cloves
1 teaspoon dry English mustard

1 teaspoon celery salt
2 drops Tabasco sauce,
   or to taste
10 peppercorns, bruised
2½ pounds shoulder or round
   steaks

> **Serves 4**
>
> Two cuts are alternatively used for London Broil: round and shoulder steaks. Round steak is more tender than shoulder steak.
>
>

1. Mix the olive oil, red wine, lemon juice, garlic cloves, whole cloves, mustard, celery salt, Tabasco sauce, and peppercorns together and pour them over the steak. Either seal with plastic wrap or place in a heavy-duty plastic bag. Turning every 2 hours, marinate for at least 4 hours.
2. Preheat the grill or prepare coals to medium-high.
3. Drain the steak and pat dry with paper towels. Broil on the hot grill, basting every few minutes with the marinade. It is okay to use the same marinade you used to baste the raw steaks, as that will burn off. Cook to desired state of doneness, about 6–8 minutes per side.
4. Be sure to rest steaks for at least 5 minutes and then slice on the diagonal, across the grain.

Meat Quality
What used to be labeled "prime" beef is mainly available to restaurants. Choice beef in supermarkets is what used to be called "Grade A." This is fine for stews, soups, burgers, and some steaks. Try to get prime for the best steaks. The higher the grading of the meat, the more fat marbles it. If you want to eat really lean beef, the best cut is round or filet mignon.

Dirty Steaks

Serves 4

This recipe requires that the steaks be cooked directly on, not over, the coals. Use wood charcoal, not briquettes.

2 prime rib eye steaks, about 2 pounds each if the bone is in

Salt and pepper to taste

1. Start the charcoal. (This cannot be done on gas or briquettes.)
2. Let the steaks reach room temperature, then dry thoroughly with paper towels and sprinkle with salt and pepper.
3. Place the meat directly on the coals and roast for 5–6 minutes per side.
4. Remove steaks from the coals and put on a platter. Brush off extra ash with paper towels. They will be very brown. Let the steaks rest, and trim off excess fat (if you wish). Then slice and serve.

Tender Herb-Crusted Rib Eye

Serves 4–6

Use steaks that are 1½ to 2 inches thick. You can also substitute a 4-pound sirloin or two 2-pound porterhouse steaks.

2 2-pound bone-in rib eye steaks or 2 porterhouse steaks
2 tablespoons unsalted butter, softened
2 tablespoons coarsely ground prepared brown mustard
1 teaspoon yellow mustard seeds

1 tablespoon Worcestershire sauce
1 teaspoon oregano, dried
2 tablespoons all-purpose flour
1 teaspoon onion powder
1 tablespoon garlic powder
Freshly ground black pepper

1. Prepare coals or light gas grill to preheat.
2. Let the steaks reach room temperature, then dry them with paper towels.
3. To make the mustard sauce, blend all other ingredients together, then paint steaks with the mustard mixture.
4. Grill to the desired level of doneness. Rest for 10 minutes, slice, and serve.

Big Sirloin Party

1 4–5-pound sirloin steak, fat
   on and bone in, cut thick

2 tablespoons Dijon-style prepared mustard
3 tablespoons A.1. steak sauce

1. Preheat gas grill or prepare coals.
2. Dry the steak with paper towels. Spread with mustard and sprinkle
   with A.1. sauce. Let steak stand until it reaches room temperature.
3. Grill to the desired state of doneness, about 8–10 minutes per side.
   Place steak on a platter in a warm oven to rest. Slice and serve.

> **Serves 6–8**
>
> It's hard to find a
> piece of meat
> boasting more flavor
> than a prime sirloin
> steak with the bone in.
>
>

Skirt and Flank Steaks

½ cup dry red wine
4 cloves mashed garlic
12 black peppercorns, bruised
   in a mortar and pestle
½ cup olive oil
2 teaspoons prepared mustard
1 teaspoon sea salt

1 teaspoon Tabasco sauce
2 teaspoons Asian fish sauce
1 1-inch strip fresh orange peel
½ inch piece gingerroot, peeled
   and minced
1 2-pound piece skirt or flank
   steak

1. Mix all ingredients except the steaks together, and pour over the meat,
   being sure to coat it completely. Place the meat and marinade in a
   closed container in the refrigerator. Marinate for 4–6 hours.
2. When ready to cook, heat grill to very hot.
3. Sear the steak on both sides. Because this is a thin cut of meat, you
   don't need to cook it for a long time. Bring the remaining marinade
   to a boil, and simmer for 10–15 minutes. Serve on the side.

> **Serves 4**
>
> These steaks are often
> fried in deep fat. Add
> chopped shallots,
> sliced onions, or chives
> to the marinade.
>
>

Philly Steak Sandwich
with Roasted Peppers and Cheese

Makes 4 sandwiches

High-quality white American cheese melts beautifully with this recipe. As a variation, you can make a Vermont cheese steak with sliced apples and sharp cheddar cheese.

2 large sweet red peppers,
  halved and seeded
2 teaspoons olive oil
4 cube steaks or 8 ¼-inch
  slices boneless sirloin
  (totaling 1½ pounds)
4 teaspoons butter (optional)

4 slices cheese
Sautéed or raw onions,
  to garnish
Italian dressing, Russian
  dressing, or steak sauce
4 hero rolls, split

1. Preheat the grill.
2. Brush the skins of the peppers with olive oil. Grill the peppers skin-side down until charred. Do not turn them.
3. Place the peppers in a plastic or paper bag. As they cool, the skins loosen and are easily removed.
4. Grill the steaks on one side for about 2 minutes; then turn the steaks and add butter and cheese. Remove and dress with onions and dressing or sauce of choice.
5. Put the rolls on the side to toast. Close the grill top to ensure well melted cheese. Remove from grill and assemble sandwiches, adding red peppers.

Pumping Iron
Some steaks can be very tough. A 5-pound metal barbell makes a wonderful pounder to flatten steak. Flatten the steak if you plan to stuff it and roll it.

Smoky Top Sirloin or Round Roast

1 teaspoon mustard seeds
1 tablespoon chili powder
1 tablespoon coarse salt
1 tablespoon black pepper,
* coarsely ground*
½ teaspoon ground cloves
½ teaspoon ground nutmeg

½ teaspoon ground coriander
½ teaspoon ground cumin
½ teaspoon ground paprika
1 teaspoon garlic powder
3–4 pounds top sirloin or top
* round roast*

Serves 6

Be sure to leave the
fat on the roast to
moisturize the meat.

1. Preheat the grill to medium-low, about 325°F or well-ashed coals.
2. Mix all the ingredients except the roast. Rub the mixture into the
   meat, and let it rest for an hour or until it reaches room temperature.
3. Brown the roast on all sides over direct heat on the grill.
4. Either set it aside on indirect heat, or turn down the gas. Close the
   lid of the grill. Roast until the internal temperature reaches 150°F.
5. Place in a warm (150°F) oven and let the roast rest for 15 minutes.
   It will continue to cook. Serve with onion mashed potatoes and packaged or canned gravy.

Finding the Right Age

*Round steaks and roasts can be exceptionally tough. Aged beef has
a full, rich flavor. Aging it involves hanging it at cool temperatures
for several days or weeks. Because the aging process requires lots
of space, restaurants that age their steaks will charge more for them.*

Kingly Veal Chops

½ cup unsalted soft butter
⅓ cup all-purpose flour
2 teaspoons balsamic vinegar
1 tablespoon white vermouth
¼ cup Dijon-style prepared mustard
2 tablespoons fresh rosemary leaves, chopped, or 1 tablespoon dried, crumbled

1 tablespoon thyme leaves, dried
Salt and pepper to taste
1 tablespoon lemon zest
1 teaspoon Worcestershire sauce
4 thick veal rib chops, 8–10 ounces each

1. Mix all ingredients except veal together.
2. Rinse the chops and pat them dry with paper towels. Pound the chops with a 5-pound weight until they have spread to double their original size.
3. Paint the "wet rub" on the chops. Arrange the chops in a glass baking pan so that they do not overlap. Cover and refrigerate for 3–6 hours.
4. Prepare the grill to medium high. Grill the chops until they are very brown on one side, about 4 minutes. Turn and continue to grill until just pink inside, about 4 more minutes.
5. Let the chops rest in a warm oven for 8–10 minutes before serving.

Lemon Zest

When a recipe calls for lemon zest, it's important to start with a fresh lemon that you have washed and dried. Then, take the fine side of a box grater and work your way around the lemon. There are also little tools for making lemon zest, but you must be careful not to get any of the white pith along with the good yellow skin. The oil is in the skin and perfumes the food you are preparing.

Mushroom Steak Sauce

1 package Asian black mushrooms (about 2 ounces)
2 tablespoons butter
2 tablespoons flour
1 shallot, minced
2 cups button mushrooms,
   brushed, stems removed,
   and sliced
1 cup porcini (Italian brown)
   mushrooms, brushed, stems
   removed, and sliced
2 cups beef broth
1 cup dry red wine
1 teaspoon Worcestershire sauce
1 teaspoon dried thyme
Salt and lots of freshly ground
   pepper

> **Makes about 2 cups**
>
> The Asian black mush-
> rooms add an amazing
> depth of flavor and
> are available in Asian
> markets and many
> supermarkets.
>
>

1. Break the dried black mushrooms in pieces and cover in cool water to soak for about 30 minutes.
2. Melt the butter over low heat and stir in the flour. Cook for three minutes, or until the flour is golden. Add the shallot and button and porcini mushrooms, stirring.
3. Warm the beef broth (to prevent the flour from getting lumpy) and stir it into the sauce. Then add the wine, Worcestershire sauce, and thyme. Simmer, stirring constantly, until the mushrooms are soft.
4. Add the black mushrooms, with their liquid; cover; and simmer for 10–15 minutes. Season with salt and pepper to taste.

Substitutions!

Green peppercorns can be used instead of ground black pepper. You can substitute packaged brown gravy for the butter, flour, and beef broth—simply sauté the minced shallot in a teaspoon of butter and omit the flour.

Lemon Pepper Steak Marinade

Makes ½ cup

This will tenderize a steak but it's also wonderful with seafood, lamb, and chicken. Adjust the heat and saltiness to taste.

Zest of 1 lemon (about ⅓ cup)
Juice of 1 lemon
1 teaspoon yellow mustard seed
1 teaspoon dried red pepper
  flakes, or to taste
1 tablespoon freshly ground
  black pepper

1 teaspoon Tabasco sauce,
  or to taste
¼ teaspoon cayenne pepper
1 teaspoon sea salt

Mix all ingredients together. Let rest for 1 hour to marry flavors. Store in the refrigerator. This will keep for at least a week.

Sweet and Spicy Steak Sauce

Makes 2 cups

The caramelized sugar in this recipe is not as sweet as it may sound. This makes a delicious barbecue sauce.

1 cup sugar
½ cup onions, minced
½ cup shallots, minced
4 jalapeño peppers, seeds and
  ribs removed, minced
½ cup lemon juice

2 cups beef broth
½ cup white wine
1 teaspoon Worcestershire sauce
Salt and freshly ground black
  pepper to taste

1. Place the sugar in a frying pan with a fairly thin bottom. Heat until the sugar melts—it's ready when it's a rich brown.
2. Add the onions, shallots, and peppers, stirring constantly. Cook over low heat until soft, about 3 minutes.
3. Add the rest of the ingredients and simmer, stirring occasionally. Reduce to about 1 cup, cool, and store until ready to serve with steak. Garnish with fresh parsley and chives.

Tomato and Vegetable Steak Topping

2 ears grilled corn, niblets cut off (see page 129)

2 sweet red peppers, grilled (see page 48) or fresh

1 sweet green pepper, grilled (see page 48) or fresh

2 ripe tomatoes, cored and chopped (yellow tomatoes work well)

1 medium (3 inches across) portobello mushroom, grilled and sliced

1 large red onion, peeled and sliced thinly

2 garlic cloves, slivered

½ cup extra virgin olive oil

¼ cup balsamic vinegar

2 tablespoons red wine vinegar

1 tablespoon lime juice (fresh only)

Red pepper flakes to taste

½ cup of a variety of fresh herbs such as basil, thyme, oregano, parsley, chives, rosemary; chopped

¼ teaspoon ground coriander

Salt and freshly ground black pepper to taste

> **Makes 2 cups
> (serves 4)**
>
> You can and should freely mix fresh and grilled vegetables. This is wonderful on steak sandwiches.
>
>

Mix all ingredients together in a large bowl. Do not worry about uniformity. Cover and refrigerate for 2 hours to settle. This keeps for a week in the refrigerator.

Aromatic Vegetables Add Flavor

The flavor base for stuffing starts with a mirepoix, which is an assortment of chopped vegetables and seasonings cooked slowly in butter, oil, or rendered bacon fat. Onions and celery are a starting point for the basic mix, along with garlic, bell peppers, leeks, carrots, fennel, and shallots.

Mushroom Ragout

½ onion, thinly sliced
1 tablespoon butter or olive oil
2 cups mixed mushrooms (shi-
    itakes, criminis, portobellos)

1 cup chicken broth
¼ cup dry red wine
Salt and pepper to taste
2 ounces heavy cream (optional)

1. Sauté onions in butter until well caramelized.
2. Add mushrooms and cook until reduced, stirring frequently.
3. Add the chicken broth and red wine, and cook until reduced to 1 cup.
4. Add salt and pepper, cream if desired.

Tropical Boneless Chicken Breasts

4 skinless, boneless chicken breasts weighing 6–7 ounces each
½ cup chili sauce
½ cup orange juice
2 tablespoons orange juice concentrate

Juice of ½ lemon
¼ teaspoon Tabasco sauce, or to taste
½ teaspoon ground cardamom
2 tablespoons vegetable oil

1. Rinse the chicken breasts in cool water, dry with paper towels, and place in a nonreactive (plastic or glass) container.
2. Whisk remaining ingredients together and pour over the chicken breasts. Marinate for 5–6 hours.
3. Heat the grill to medium heat—about 350°F.
4. Sear the chicken and then move off direct heat or lower gas.
5. Use remaining marinade to baste in the first few minutes—the marinade will burn off when you cook it. Discard any remaining marinade. Continue to sear the chicken until done. Serve on a bed of greens. Garnish with fresh orange slices.

Keeping It Juicy and Delicious

There is a fine line between juicy and delicious and all dried out. Cooking time varies according to the thickness of the breasts and the heat of the grill. Cut into the breast and make sure that it is densely white all the way through. If it looks even a bit gelatinous, put it back on the grill.

Stuffed Boneless Chicken Breasts

4 boneless, skinless chicken breasts, 6–7 ounces each
Salt and pepper to taste
2 shallots, minced
4 small porcini mushrooms, cleaned and chopped
½ cup extra virgin olive oil
⅛ pound prosciutto or Virginia ham, minced
1 teaspoon rosemary, dried, or 2 teaspoons fresh, chopped
1 teaspoon oregano, dried, or 2 teaspoons fresh
2 tablespoons fresh parsley, chopped
Freshly ground black pepper to taste
⅔ cup fresh, soft breadcrumbs from a loaf of French or Italian bread
2 tablespoons vegetable oil

> **Serves 4**
>
> This delicious entrée can be partially cooked in advance, with the final cooking done in the oven. Omit salt because the ham is already salty.
>
>

1. Rinse and dry the chicken breasts. Place them, one at a time, between two layers of waxed paper. Pound them until they are quite thin, about ⅓ inch thick.
2. Sprinkle the breasts on both sides with salt and pepper.
3. To make the stuffing, sauté the shallots and mushrooms in olive oil until soft, then add the ham and herbs. Mix the crumbs into the stuffing. Season with pepper. If it seems dry, add a tablespoon or two of olive oil.
4. To assemble for grilling, place 1 tablespoon stuffing on each chicken breast. Roll the breasts and secure with wooden toothpicks.
5. Prepare the grill to medium.
6. Brush the breasts with oil, then grill until brown on all sides. Finish cooking at 275°F for 20 minutes.

Apples for Mushrooms?

You can substitute ½ tart apple, chopped, for the mushrooms in this recipe. For a great big calorie splurge, spoon on Fast Perfect Hollandaise Sauce (page 240). Serve with rice or orzo (rice-shaped pasta) and grilled baby artichokes.

Lemon Garlic Chicken Legs and Thighs

Serves 4

This is excellent with potato salad (see page 252 or 253). Cooking slowly is important— the apple butter will brown quickly and could burn.

4 cloves garlic, peeled and chopped
1–2 jalapeño peppers, cored and chopped, or if you like it really hot, 2 red chili peppers
2 tablespoons butter
2 cups canned crushed tomatoes, drained
2 tablespoons tomato paste
½ cup apple butter
Juice of 1 lemon
Zest of ½ lemon
½ teaspoon celery salt
Salt, ground black pepper, and red pepper flakes to taste
4 chicken leg and thigh pieces

1. Sauté the garlic and peppers in butter over medium-low flame, until soft.
2. Add the rest of the ingredients (except the chicken). Taste for seasonings, adding salt if necessary. Simmer on very low heat until reduced to 1¼ cups.
3. Prepare your grill until coals are ash-covered, or set the gas at 350°F.
4. If the chicken pieces are large, separate the drumsticks from the thighs. Brush the legs and thighs with sauce. Grill well above the coals or flames.
5. Keep brushing with sauce and turning. To check if chicken is done, insert a meat thermometer and make sure the internal temperature is at least 155°F at the thickest part of the chicken.

Making Broth
You will find that making broth with the necks and innards of chickens and game hens provides a useful addition to soups and sauces. Adding a little white wine, a piece of onion, and half a stalk of celery will enhance the flavor.

Hot-Hot Football Wings

1 cup vegetable oil
1 pound butter
1 cup of your favorite hot sauce (Tabasco, Red Pepper, Pikapepper, or African hot sauce)

1 tablespoon salt or celery salt
¼ cup cider vinegar
2 tablespoons Worcestershire sauce
10 pounds wings

Serves 4 to 6

These are just what you want with beer or soda when watching an afternoon game.

1. Mix all of the ingredients (except the wings) together and keep warm in a large saucepan.
2. Rinse the wings and dry them on paper towels. Brush the wings with vegetable oil on both sides.
3. Set the grill to medium-high.
4. Grill until just lightly browned. These are done in just about 3 minutes per side. Use tongs to take the wings off the grill. Dip in the sauce and serve with lots and lots of paper napkins.

Not Too Hot!

You can lessen the heat by cutting down on the hot sauce if your crowd is young. Try to put out something bland and cool, like an artichoke or spinach dip with lots of sour cream, to counteract the heat of the wings.

Devilishly Good Deviled Cornish Game Hens

Serves 4

Make extras and serve cold for lunch the next day. Potato salad (page 252 or 253) or Colorful Coleslaw (page 247) is a perfect accompaniment.

2 large or 4 small Cornish game hens
2 tablespoons dry English mustard
2 tablespoons cold water
Coarse salt and black or white pepper to taste

½ cup dry (white) vermouth
2 tablespoons quick-blending flour (Wondra)
2 tablespoons soft butter
2 tablespoons honey (optional)
1 teaspoon thyme or rosemary, dried, crumbled

1. Rinse the hens and pat them dry. If large, cut them in half. Reserve the necks, livers, hearts, and gizzards for broth or sauce base.
2. In a bowl, make a paste with the mustard and water, stirring until well blended. Whisk the rest of the ingredients (except hens) into the bowl. Paint the deviling mixture on the birds on both sides. Rest in a pan in the refrigerator until ready to cook.
3. Set the grill to medium-low or wait until coals are covered with white ash.
4. Grill with skin-side down first, until brown. Then turn and grill the cut side until brown. The cooking time will depend on the size of the birds. Check for doneness with a meat thermometer. When they reach 155°F, the hens are done. Place hens on a platter and let rest for 10 minutes.

Game Hen Size

Game hens come in two sizes: Large ones run about 1 to 1½ pounds each; small hens are under 1 pound each. If you get the smaller ones, serve a hen per person. The larger ones, cut in half, will serve 2. Large or small, hot or cold, they are terrific.

Classic Cornish Game Hens
with Orange Glaze

2 large or 4 small game hens
2 tablespoons butter
4 scallions, chopped
2 teaspoons fresh gingerroot,
  peeled and minced
4 tablespoons dry white wine

1 teaspoon hot sauce such as
  Tabasco
1 tablespoon Worcestershire
  sauce
½ cup marmalade
Coarse salt to taste

Serves 4

This recipe is unbelievably good!
Serve with rice and
a salad of watercress
and sprouts.

1. Cut the game hens in half. Rinse and pat dry with paper towels.
2. To make the glaze, melt the butter; add the scallions and ginger. Add the rest of the ingredients (except game hens) and heat in a small saucepan, stirring until the marmalade melts.
3. Set the gas grill at medium, or for a charcoal grill, mound the coals on one side. Set the grill 5–6 inches above the flame or coals.
4. Broil the hens over direct heat, cut-side down, for 8–10 minutes, depending on their size. Brush the skin with glaze.
5. Turn the hens, skin-side down. Grill until very brown; then, turn and place on indirect heat and close cover. Do not burn but make sure the internal temperature reaches 155°F.

The Importance of a Meat Thermometer

It is most important to use a meat thermometer to check the doneness of all poultry. Poultry carries a nasty bacteria called salmonella, which can cause diarrhea in an adult and can kill a small child. Salmonella is eliminated by heat, so it is essential to heat all parts of the poultry to a temperature (155°F) high enough to kill the bacteria.

Southeast Asian Cornish Game Hens with Tamarind Glaze

Serves 4

Serve with couscous or rice and grilled eggplant or a lentil salad.

½ cup (4 ounces) tamarind paste
1 cup orange juice
3 tablespoons light brown sugar
Juice of 2 fresh limes
Juice of 1 fresh lemon
Salt to taste
1 teaspoon Tabasco sauce, or to taste
2 large or 4 small game hens
Salt and pepper

1. Mix all of the ingredients except the last two in a saucepan and simmer until smooth and thickened, about 15 minutes. Set aside.
2. Split the hens, if large; rinse; and dry on paper towels. Sprinkle both sides with salt and pepper.
3. Set grill to 325°F or prepare coals for both direct and indirect heat.
4. Start the hens over direct flame, cut-side down. Grill for 10 minutes or until well browned.
5. Turn and brush on glaze. Grill until well browned. Place off direct heat and cover the grill. (Because of the sugar in the glaze, these hens will burn easily.) When internal temperature reaches 155°F, arrange the hens on a large, warm platter. Spoon tamarind sauce over hens and serve.

Tart Tamarind

Tamarind is very popular in Asian, Middle Eastern, and Hawaiian cooking. Tamarind is a delicious pulp, made from a pod. It has a tart and exotic flavor. It's available in Asian and Middle Eastern markets and some supermarkets. Tamarind paste comes in hard, 8-ounce blocks or jars of about 1 pound. Be sure that you buy the seedless paste; otherwise, it must be strained. The process is to cut a cube off the block and soak it until it softens. Then, you can use it in a number of delicious ways.

Grilled Turkey Breast with Bacon

1 turkey breast, about 6 pounds
1/2 teaspoon ground cloves
1 teaspoon dried thyme leaves,
    crumbled
1 teaspoon dried rosemary
    leaves, crumbled

1/2 teaspoon salt
Freshly ground black pepper
    to taste
3/4 stick unsalted butter,
    at room temperature
3–4 slices bacon

Serves 8–10

Serve hot with commercial gravy or salsa. Leftover turkey breast can be transformed the next day into turkey salad, turkey sandwiches, or turkey à la king!

1. Rinse the turkey breast and pat dry with towels. Split the breast lengthwise but leave sides connected.
2. In a small bowl, mix together the cloves, thyme, rosemary, salt, and pepper. Using a fork, mash the herbs and spices with softened butter.
3. Tease 3/4 of the mixture under the skin of the turkey and rub the rest into both sides of the bird.
4. Drape the turkey with strips of bacon and secure them with skewers.
5. Roast the turkey for about 20 minutes per pound at 350°F, if you have a gas grill, or medium-hot coals, lid closed. Don't try to save the bacon; it will get too brown to eat. It will keep the bird moist, though.

Better Butter

Why use unsalted butter instead of lightly salted butter? Unsalted butter does not burn as easily as that with salt in it. The cream used in sweet butter is also fresher and of better quality. Salt acts as a preservative and masks flavors. You can always add salt for flavor.

Grilled Duck Breasts
with Calvados and Apples

Serves 4

The marinade makes this delicious and elegant. The recipe calls for a luscious sauce made from the marinade.

For marinade:
½ cup Calvados or other
   apple brandy
1¾ cups chicken broth
½ cup chopped onion
1 teaspoon dark brown sugar
1 tablespoon currant jelly
1 teaspoon dried sage, or 4
   fresh sage leaves, chopped
¼ teaspoon ground cloves
Salt and pepper to taste

2 tart apples, peeled, cored,
   and chopped
4 boneless, skinless duck
   breasts, ¼ to ⅓ pound
   each
Salt, pepper, and ground
   coriander to sprinkle over
   breasts
½ cup heavy cream
2 tablespoons butter, melted

1. Bring all marinade ingredients to a boil. When the apples are very soft, remove from heat and cool.
2. Rinse the duck breasts in cool water and dry on paper towels. Sprinkle with salt, pepper, and ground coriander. Place the duck breasts in a glass pan or other nonreactive pan and cover with half the marinade, which should be about 1 cup. Cover with plastic wrap and marinate the duck breasts in the refrigerator for 4–6 hours, turning once halfway through.
3. Set grill on high, about 475°F. While heating, make the sauce by bringing the marinade that has not been used on the duck to a boil. Add heavy cream and set aside.
4. Brush the ducks with melted butter or oil and grill for about 3 minutes per side or until well browned. Place off direct heat to rest and then add the sauce. Garnish with sprigs of fresh parsley, chopped roasted chestnuts, or toasted walnuts.

Silky Grilled Duck Liver Spread (Foie Gras)

*1 pound fresh or frozen duck
  livers*
2 tablespoons olive oil
Nonstick cooking spray
¼ teaspoon ground cloves
¼ teaspoon ground allspice

¼ teaspoon ground nutmeg
2 tablespoons good sherry
½ cup unsalted butter, softened
*1 tablespoon onion, finely
  minced*
Salt and pepper to taste

1. Brush the livers with olive oil.
2. Prepare the coals or set the gas on medium-high. Spray a piece of grilling mesh with nonstick spray.
3. Place the duck livers on the grill, and grill for about 2 minutes on each side. Cut one open to make sure that it is barely pink in the center. Remove from heat and cool.
4. Place the cooled livers in a food processor. Add the rest of the ingredients and whirl until smooth. Pack in a jar and chill. When ready to eat, spread on sliced baguettes or toast points. Enjoy with gherkins.

Poultry Loves Herbs
There is hardly an herb that does not go well with chicken, duck, game hens, and so forth. Some mixtures make wonderful accompaniments and add dimension to sauces. Try mixing sage and oregano. Italian flat-leaf parsley is tastier and more intense in flavor than curly parsley. When you are making a gravy or cream sauce, throw in some dried lavender flowers for a pungent and different flavor.

Serves 10 as canapés

This is very rich, so make sure you put out raw vegetables, grilled vegetables, and nice light dips made with low-fat yogurt.

Holiday Grilled Pheasant
with Currant Glaze

Serves 4

Serve with wild rice salad in the summer and hot wild rice in the winter. Try some grilled squash on the side, too.

1 cup currant jelly
½ cup claret
2 bay leaves
1-inch strip orange peel

⅛ teaspoon ground cloves
2 pheasants, 3–3½ pounds each,
    cut into 4 quarters each
4 strips bacon

1. Mix all of the ingredients except the pheasants and bacon in a saucepan. Simmer over low heat until reduced by half. Remove bay leaves and set glaze aside.
2. Set the gas grill to medium or prepare the coals.
3. Rinse the pheasant pieces and dry on paper towels. Cut the strips of bacon in half and wrap them around the pieces of pheasant, securing them with small metal skewers.
4. Grill pheasant until the bacon is charred. Then place the pheasant pieces on a platter and remove the bacon. Brush the pheasants with glaze and return to the grill, setting them over indirect heat or reducing the temperature of the gas.
5. Continue to grill, basting with glaze, until the glaze begins to caramelize. Place on a warm platter and serve.

Delicate Pheasant

Because pheasants are so very lean, they must be treated very carefully on the grill or they will dry out and toughen.

Grilled Turkey Legs and Thighs with Herb Butter

1 turkey leg and thigh quarter (about 3–4 pounds)
½ cup butter, softened
¼ cup fresh Italian flat-leaf parsley, minced

2 teaspoons dried thyme
2 teaspoons dried basil
½ teaspoon anise seeds
1 teaspoon lemon peel, minced
Freshly ground white pepper

1. Rinse the turkey and dry on paper towels.
2. Mix the rest of the ingredients together.
3. Prepare coals on one side of the grill, placing a drip pan under where the turkey will cook. Reduce the heat to medium-low.
4. Gently pull the skin of the turkey away from the thigh and tease the butter mixture in between the skin and the meat, pushing it all the way into the leg. Be careful not to tear the turkey skin. Rub the outside of the turkey's skin with some of the butter-and-herb mixture.
5. Grill until the internal temperature reaches 155°F. Then let the bird rest for 10 minutes and serve.
6. To make gravy with the drippings, add quick-blending flour and 1 cup of chicken broth to the drip pan.

> **Serves 4–6**
>
> This is an inexpensive meal that tastes like a million! Serve it with grilled corn salad and make some nice creamy mashed potatoes.
>
>

Water Birds

Ducks and geese are water birds—they swim as well as fly. Thus, they have a coating of fat under their skin to keep them warm and afloat. There are many ways of dealing with all this fat. When roasting, you may pour boiling water over the duck or goose and prick it with a fork. This procedure makes the fat run out. However, it is not practical to pour water on your grill or to have fat spritzing on the coals or gas. To reduce flame, move meat away from flame. (Pheasants are quite the reverse of ducks. They have practically no fat at all.)

Roasted Cornish Game Hens with Stuffing

4 small game hens
4 teaspoons vegetable oil
2 large pears, peeled, cored, and coarsely chopped
2 cups corn bread stuffing mix
2 teaspoons dried sage, crumbled, or four fresh leaves, shredded
½ cup chicken broth for stuffing
½ cup dry white wine
Zest of ½ lemon
½ cup celery tops, rinsed and chopped
1 teaspoon celery salt

2 ounces (½ stick) butter, melted, for stuffing
2 tablespoons butter for sauce
2 shallots, minced
2 tablespoons quick-blending flour (Wondra)
2 teaspoons Dijon-style prepared mustard
½ cup warm chicken or hen broth for sauce
½ cup heavy cream
⅛ teaspoon ground nutmeg
Salt and freshly ground white pepper to taste

1. Rinse the game hens and pat dry with paper towels. Salt and pepper the cavities of the hens. Rub with vegetable oil and set aside.
2. To make fresh broth, simmer the necks and innards in salted water to cover, over low heat, for 20 minutes. Set aside for use in sauce.
3. In a bowl, mix together the pears, cornbread stuffing mix, sage, chicken broth, wine, lemon zest, celery tops, celery salt, pepper, and melted butter. The stuffing should be very moist but not runny. Check for moistness and add more broth if necessary.
4. Divide the stuffing between the birds, pressing into the cavities from the rear. Using small metal skewers, close the cavities.
5. Roast over medium-low heat coals or set gas to 325°F. Roast, browning hens nicely for 20 minutes, with the top of the grill closed. Turn the hens and roast for another 15 minutes. Make sure a meat thermometer reaches at least 155°F in the thickest part of the thigh. Remove from grill and rest the hens on a warm platter for 10 minutes. Remove the skewers.

6. To make the sauce, melt the butter and add the minced shallots over medium heat. When the shallots are soft, whisk in the flour and mustard to make a smooth paste.
7. Stir in the broth and simmer gently until thickened and reduced.
8. Add the cream and warm. Remove from the heat. Season with nutmeg and salt and pepper. Serve sauce on the side with the hens.

Are You Game?

Ducks, geese, and pheasants used to be considered game birds. Today, they can be considered either because they are farmed, just like chickens.

Chunky Fruit and Herb Sauce for Poultry

½ cup dried cherries
½ cup dry white wine
⅓ stick cinnamon
2 bay leaves
2 tablespoons fresh parsley, rinsed and chopped
4 fresh sage leaves, shredded, or 1 teaspoon dried

6 fresh basil leaves, shredded, or 1 tablespoon dried
½ teaspoon dried tarragon
2 tablespoons butter
2 tablespoons shallots, peeled and minced
2 tablespoons flour
1 cup chicken broth

> **Makes 1½ cups**
>
> This sauce is good on any chicken, duck, turkey, or other poultry dish. It's simple to make and can be frozen for up to three months.
>
>

1. Mix the cherries, wine, cinnamon, bay leaves, parsley, sage, basil, and tarragon in a saucepan. Bring to a boil, then turn off the heat. Set aside.
2. Melt the butter and add the shallots. Stir until shallots soften, about 4 minutes. Stir in the flour and cook for another 3 minutes.
3. Mix in the chicken broth and the cherry/wine mixture. Stir and cook until thick and delicious. Remove bay leaves. Serve with any poultry.

Chestnut Cranberry Poultry Sauce

Makes 4 cups

This delicious variation on a classic is a versatile addition for any occasion, from holidays to everyday fun.

2 bags cranberries, washed and picked over to remove stems
2 hot chilies (such as jalapeño or Scotch bonnet)
Water to cover
1½–2 cups sugar

1-inch piece gingerroot, peeled and chopped
½ orange, seeded and chopped
2 pounds chestnuts, scored and roasted until they pop

1. Place the cranberries, chilies, water, and sugar in a large pot. Bring to a boil and then reduce heat to a simmer.
2. After about 10 minutes, add the gingerroot and orange.
3. While the cranberries are cooking, remove shells and skins from the chestnuts. Chop the chestnuts coarsely. Add chestnuts and cook until thick and syrupy, about 30 minutes.
4. Jar and store in the refrigerator for up to 3 weeks.

Orange-Cranberry Relish for Poultry

Makes 6 cups

In the days of the hand grinder, this took most of a day. My friend Nancy's great-great-grandmother taught me this one.

2 bags cranberries, rinsed and picked over for stems
2 sweet, thick-skinned oranges, seeded and chopped
½ grapefruit, seeded and cut into chunks

1 lemon, cut into quarters and seeded
3 cups sugar

Put the fruit in a food processor and chop coarsely (but do not purée). Then scrape it into a big, nonreactive bowl. Add the sugar, stir, cover, and refrigerate. Let the relish ripen for a week before using.

Lamb

Herb-Crusted Baby Rack of Lamb

2 racks of lamb, about 8 ribs each, well trimmed
Slice of fresh lemon
Salt and pepper
1 cup soft (homemade) breadcrumbs
½ cup olive oil or melted butter
2 cloves garlic, minced

2 scallions (both green and white parts), chopped
½ cup Italian flat-leaf parsley, chopped fine
4 fresh sage leaves, shredded, or 1 teaspoon dried sage
Plenty of freshly ground pepper

1. Rub the lamb with the cut lemon. Sprinkle the lamb with salt and pepper.
2. Set gas grill on high. If using coals, mound them on one side of the grill basin so that you will provide both direct and indirect heat.
3. Mix together the breadcrumbs, oil or butter, garlic, scallions, herbs, and pepper. Depending on the dryness of the crumbs, you may want to add more oil or butter. Set aside.
4. Grill the lamb over direct heat, bone-side down, for 5 minutes. Turn and grill, meat-side down, over direct heat for five minutes.
5. Move the lamb to the indirect heat or reduce the heat of the gas grill. With the lamb meat-side up, press the crust onto the meat. Cover with the lid and roast at about 400°F for 10 minutes. The lamb should be pink on the inside and the crust delicious and crisp. Cut chops apart gently before serving.

Distinguishing Lamb and Mutton

Mutton comes from a full-grown sheep. Though popular in England, it is strong to American tastes and much tougher than young lamb. If you can find a Greek, Italian, or Middle Eastern butcher, you may be able to get really young lamb. It's worth the extra trouble and expense for its fine flavor and tenderness. Lamb fat is strong and must be removed before cooking. Also, lamb is better served medium-rare, as overcooking toughens it.

Nut-Crusted Baby Rack of Lamb

2 racks of lamb, about 8 ribs each, well trimmed
1 slice of fresh lemon
Salt and pepper
¾ cup soft (homemade) breadcrumbs
½ cup hazelnuts, finely chopped
⅔ cup unsalted butter, melted
1 teaspoon ground coriander seeds
½ teaspoon dried red pepper flakes, or to taste
1 teaspoon fresh lemon zest, finely minced

> **Serves 4**
>
> Baby rack of lamb is perfect for a special family occasion.

1. Rub the lamb with the cut lemon. Sprinkle the lamb with salt and pepper.
2. Set gas grill on high. If using coals, mound them on one side of the grill basin so that you will provide both direct and indirect heat.
3. Mix the breadcrumbs, nuts, butter, coriander, red pepper flakes, and lemon zest. Depending on the dryness of the crumbs, you may want to add more butter. Set aside.
4. Grill the lamb over direct heat, bone-side down, for 5 minutes.
5. Turn and grill, meat-side down, over direct heat for five minutes.
6. Move the lamb to the indirect heat or reduce the heat of the gas grill. With the lamb meat-side up, press the crust onto the meat. Cover with the lid and roast at about 400°F for 10 minutes. The lamb should be pink on the inside and the crust golden, delicious, and crisp. Cut chops apart gently to keep crust on securely.

Tenderizing the Lamb

Lamb works exceptionally well with lemons, tomatoes, all kinds of wines, garlic, and most herbs. Really young lamb does not need tenderizing, but an older one will need a good soak in a marinade. The citrus and wine break down the tough fibers while adding to the flavor.

Sicilian-Style Lamb Steaks

Serves 4

This recipe is based on a classic marinating technique to produce a delicious flavor!

2 1½-inch-thick lamb steaks, about a pound each, bone in
Salt and ground pepper to taste
2 cloves garlic, mashed
½ medium onion, peeled and sliced
Tops from a small bunch of celery
2 bay leaves
½ lemon, sliced thinly
½ teaspoon ground coriander
1 teaspoon dried thyme
3 whole cloves, bruised
1 teaspoon Tabasco sauce
⅔ cup dry red wine such as burgundy
½ cup olive oil

1. Sprinkle the steaks with salt and pepper.
2. Mix the rest of the ingredients together in a glass pan to make marinade. Place steaks in pan, cover, and marinate overnight, turning them a few times while they marinate.
3. Set grill to medium heat.
4. Grill the steaks for 5 minutes per side, basting frequently with the marinade. You may use the same marinade you used to soak the steaks, just make sure that it all burns off on the grill.
5. Place the steaks on a platter and keep warm for 10 minutes in a 150°F oven. The meat will continue to cook and become more juicy if it's allowed to rest. Slice thinly on a slant and serve.

The Pleasures of Lamb Steaks

Lamb steaks are cut from the leg and are tastier and more tender when marinated. Lamb is fine with rice, potatoes, and any greens.

Stuffed Rib Lamb Chops

*4 double rib lamb chops, about
    ½ pound each, trimmed of fat
4 thin slices lemon, with peel
4 half-cloves garlic, cut lengthways*

*4 leaves fresh mint
Salt and pepper
4 thin pats unsalted butter*

1. Have the butcher make a long slit through the thickest part of the chops, following the bone. Fill the slits with the lemon slices, garlic, and mint leaves. Sprinkle with salt and pepper to taste, and put a pat of butter on top of each chop.
2. Set grill to medium-high heat.
3. Grill about 7 minutes per side, or until the chops are well browned on both sides.
4. When the chops are almost ready to serve, place on a platter in a 150°F oven to rest and finish cooking.

Serves 4

This is one of the most delicious cuts of lamb, slightly more mature than a baby rack. Serve with creamy whipped potatoes and green vegetables.

Mint-Butter Sauce for Lamb

*½ cup unsalted butter
2 teaspoons fresh chives, minced
¾ cup fresh mint leaves,
    chopped and loosely packed*

*½ cup white (dry) vermouth
2 tablespoons lemon juice
Salt and pepper to taste*

Heat the butter in a saucepan and add the herbs. Add the rest of the ingredients and bring to a boil. Serve warm.

Makes 1 cup

This is wonderful with any of the lamb recipes in this chapter. It is also good with chicken.

Italian Easter-Style Leg of Lamb

1 6-pound leg of lamb,
   trimmed of all fat
Salt and pepper
Ground coriander
6 cloves garlic, peeled and
   slivered the long way
2 cups white vermouth
½ cup olive oil
2 sprigs fresh thyme

2 sprigs fresh parsley
2 sprigs fresh rosemary
1 whole lemon, sliced
½ onion, peeled and sliced
1 rib celery with leaves,
   coarsely chopped
2 anchovy fillets
2 slices bacon

1. Make sure that all of the fat is trimmed from the lamb. Sprinkle with salt, pepper, and ground coriander, rubbing them into the flesh. Make slits along the leg bone and here and there in the meat, sticking the halved garlic cloves in as deeply as possible.
2. Mix together the rest of the ingredients (except the bacon) to make the marinade. Place the lamb in a large glass pan and pour the marinade over it. Cover and refrigerate overnight. During the night, turn the lamb occasionally. Two hours before cooking, take the lamb out of the refrigerator and let it come to room temperature.
3. Prepare grill to medium-high. If using coals, mound so that you can use both direct and indirect heat.
4. Put the remaining marinade from the lamb in a saucepan and reduce. This will be used as a basting sauce.
5. Remove the lamb from the marinade and place it on a piece of aluminum foil on the grill over direct heat. When the lamb is brown on one side, turn it and brown the other side, keeping a piece of foil directly under the meat. Add the bacon after turning meat.
6. Baste occasionally with the marinade. Place on indirect heat and continue to roast, covered, for 16 minutes per pound for medium.
7. Place on a platter and keep warm in a low oven until ready to serve.

Young Leg of Lamb Marinated in Sweet Vermouth

*4 cloves garlic, peeled and cut
    in half*
*5–6 pounds young leg of lamb,
    fat trimmed away*
Salt and pepper
6 bay leaves

1 teaspoon mustard seeds
*1 cup Italian (sweet red)
    vermouth*
Juice of 1 lemon
¼ cup olive oil

> **Serves 6–8**
>
> The marinade can also be used (make extra!) to glaze new potatoes, cut in half and grilled.
>
>

1. Stick the garlic into slits cut in the lamb. Sprinkle with salt and pepper. Soak the bay leaves in a little water. Add the remaining ingredients to a glass baking pan, and add the lamb and the soaked bay leaves.
2. Turn the lamb in the marinade to make sure it is well coated. Cover and marinate for 8 hours, turning every 2 hours.
3. Set grill to medium.
4. Brown the lamb on all sides and move it off direct flame. Grill for 18 minutes per pound, basting occasionally.
5. Remove from the heat when the internal temperature reaches at least 145°F for rare, 155°F for medium, or 170°F for well done. Let rest in a warm oven for 15 minutes before carving.

An Ancient Spice

Mustard recipes have been closely guarded secrets for hundreds of years. An ancient spice, the Greeks ate the leaves as a vegetable and rubbed the seeds into their meat and seafood. The Romans brought mustard to Gaul, where it was adopted. The English are famous for their hot yellow mustard powder. Mustard grows wild, a weed in many areas of the United States

Spinach-Stuffed Boneless Leg of Lamb

5-pound boneless leg of lamb,
  all fat removed
Salt and pepper
Juice of 1 lemon
2 tablespoons butter
2 cloves garlic, minced

½ cup sweet onion, chopped
1 package frozen spinach,
  thawed and drained
¼ teaspoon ground nutmeg
½ cup fine breadcrumbs
¼ cup olive oil

1. If the lamb is rolled and tied, unroll it. Trim any fat and gristle from the lamb and place lamb on a large piece of waxed paper. Sprinkle the lamb with salt, pepper, and lemon juice on both sides.
2. Melt the butter in a saucepan, and add the garlic and onion. Sauté the garlic and onion until soft, about 5 minutes. Be sure *not* to brown or burn.
3. Add the spinach and cook, stirring for 5 minutes. If dry, add more butter to keep it moist.
4. Add the nutmeg and breadcrumbs. Stir until well mixed and hot.
5. Spread the spinach mixture over the lamb. Roll the lamb and tie with kitchen string. At this point, you can refrigerate for 6–8 hours and cook later. Be sure to let the lamb stand until it comes to room temperature before cooking.
6. Heat the grill to medium.
7. Sprinkle the lamb with olive oil. Brown the lamb all over. Set off direct flame and cover the grill. When the internal temperature is at least 150°F, place in a warming oven to rest (it will continue cooking). Serve when it reaches 155°F.

And to Accompany Your Lamb . . .

Lamb is versatile and can stand up to all kinds of flavorings. Perhaps old-fashioned mint jelly is the worst thing to serve with lamb. It's terribly sweet and overpowering. Any commercial chutney (Major Grey's is readily available) is better. Try a nonsweet, tangy Mint-Butter Sauce (page 75) or a sweeter Apricot Salsa (page 80). You can make a fine gravy using lamb drippings and packaged beef or chicken gravy.

Lemon-Rosemary Stuffed Leg of Lamb

5–6-pound boneless leg of lamb
Salt and pepper
4 ounces unsalted butter
4 cloves garlic, peeled and
*   sliced thinly*
2 tablespoons fresh parsley,
*   chopped*

2 foot-long stalks rosemary,
*   leaves stripped from 1 stalk*
1½ cups breadcrumbs
1 teaspoon freshly ground
*   black pepper*
1 lemon, sliced thinly
2 strips bacon

Serves 6–8

This lamb is bursting with flavor. The smoke from the rosemary adds a great deal of flavor to the lamb.

1. If the lamb is rolled, unroll it. Make sure that there is no fat remaining on the lamb. Lay it on a large piece of waxed paper. Sprinkle both sides with salt and pepper.
2. Melt the butter in a saucepan over low heat and add garlic. Sauté gently for 5 minutes.
3. Add the parsley and 1 tablespoon rosemary leaves. Stir in the breadcrumbs and pepper. Spread on the lamb, and arrange half of the lemon slices across the meat.
4. Roll the lamb and tie with kitchen string. Rub the remaining rosemary leaves into the meat.
5. Set your grill on medium or make a fire with coals. Add the stripped rosemary stalk and the one with the leaves still on it to the fire, whether charcoal or gas.
6. Lay the bacon over the lamb while grilling. Brown the lamb. Close the lid and roast it until it reaches an internal temperature of at least 150°F. Let the lamb rest in a low (150°F) oven for 15 minutes before carving.

Moroccan-Style Loin Lamb Chops

4 thick loin lamb chops, about 6 ounces each
1 teaspoon ground cloves
2 teaspoons ground cumin
3 tablespoons sweet paprika
2 teaspoons hot paprika
½ teaspoon cayenne pepper
1 teaspoon ground coriander
1 teaspoon orange zest
1 teaspoon sea salt
1 teaspoon freshly ground black pepper

1. Remove the fat from the chops. Mix the rest of the ingredients together in a bowl, then rub the mixture into the chops on all sides. Let the rub permeate the chops for 1–2 hours.
2. Heat the grill to high heat, about 425°F. Grill the chops fast and hot until brown, but do not burn—about 5 minutes per side.
3. Place the chops on a platter to rest for 6 minutes.

Apricot Salsa

1 cup dried apricots, quartered
⅔ cup dry white wine
1 tablespoon olive oil
2 hot chilies, cored, seeded, and chopped
1 teaspoon cumin
1 teaspoon ground coriander seeds
Juice of ½ lime
4 tablespoons dark brown sugar
1 teaspoon salt
2 teaspoons fresh cilantro, chopped (optional)

1. Put the cut apricots in the wine to soak for 30 minutes.
2. Warm the olive oil in a saucepan. Add the chilies and cook for 5 minutes over medium heat.
3. Stir in the rest of the ingredients, including the apricots, and bring to a boil. Then reduce heat to a simmer. Cook for 10 minutes or until the apricots are very soft. Serve warm or cold, in a bowl.

CHAPTER 7
Pork and Ham

Old-Fashioned Barbecue Baby Back Ribs

Serves 4

Make extra sauce—
it will keep in the
refrigerator for
2 weeks.

2 tablespoons vegetable oil
1 small onion, chopped
2 cloves garlic, minced
2 jalapeño peppers, cored,
 seeded, and minced
2 tablespoons cider vinegar
½ cup dark brown sugar, or
 to taste
2 cups commercial chili sauce

1 teaspoon orange juice
 concentrate
1 teaspoon ground cloves
1 teaspoon ground cumin
1 teaspoon ground coriander
 seeds
Salt and pepper
4 pounds spareribs

1. Heat the oil in a saucepan. Add the onion, garlic, and peppers and sauté over medium heat for five minutes.
2. Add the rest of the ingredients (except the ribs), cover, and simmer for 20 minutes. Remove from heat. Put half of the sauce in a jar for future use.
3. Prepare the grill for indirect heat.
4. Add some water-soaked mesquite, hickory, or other wood chips for a smoky flavor.
5. Grill the ribs on low heat for 2 hours.
6. Brush with sauce. Then grill an additional 10–15 minutes per side, over direct medium-high heat. Ribs should be caramelized but not burned.

Variations on a Theme
There must be 100,000 or more variations on the theme of barbecue sauce. The old-style one here is very easy to make, satisfying, and not as harsh as some you can buy. It's generic, too! You can use it with chicken, beef, or whatever, and you can adjust the heat to your family's taste.

Hot Southwestern-Style Baby Back Ribs

1 tablespoon cayenne pepper

2 teaspoons red pepper flakes

1 teaspoon ground black
   pepper

1 teaspoon ground cumin

½ teaspoon ground cloves

½ teaspoon ground cinnamon

½ teaspoon ground allspice

1 teaspoon dried thyme

2 teaspoons salt

5–6 pounds baby back ribs or
   spareribs

½ cup vegetable oil in a spray
   bottle

> **Serves 4 (1 pound per person, more if for a ball game!)**
>
> This method requires the ribs to be prepared with a rub, then grilled after the rub has permeated the meat. Be warned: This is very, very spicy!

1. Mix all of the spices together. Wearing rubber gloves (this stuff can burn), rub it into the meat. Cover and refrigerate overnight.
2. Prepare the grill to medium with plenty of room for indirect heat.
3. Grill the ribs over indirect heat for 20 minutes per side.
4. Spray with vegetable oil and finish grilling until nicely browned.

About Hot Peppers

It's no joke that very hot peppers can actually burn off your taste buds! As your taste buds are burned, you require more and more hot stuff in order to taste it. Anything subtle will completely escape your taste buds. So, be careful. Be sure to drink plenty of fluids with very hot food. And, if you keep adding hot sauce, you'll know that you've lost a good part of your sense of taste.

Asian-Style Baby Back Ribs

4 pounds baby back ribs
Generous amount of salt and black pepper, or to taste
1 cup soy sauce
Juice of 1 lime
2 cloves garlic, peeled and minced

2 teaspoons fresh gingerroot, minced
2 teaspoons sesame seed oil
½ teaspoon five-spice powder
2 tablespoons honey
1 teaspoon chili-pepper oil, or to taste

1. Sprinkle the ribs with salt and pepper.
2. Mix all the rest of the ingredients together, and paint on the ribs. Let marinate for 5 hours.
3. Prepare grill for indirect cooking.
4. Grill ribs, covered, over indirect heat for 20 minutes per side or until browned but not burned.

Hawaiian-Style Ham Steaks

1 tablespoon fresh gingerroot, peeled and minced
1 mango, peeled and chopped fine
½ cup soy sauce
1 tablespoon sugar

1 24–30 ounce thick-cut smoked, precooked ham steak
1 large fresh pineapple, peeled and cored, cut in rings ½ inch thick

1. Set the grill for high, indirect cooking.
2. In a blender, whirl the gingerroot, mango, soy sauce, and sugar until smooth. Then paint the purée on the ham steak.
3. Grill the ham steak and the pineapple, turning once.
4. Cut into serving pieces and arrange the pineapple over the ham.

Sweet and Smoky Ham Steaks

2 large tart apples, peeled and
    cored
2 pears, peeled and cored
½ cup white wine
2 tablespoons golden brown
    sugar
½ teaspoon nutmeg
1 teaspoon ground cinnamon
Juice of ½ lemon and ⅛-inch
    slice of fresh lemon with peel
1 24–30-ounce thick-cut smoked,
    precooked ham steak

Caramel rub:
¼ cup butter, softened
½ cup golden brown sugar
½ teaspoon ground cloves
¼ teaspoon ground nutmeg
1 teaspoon dry mustard

Serves 4

Since ham steaks are
precooked, this
doesn't take as long
as it does to cook
raw meat.

1. To make the fruit sauce, coarsely chop the pears and apples. Mix
   them with the wine, sugar, nutmeg, cinnamon, and lemon slice. Cook
   over low heat in a saucepan until the fruit is very soft. Remove from
   heat, and remove the lemon peel before serving. (This can be made
   up to two days in advance and stored in a plastic or glass container,
   covered, in the refrigerator.) Serve hot or cold with the ham.
2. To make the caramel rub for the ham: In a separate bowl, mix butter,
   sugar, cinnamon, nutmeg, and mustard.
3. Press the caramel rub into the ham steak.
4. Prepare the grill for direct heat, on medium. Make sure the rack is
   well above (9 inches above) the coals or flame.
5. Grill the ham for about 4 minutes per side, letting the caramel rub
   brown but not blacken. Cut the ham in serving pieces and serve with
   the fruit sauce on the side.
6. Grill the ham until the sugar caramelizes and starts to run, about 8
   minutes. Turn and repeat on other side.

Ham Steaks with Nectarines or Peaches

1 24–30 ounce thick-cut smoked, precooked ham steak
1 cup honey-mustard salad dressing
4 ripe nectarines or peaches, halved and pitted, skins on

4 teaspoons lemon or orange juice
Salt and pepper to taste

1. Prepare the grill for direct heat.
2. Paint the ham with honey-mustard dressing.
3. Sprinkle the nectarines or peaches with lemon or orange juice and salt and pepper. Grill the fruit, cut-side down, until you see the marks of the rack, about 5 minutes.
4. Set the ham on the grill and grill until sizzling hot.
5. Cut the ham into serving pieces and arrange the fruit around the ham.

Ham—Sugary, Salty, or Smoky?

Ham is cured in a number of different ways. Maple is a northeast favorite and smoking is a wonderful flavor. Ham that has been soaked in brine or injected with briny water is often seemingly cheaper than other hams, but you are paying for water weight. A good smoked ham from Virginia, also called country ham, does tend to be salty and needs to be soaked in water for a day or two before roasting. Check the labels to find out if the ham is all meat or includes water.

Game-Time Fresh Ham

1 8–10-pound fresh ham, bone in, ¼ inch fat left on

½ cup Dijon-style prepared mustard

½ cup butter, softened

1 tablespoon dried sage, or 5 sage leaves, shredded

1 teaspoon dried thyme, or 2 tablespoons fresh, chopped

1 tablespoon Worcestershire sauce

2 tablespoons quick-blending flour (Wondra)

1 teaspoon parsley

½ cup unsalted butter

¼ cup all-purpose flour

2 teaspoons dry English mustard

½ cup chicken broth, warmed

½ cup dry white wine

½ cup heavy cream

Salt and pepper to taste

Serves 14–16

This dish is often served with sides of cornbread stuffing, sweet relishes, and big mounds of mashed potatoes, winter squash, and, of course, applesauce.

---

1. Let the ham stand at room temperature for 1 hour while you prepare the grill for indirect cooking and make the coating and sauce.
2. For the coating, mix together the mustard, butter, sage, thyme, and Worcestershire sauce into a thick paste. Add Wondra and stir. Coat the ham with the mustard mixture and place it on the grill. Roast the fresh ham until the internal temperature is 170°F. Reapply the coating from time to time. The outer fat should become very crisp and delicious.
3. To make the sauce, melt the butter in a saucepan over medium heat. Whisk in the all-purpose flour and 2 teaspoons dry English mustard and let cook for three minutes.
4. Whisk in the warm chicken broth and cook until very smooth. Beat in the wine and cook until thickened. Reduce the heat to a simmer.
5. Add the cream and parsley; cook until hot and thick. Stir in salt and pepper to taste.
6. Remove the roast from the grill and let stand for 20 minutes to retain juices. Carve and serve on a warm platter with the creamy mustard sauce on the side.

Apple-Stuffed Pork Rib Chops

Serves 4

Have your butcher make a pocket in each chop, or use a sharp knife and make the pockets yourself. Serve with any grilled fruit on the side.

1 fennel bulb, core and brown parts removed, chopped
1 tart apple, peeled, cored, and chopped
½ cup white wine
1 tablespoon butter
½ teaspoon caraway seeds
Salt and pepper to taste
½ cup sour cream (optional)
1 tablespoon vegetable oil
½ cup celery, finely chopped
2 tablespoons onion, minced

1 apple, peeled, cored, and chopped
2 teaspoons dried rosemary or 2 tablespoons fresh, chopped
½ cup dry breadcrumbs or stuffing mix
4 double-thick pork rib chops (7–8 ounces each)
8 wooden toothpicks, soaked in water for ½ hour

1. Cook the fennel and apple in the wine, covered, for about 20 minutes. Be sure to keep it wet by adding liquid as needed. Don't let it dry out.
2. When the fennel and apple are very soft, add the butter, caraway seeds, salt and pepper, and sour cream. Stir lightly; then remove from heat. Set aside.
3. Heat the vegetable oil in a skillet over medium heat. Add the celery, onion, apple, and rosemary. Cook about two minutes; then mix in the breadcrumbs or stuffing mix.
4. Fill the pockets of the chops with the breadcrumb mixture, securing openings with toothpicks.
5. Set the grill to medium and brown chops over direct heat.
6. Place on indirect heat, cover, and grill for 15 minutes per side. Spoon some fennel sauce onto each chop before serving.

Two Ways of Cooking

You can either parboil the ribs for 20 minutes, or grill them over indirect heat for about 35 minutes before adding the sauce. Make extra and it will keep in the refrigerator for 2 weeks.

Classic Pork Rib Chops

4 double-thick pork rib chops
Salt and pepper
½ cup dried apricots, chopped
½ stick butter
2 shallots, peeled and minced
1 teaspoon dried thyme
1 teaspoon dried sage
1 teaspoon dried rosemary

1½ cups chicken broth,
  warmed
½ cup dry white wine
1 cup soft breadcrumbs
2 tablespoons flour
8 wooden toothpicks, soaked
  in water for 30 minutes

1. Cut pockets into each chop using a sharp knife. Sprinkle the chops with salt and pepper.
2. Soak the apricots in 1 cup hot water for about 30 minutes.
3. Melt the butter in a skillet and sauté the shallots until soft.
4. Add the herbs and blend in the broth. Stir until smooth, then add the wine and keep cooking. Add flour and stir until thick. Combine half of the sauce with the softened apricots and the breadcrumbs. Reserve remaining half of the sauce to serve with the chops.
5. Prepare the grill to medium-high and have plenty of space for indirect, low cooking.
6. Stuff the chops with the breadcrumb mixture and secure with toothpicks. Brown the chops over direct heat, then place on indirect heat. Cover and grill until they reach 165°F inside.
7. Place the chops on a warm platter and let them rest in a warm oven for 8–10 minutes before serving. Serve with reserved sauce.

Chinese-Style Pork Tenderloin

Serves 4–5

Tenderloins usually come in packages of two and each weighs about 1¾ pounds. This recipe is easy to cook and very versatile.

½ cup soy sauce

½ cup sweet sherry

2 tablespoons orange juice concentrate

1 tablespoon fresh gingerroot, peeled and minced

2 garlic cloves, peeled and minced

1 teaspoon anise seed

½ teaspoon Tabasco sauce, or to taste

2 whole pork tenderloins, rinsed and dried

2 large sweet, thick-skinned oranges

1. Mix all of the ingredients except meat and oranges together and place them in a nonreactive (glass or ceramic) baking dish. Add the pork and turn to coat. Cover with plastic wrap and refrigerate for 6–8 hours.
2. Set the grill for indirect heat on one side and flame on the other.
3. Pat the tenderloins dry and place on grill over direct heat. Quickly brown on both sides. Brush with the marinade before turning. After brushing the marinade on the meat twice, discard the marinade. Move the meat to the indirect side of the grill and roast until the meat reaches 150°F.
4. Cut the oranges horizontally into ½-inch slices. Grill the oranges for about 3–4 minutes per side over direct heat.
5. Let the meat rest on a platter in a warm oven. Cut in thin slices on the diagonal and serve with rice. Arrange the oranges on the plates or serving platter.

Double Dip

Some of these marinades make wonderful dipping sauces. If you want to have a dipping sauce, simply make a double recipe. Store half of it in the refrigerator until you are ready to use it as a sauce.

Fruit-Stuffed Pork Tenderloin

8 pitted prunes, cut up
8 dried apricots, cut up
1 cup port wine
½ cup walnuts

½ fresh apple, peeled, cored,
  and chopped
2 pork tenderloins, each
  weighing about 14 ounces

1. Mix the prunes and apricots with the port wine and bring to a boil in a saucepan.
2. Toast the nuts in a pan over low heat.
3. Mix the fruit mixture, nuts, and apple together. Remove from heat and let expand for about 15 minutes.
4. Using a large knitting needle or the end of a long wooden spoon, poke a tunnel into the meat to provide an area for you to place the stuffing. You can increase the size of the tube with the handle of a knife, inserted into the opening.
5. Poke the stuffing into the tenderloins.
6. Set grill on medium and quickly brown the meat.
7. Place the loins off direct heat and cook until they reach 155°F.

Mixing the Sweet and Savory

There's much to be said for the use of fresh or dried fruit in sauces. Using citrus and other fruit juices such as apple, apricot, and pear, among others, can change a recipe for the better.

Serves 4–5

All kinds of fresh and dried fruits, aromatic vegetables, dressings, and nuts make creative and exciting stuffings. Stuffed tenderloin is very pretty when carved.

Autumn-Flavored Pork Tenderloin

Serves 4–5

This is so easy and delightful! Serve with any good commercial chicken or turkey gravy.

2 pork tenderloins, about 14 ounces each
Salt and pepper
5 teaspoons unsalted butter
1 medium sweet white onion, peeled and chopped
½ teaspoon dried savory
1 teaspoon dried rosemary
2 teaspoons fresh parsley, rinsed and chopped

4 fresh sage leaves, shredded, or 1 teaspoon dried sage
2 6-ounce corn muffins, crumbled
½ teaspoon cayenne pepper, or to taste
2 tablespoons olive oil

1. Rinse the tenderloins and pat them dry with paper towels. Sprinkle them with salt and freshly ground black pepper and set aside.
2. Make the tunnels in the tenderloins by taking a dull knife and poking it through the tenderloin on each side. Then, poke and twist the back of the dull knife through the tube so you have hollowed out a ½- to ¾-inch tunnel to stuff.
3. Heat the butter in a skillet and add the onion. Sauté the onions until very soft. Add the herbs and turn off the stove. Let the herbs steep in the onion/butter mixture for 5 minutes. Add pepper.
4. Add the muffin crumbs and mix thoroughly. Stuff the mixture into the tunnels in the tenderloins. Brush the tenderloins with olive oil.
5. Grill on medium until the internal temperature reaches 155°F. Let rest in a warm oven to keep juicy, then carve on the diagonal. Serve with applesauce or mustard sauce.

You Can't Be Too Careful!

Whenever you've marinated a piece of meat, fish, or poultry, be sure to discard the marinade after basting once or twice. Wash the bowl or pan that you've used to marinate the food in using very hot soapy water, or run it through the dishwasher.

Hungarian-Style Pork Tenderloin

2 pork tenderloins
2 tablespoons sweet Hungarian
   paprika
1 tablespoon hot Hungarian
   paprika
1 teaspoon garlic powder
1 teaspoon salt

1 teaspoon freshly ground
   black pepper, or to taste
1 teaspoon caraway seeds,
   bruised in a mortar and
   pestle
1 8-ounce jar basic tomato
   sauce

> **Serves 4–5**
>
> This is easy to make and is excellent comfort food. You can use commercial tomato sauce, sour cream, and sauerkraut or red cabbage.
>
>

1. Mix together the paprikas, garlic powder, salt, black pepper, and caraway seeds.
2. Rinse the tenderloins and pat dry with paper towels. Rub the dry spice mix into the meat and let rest, covered and refrigerated, for 1–2 hours.
3. Heat the grill to medium.
4. Brown the meat over direct flame and then move off the flame; cover the grill and cook gently until the internal temperature of the meat reaches 155°F degrees.
5. Heat the tomato sauce.
6. Slice the pork and serve with spoonfuls of tomato sauce and dollops of sour cream.

The Joy of Marinating

Any acid in a marinade will act to tenderize the meat. Orange, lemon, and lime juice make excellent tenderizers. Red or white wine are good, too. (Bourbon and other whiskeys aren't acidic enough to tenderize.) Just about any herb is good mixed into the liquid—oregano, basil, parsley, and rosemary are fine additions. You can also add dried, bruised juniper berries (available in gourmet shops), capers, or chopped olives to your marinade. Experiment with the flavors, pick tastes you enjoy, and come up with your own special signature concoction.

South Carolina BBQ Sauce for Pork

3 tablespoons bacon fat
1 large onion, minced
2 cloves garlic, minced
1 cup Dijon-style mustard
Salt and freshly ground black
   pepper to taste
½ cup white wine vinegar
½ cup molasses or honey

Heat the bacon fat in a large, heavy saucepan. Sauté the onion and garlic over low heat about 6 minutes until the onions are softened. Add the rest of the ingredients and bring to a boil. Chill overnight in the refrigerator before using.

Prune Sauce for Pork or Ham

16 pitted prunes cut in half
1 cup ruby port wine
1 tablespoon olive oil
2 shallots, peeled and minced
Juice of ½ fresh lemon
1 tablespoon dry English
   mustard
⅔ cup heavy cream
Salt and pepper to taste

1. Put the prunes in a bowl with the port wine covering them and set aside for 1 hour.
2. Heat the olive oil and add the shallots. Sauté for 5 minutes.
3. Add the lemon juice and mustard and whisk until well blended. Then add the prunes and their liquid and bring to a boil.
4. Stir in the cream and remove from heat; season with salt and pepper. Serve in a sauceboat.

CHAPTER 8
From the Sea

Juicy Chilean Sea Bass
with Tomato Coulis

Serves 4

Chilean sea bass is one of the most popular fish entrées in restaurants and for home cooking.

4 fillets Chilean sea bass
¼ cup canola oil
Salt and pepper to taste
Paprika
4 medium tomatoes, quartered,
    stem end removed
1 clove garlic, peeled
2 scallions, whole

2 celery tops, rinsed
Zest of ½ lemon
Juice of ½ lemon
1 teaspoon Tabasco sauce
¼ cup extra-virgin olive oil
2 tablespoons fresh parsley,
    chopped

1. Rinse the fish in cold water and pat dry on a paper towel. Sprinkle the fish with oil, salt, pepper, and paprika.
2. Heat the grill to 400°F.
3. While the grill is heating, make the coulis. Place tomatoes, garlic, scallions, celery tops, lemon zest, lemon juice, Tabasco sauce, olive oil, and parsley in the jar of your blender and whirl until very smooth.
4. Paint the fish with coulis and place on grill. Time each side to about 5 minutes per inch of thickness. Do not let it burn.
5. Let the fish rest in a warm oven for 5 minutes. Place on a warm serving platter or warmed dishes.

Buying Fish

Always go by your nose—any fishy smell is a sure sign that the fish has been too long out of the water. Look at the eyes—they should be shiny and clear, not glazed and clouded. The skin or scales should also be very shiny, not dull.

Wild Striped Bass Fillets with Herbs

*1 large or 2 medium fillets of
striped bass, 1½ pounds,
skin on*
1 cup fine breadcrumbs
*½ cup fresh parsley, finely
chopped, or 1 tablespoon
dried*

*½ teaspoon sage leaves, dried
and crumbled*
½ teaspoon oregano, dried
*Salt and freshly ground pepper
to taste*
½ cup unsalted butter, melted

Serves 4

Striped bass is a lean
and delicious fish with
a delicate, buttery
flavor. It does not
need to be overpow-
ered with garlic, mus-
tard, or any strong
aromatic.

1. Rinse the fish and dry it on a paper towel.
2. Mix the rest of the ingredients together in a bowl.
3. Heat the grill to medium.
4. Spread the herb/breadcrumb mixture on the fish and grill until it just begins to flake. Timing depends on the thickness of the fish.
5. Finish by toasting the topping under the broiler until golden brown.
6. Place on a warm serving platter or warm dishes.

When Is a Fish Done?

*"Cook until done" is a common instruction and a terrible way to tell
a new cook how to do fish. Generally, fish is done when it flakes a
bit when gently poked with a fork—except for Chilean sea bass or
fresh tuna. They will toughen if you cook them to this point. Practice
is the very best teacher. Try to give each side 4–5 minutes per inch
of thickness.*

Rich Brown Bluefish Fillets Asian Style

Serves 4

American bluefish is a fine, fatty fish with a marvelous taste. This is great with rice, sautéed bean sprouts, and/or snow peas.

4 small or 2 large fillets of bluefish totaling 1½ pounds, skin on
¼ cup soy sauce
1 clove garlic, minced

2 ounces white (French) vermouth
1 tablespoon lemon juice
1 teaspoon sesame seed oil
Slices of lemon or lime

1. Rinse fish and pat dry on paper towels.
2. Mix the rest of the ingredients (except lemon or lime slices) together and spoon over the fish.
3. Grill, skin-side down, over medium heat until the fish flakes.
4. Place on a warm serving platter or warmed dishes and garnish with slices of lemon or lime.

Spanish-Style Halibut with Anchovy Butter

Serves 4

Any recipe that is good for cod is also good for halibut. Steaks or fillets may be used in this or any halibut recipe.

4 halibut steaks, skin on
½ cup unsalted butter, melted
1 inch of anchovy paste, more to taste
1 tablespoon Tabasco sauce

Juice of ½ fresh lemon
Garnish of ½ cup fresh celery tops, pale leaves, rinsed and chopped

1. Preheat the grill to medium-high.
2. Rinse the fish in cold water and pat it dry on paper towels.
3. Whisk together the melted butter, anchovy paste, Tabasco sauce, and lemon juice, and paint the fish on both sides with the anchovy butter.
4. Grill the fish, painting it often with the sauce, until golden on each side with nice brown marks from the grill.
5. Peel off the skin. Serve on a warm platter with chopped celery leaves as a tasty garnish.

Catfish Cajun Style

4 catfish fillets, about 6 ounces each

4 teaspoons vegetable oil

1 tablespoon cayenne pepper

1 tablespoon fresh ginger, minced

1 tablespoon dry English mustard

¼ teaspoon ground cinnamon

¼ teaspoon ground cloves

1 teaspoon garlic powder

1 teaspoon sea salt, or to taste

½ teaspoon freshly ground black pepper

Wedges of lemon or lime and sprigs of parsley or watercress (for garnish)

Serves 4

For grilling catfish, you need a nice thick piece of fish. It is important to put a piece of aluminum foil under the fish to keep it together.

1. Set the grill to medium-high or wait until the coals are white.
2. Cut pieces of heavy-duty foil to fit each fillet, and brush each fillet with vegetable oil.
3. Mix the rest of the ingredients (except for garnish) together to make a rub. (Alternatively, you can use a commercial Cajun spice rub.) Spread and press it into the fish.
4. Grill over medium-hot coals or gas until the fish just starts to flake. Place on a warm serving platter or warmed dishes. Serve with lemon or lime wedges and sprigs of parsley or watercress.

Catfish (and Dogfish) Facts

The Encyclopedia of Southern Culture *says, "Southerners have never aligned themselves as closely with any cold-blooded creature as they have with the feline-looking catfish." Catfish are also included in aquariums as scavengers, to help keep the tank clean. One family of catfish has even developed air-breathing organs, and another can migrate across land! Dogfish, meanwhile, are small, spiny sharks whose meat is often used in England for fish and chips.*

Nova Scotia–Style Cod Steaks

4 thick codfish steaks, about 6 ounces each, skin on
½ cup extra-virgin olive oil
1 tablespoon green peppercorns
1 tablespoon white wine vinegar
1 tablespoon fresh oregano leaves or 1 teaspoon dried
Salt and freshly ground pepper to taste

1. Rinse the fish and dry on a paper towel.
2. Mix all of the rest of the ingredients together, bruising the green peppercorns with a pestle or heavy spoon. If you make this the day before, you'll get more flavor.
3. Pour sauce over fish and let rest for 1 hour or longer, turning once.
4. Preheat the grill to medium-high.
5. Grill the fish until you get nice brown marks on one side, then turn and grill on the other. Timing depends on the thickness of the fish. For 1-inch-thick pieces of cod, allow about 4 minutes per side. Use the marinade to baste the fish.
6. Peel off the skin and serve on a warm platter; garnish with sprigs of fresh arugula.

Cod and Potatoes

Cod is a favorite for fish and chips. In the British Isles, a "chip" is not a potato chip, but a fried potato. You can make low-fat fish and chips by serving fried potatoes with grilled cod or scrod. A scrod is a young codfish. Cod is wonderful with any potatoes—fried, mashed, or scalloped. One of the best Irish pubs makes fish and chips with Yukon Gold potatoes, which stand up well to frying. And, you can't go wrong with baby string beans or broiled tomatoes.

Refreshing Salmon Salad

4 grilled salmon steaks, chilled
1 cup celery, finely chopped
4 scallions, finely chopped
⅔ cup whole mayonnaise
Juice of ½ lemon

2 tablespoons capers
2 tablespoons fresh dill weed,
* finely chopped, or 1 tea-*
* spoon dried*

Remove the skin and bones from the salmon, and break into chunks. Add the celery and scallions to the salmon. Mix the rest of the ingredients together and dress the salad, tossing gently. Serve well chilled. This can be made a day in advance.

Serves 4

This salad is great as a quick and light lunch or supper. Serve the salad over shredded lettuce. Deviled eggs make an excellent side dish.

Salmon with Juniper Berries

4 salmon steaks, ⅔ pound each
24 dried juniper berries
4 teaspoons butter, melted

1 lemon, quartered
4 teaspoons parsley, chopped

1. Rinse salmon steaks in cold water and pat dry with a paper towel.
2. Press 6 juniper berries into each steak as deeply as possible. Then brush both sides of each steak with melted butter.
3. Broil over medium flame for 3–4 minutes.
4. Turn and brush with more butter. Grill for 3–4 minutes more.
5. Place on plates or serving platter. Sprinkle with fresh lemon juice and chopped parsley.

Serves 4

Native Americans and Scandinavians are very fond of using juniper berries in their cooking. Juniper berries are available in most gourmet shops, or order them online.

Salmon with Dill Cream and Cucumber Sauce

Serves 4

This is a fine lunch or supper dish. Garnish with yellow and red cherry tomatoes and extra sprigs of fresh dill.

4 cups mixed lettuce and spicy greens such as watercress or arugula, shredded

4 grilled salmon steaks, chilled, bones and skin removed

1 extra-long English cucumber, peeled and chopped

½ cup sweet red onion, finely chopped

4 tablespoons fresh dill, finely chopped, or 1 teaspoon dried

⅓ cup mayonnaise

⅓ cup sour cream

Juice of ½ lemon

1 clove garlic, peeled and minced

Salt and pepper to taste

1. Rinse and dry the greens. Arrange them on serving plates.
2. Break the boned and skinned salmon into chunks and place in a chilled bowl. Add the chopped cucumber and onion and mix lightly.
3. Whisk the rest of the ingredients together and spoon over the salmon and cucumbers. You can make this 2–3 hours in advance and keep refrigerated.

A Perfect Combination

This is a marriage made in heaven! Dill is wonderful with halibut, haddock, shrimp, monkfish, and more. If you aren't making a cream sauce, just mix it with some mayonnaise, or butter when you cook your fish. You can also use dill seeds for a delightful flavor. Try chopping a little dill pickle into your seafood salad and it will be a hit!

Herb-Crusted Salmon

4 6-ounce salmon steaks
Salt and freshly ground black
    pepper to taste
1 egg white, well beaten
Juice of ½ lemon

Zest of ½ lemon
2 tablespoons fresh parsley,
    chopped
1 tablespoon fresh dill, chopped
1 teaspoon dried oregano

Serves 4

Serve with
German Potato Salad
(page 253).

1. Rinse the salmon in cold water and pat dry on paper towels. Sprinkle the salmon with salt and pepper. Paint the salmon on both sides with the egg white.
2. Mix the rest of the ingredients together and press them into the fish. Let stand for a few minutes.
3. Heat the grill to medium-low.
4. Grill the salmon slowly for about 4–5 minutes per side, depending on the thickness.

Shark Fillets with Citrus Marinade

1 ½-lb. shark fillet
Zest of ½ orange, finely minced
Zest of ½ lemon
½ teaspoon red pepper flakes
Juice of ½ fresh lime
1 tablespoon fresh scallion,
    white part peeled, minced

¼ teaspoon ground coriander
    seeds
Salt and pepper to taste
½ cup chili sauce
¼ cup olive oil

Serves 4

Always remove the
skin before eating
shark, as it's rough
and tough. This is
excellent with grilled
fruit (page 221) in
the summer.

1. Rinse the shark and pat dry. Mix the rest of the ingredients together in a nonreactive dish, and place the shark in it. Marinate the shark for 2–4 hours, covered, in the refrigerator.
2. Heat the grill to medium-high—about 375°F.
3. Grill the shark quickly; do not let sit on the heat or it will toughen and dry out. Serve on a warm platter with parsley for garnish.

Swordfish Steaks with Hot Orange Sauce

4 6-ounce swordfish steaks
2 ounces orange juice
    concentrate
2 ounces white vermouth
1 teaspoon Worcestershire sauce
1 tablespoon dry English
    mustard
1 tablespoon Tabasco sauce,
    or to taste
Salt and pepper to taste

1. Rinse the fish and dry it on paper towels.
2. In a bowl, mix together the rest of the ingredients. Paint it on the fish before grilling.
3. Set the grill on medium.
4. Sear the fish until golden on both sides—about 4 minutes per side. The sugar in the orange juice will make this brown quickly. Check for doneness by pricking the fish with a fork to see if it flakes. Serve on warm plates and garnish with parsley or cilantro.

Stuffed Freshwater Trout

4 whole trout, heads on or off
2 teaspoons unsalted butter,
    melted
Salt and pepper to taste
8 fresh sage leaves
8 sprigs parsley
4 strips hickory-smoked bacon

1. Have your fishmonger clean the fish. You will have a cavity down the center of the belly. Rinse the fish in cold water and dry on paper towels.
2. Brush the insides of the fish with butter and sprinkle with salt and pepper. Put the sage and parsley inside the fish.
3. Wrap each fish with a strip of bacon and secure the fish closed and the bacon on with presoaked toothpicks.
4. Set grill to medium-low and roast the fish until the bacon is crisp and the fish cooked. Fish should be lightly browned on the outside.

Tangy Sea Trout with Watercress

1 sea trout fillet, about 1½ pounds
Salt and pepper to taste
1 bunch watercress, tops only, washed and dried

2–4 teaspoons cold butter, cut into pieces
½ lemon, sliced thinly

1. Rinse and pat fish dry with paper towels. Sprinkle the fillet with salt and pepper.
2. Spread the watercress leaves over the fillet and dot with butter. Arrange the lemon slices on top of the watercress.
3. Heat grill to 400°F.
4. Grill until the fish softens and the skin is crisp. Cut into pieces and serve on warm plates.

> **Serves 4**
>
> Sea trout has lovely pink flesh; it's mild yet flavorful. Serve this dish with a big bowl of potato salad (page 252 or 253).
>
>

Traditional Grilled Lobsters

1 pound unsalted butter
2 fresh lemons, quartered

4 lobsters—1½–2 pounds each

1. Set the grill to medium.
2. Make clarified butter by putting the pound of butter in a large oven-proof bowl or quart measuring pitcher. Place in a warm (200°F) oven until the butter melts and the solids fall to the bottom. Strain the butter through a piece of cheesecloth, and it's ready to use with your lobster.
3. Kill the lobsters and then remove the claws and legs. Crack the claws with a cracker or mallet and put them on the grill, turning after 5 minutes.
4. Cut through each lobster lengthwise with a serrated knife, splitting it. Brush the meat with some of the clarified butter.
5. Grill the lobsters, cut-side down, for 8–10 minutes—until they turn reddish orange. Serve with lemon quarters and clarified butter.

> **Serves 4**
>
> Kill the lobsters before you cut them up and grill them. This is done humanely by inserting a sharp knife behind the head. Never use a lobster that's limp or "dead."
>
>

Sesame-Crusted Tuna with Wasabi

Serves 4

Tuna comes in various grades, the best being "sushi grade," which is eaten raw. This dish is great over baby spinach, raw or lightly sautéed.

4 tuna steaks, skinless and boneless
½ cup soy sauce
¼ cup white vermouth
Juice of ½ lemon
2 cloves garlic, minced
1-inch knob fresh gingerroot, peeled and minced

1 tablespoon sesame seed oil
1 teaspoon Tabasco sauce
¾ cup sesame seeds
2 teaspoons wasabi powder mixed with 2 teaspoons water

1. Rinse the tuna steaks and pat dry with paper towels.
2. In a large bowl, mix the soy sauce, vermouth, lemon juice, garlic, ginger, sesame seed oil, and Tabasco. Add the tuna to the marinade, making sure it's completely covered. Cover and refrigerate for 1 hour.
3. Spread the sesame seeds on a large piece of waxed paper. Drain the tuna but don't dry it. Coat the tuna with the seeds, pressing them into the meat.
4. Set grill to medium. Grill the tuna steaks until the seeds are brown and crunchy, about 4 minutes per side. If you want your tuna more done, place in a 275°F oven for another 10 minutes.
5. Slice the tuna thinly and place over mixed greens or baby spinach. Place ½ teaspoon of the wasabi sauce on the edge of each plate before serving.

Was-a-bi!

The ground root of the wasabi plant is sold in different forms, including in a tube as wasabi paste, "wasabi ko" for sushi, and as powder. You can find it at Asian markets. The ground root flavors many foods in Japanese cuisine and its bright green color adds color contrast, which Japanese dishes are famous for. Other parts of the wasabi plant are also used. The leaves and petioles are picked or can be powdered for use as wasabi flavoring, used now in many foods. Some sushi chefs will only use a sharkskin grater, which is said to give the wasabi a smooth, soft, and aromatic finish. Be warned: Wasabi is one of the hottest substances known, so be very careful with it.

Barbecued Littleneck Clams in Cocktail Sauce

24 littleneck clams (about 1 inch across)
1 cup chili sauce
1 tablespoon prepared horseradish
Juice of ½ lemon
1 teaspoon Worcestershire sauce

1 teaspoon orange bitters
½ teaspoon celery salt
1 teaspoon Tabasco sauce, or to taste
Salt and freshly ground pepper to taste

> **Serves 4 as an appetizer**
>
> Littlenecks are very delicious eaten raw or grilled. Make extra sauce for dipping and use with other seafood such as oysters and shrimp.
>
>

1. Scrub the clams and tap (see below) to weed out dead clams.
2. Mix the rest of the ingredients together to make the sauce.
3. Set the grill on high heat.
4. Place clams on grill. You can either put them on a layer of aluminum foil or put them directly on the grill. Close grill.
5. Check the clams after 3 minutes. As soon as they open, add a teaspoon of sauce to each clam. Let heat on grill for about 1 minute and serve with extra sauce.

Preparing Shellfish

Clams, mussels, and oysters need to be rinsed in cold water and scrubbed with a vegetable brush. Once the shellfish are clean, discard any that are open unless they are alive, closing quickly when tapped. Discard any with cracked or broken shells. To test for life and safety (never eat dead shellfish), tap two clams together. If you hear a hollow sound, one is dead—you should hear a sharp click. The click, like the sound of two stones being hit together, means the shells are tightly closed and the mollusks are alive. This same test works equally well with mussels and oysters.

Grilled Cherrystone Clams Piquant

Serves 6–8 as an appetizer

You can use either cherrystones or littlenecks for this dish—double the quantity of littlenecks. The topping should be made before you grill the clams.

24 cherrystone clams
8 slices bacon
4 tablespoons unsalted butter
¾ cup onion, chopped fine
½ cup sweet red pepper, chopped fine
½ cup Italian flat-leaf parsley, rinsed, dried, and minced

Pepper to taste
1 teaspoon orange juice concentrate
Juice of ½ lemon
½ cup fine breadcrumbs
4 tablespoons butter (½ stick), cut into pieces

1. Scrub and tap clams. Using a clam knife, open the clams. Discard the top shells. Save all the juices. Set the clams on a metal tray.
2. Cook the bacon in a skillet until almost crisp and set aside on paper towels.
3. Wipe out the skillet after cooking the bacon and add 4 tablespoons butter. Add the onion and pepper. Sauté for 6–8 minutes or until soft.
4. Crumble the cooked bacon into the skillet and mix in the parsley, black pepper, orange juice concentrate, lemon juice, and breadcrumbs. Mix them up and remove from heat.
5. Put a teaspoon of filling on each clam. Add any residual clam juice. Dot with butter.
6. Preheat the grill to medium. Place the metal tray with the clams on it on the grill and close the lid.
7. Roast until the clams are just beginning to bubble and the topping is golden—about 10 minutes depending on the heat of the grill. Serve with chunks of toasted French or Italian bread for sopping up the wonderful juices.

Clam Liquor

Whether the liquor comes from raw or cooked clams, save it! It's useful in chowders, mixed with tomato juice for Bloody Marys, and there are people who simply drink it plain.

Buttery Soft-Shell Crabs in Packets

8 tablespoons butter (1 stick)
1 inch anchovy paste
4 tablespoons dry white wine
4 teaspoons lemon juice
4 tablespoons parsley, rinsed
    and minced, or 4 table-
    spoons fresh sorrel

Salt and freshly ground black
    pepper to taste
8 jumbo soft-shell crabs

> **Serves 4**
>
> Soft-shell crabs are delicate creatures—don't overcook. Serve with rice or couscous. You can increase the quantity of sauce and serve them over linguini.
>
>

1. Set the grill to medium.
2. Melt the butter and mix with the rest of the ingredients (except the crabs) to make the sauce.
3. Tear off 4 large sheets of heavy-duty aluminum foil, and place 2 crabs on each sheet. Pull up corners to hold in sauce.
4. Divide the sauce, spooning it over the crabs. Close the packets, leaving a small "chimney" on top for the steam to escape.
5. Put the crabs on the grill. They are done as soon as they have steamed for 5 minutes.

A Sign of Spring

Soft-shell crabs once were a sure sign of spring. Now they are farmed, which makes them available from spring through summer. The Maryland soft-shell crab is of the blue (as opposed to brown) crab family. They are soft-shells right after they shed their hard shells. As the hard shells grow back, the coverings are first tender, then leathery, and finally downright hard.

Classic Lord Baltimore's Crabmeat in Ramekins

2 tablespoons butter
2 shallots, peeled and minced
½ cup celery, chopped finely
1 cup mushrooms, sliced, or tiny button mushrooms
2 tablespoons flour
1 cup heavy cream
¼ teaspoon nutmeg

½ teaspoon dill weed
2 tablespoons sherry
Salt and pepper to taste
1 pound lump Maryland crabmeat, picked over for shells and cartilage
Soft breadcrumbs to cover tops of ramekins

1. Melt the butter in a large skillet. Sauté the shallots and celery until soft, about 4 minutes. Add the mushrooms and flour and blend.
2. Warm the cream so it will blend with the flour without making lumps, then beat it into the mixture. Mix in the rest of the ingredients (except breadcrumbs) and stir until thickened. Remove from heat.
3. Heat the grill to medium and arrange for indirect heat. You can use 6-ounce ramekins, soufflé cups, or huge scallop shells; treat them with nonstick spray.
4. Divide the crabmeat mixture between the ramekins. Sprinkle the tops with breadcrumbs.
5. Place on the grill, on indirect heat, and close lid. Bake for 15 minutes, or until the crumbs are browned and the mixture is very hot.

Sizing up Soft-Shell Crabs

Most soft-shell crabs are either medium, 2–3 ounces, or jumbo, running about 5–6 ounces. The smallest ones usually end up fried or sautéed and served on hamburger buns with lettuce and tartar sauce. The jumbo crabs are wonderful fried or grilled. If you are using the small ones, allow three per person. Two jumbo crabs will make up one serving.

New England Grilled Lobster Flamed with Brandy

1 pound unsalted butter
4 lobsters—1½–2 pounds each

1 cup brandy or cognac
2 fresh lemons, quartered

1. Set the grill to medium.
2. Make clarified butter by putting the pound of butter in a large oven-proof bowl or quart measuring pitcher. Place in a warm (200°F) oven until the butter melts and the solids fall to the bottom. Strain the butter through a piece of cheesecloth, and it's ready to use with your lobster.
3. Kill the lobsters and then remove the claws and legs. Crack the claws with a cracker or mallet and put them on the grill, turning after 5 minutes.
4. Use a serrated knife to split the lobster lengthwise. Cut through the lobster, being careful not to leave the intestinal tract. Brush the meat with the clarified butter.
5. Grill the lobsters, cut-side down, for 8–10 minutes. When the lobsters are almost done, pour brandy over the open areas of meat in the bodies and tails.
6. Standing well away from the grill, light with a long-handled match. As soon as the brandy stops flaming, serve with clarified butter and lemon quarters.

Plain or Fancy?

Purists eat it plain, boiled, broiled, or grilled with nothing more than lemon and butter. Lobster is sweet and delicate. It's tender when it's not overcooked. So, start with the purist approach; then, if you like, try something fancier.

> **Serves 4**
>
> This is a very good way to have some fun with your guests. By flaming the lobster with brandy, you get a distinctive and delightful flavor.
>
>

Grilled Lobster Tails with Vermouth

Serves 4

These small, frozen lobster tails are so convenient when company shows up unexpectedly. You need 3 or 4 per person.

16 small lobster tails
½ pound unsalted butter
½ cup sweet, red vermouth
Salt and pepper to taste

2 bunches watercress, rinsed, stems removed
1 cup French dressing
Lemon wedges

1. Set the tails on a metal tray to defrost.
2. Melt the butter in a small saucepan; then add the vermouth.
3. Cut the tails down the middle and open them. Paint the tails with the butter and vermouth sauce, and sprinkle them with salt and pepper to taste.
4. Set the grill to medium. Grill the tails for about three minutes, shell-side down.
5. Arrange the tails on a platter. Toss the watercress in French dressing and arrange around the lobster tails. Serve with lemon wedges.

French-Style Oysters with Almonds

**Serves 4
as an appetizer**

Herbs de Provence are available at most grocery stores and specialty shops.

½ pound unsalted butter (2 sticks), softened
1 cup toasted almonds, ground
½ cup breadcrumbs, commercial is okay
1 teaspoon lemon zest, minced

1 teaspoon herbs de Provence
½ teaspoon dried red pepper flakes or cayenne to taste
12 large or 16 small oysters, opened, on ice

1. Cream the butter and beat in the rest of the ingredients (except the oysters).
2. Set the grill to medium.
3. Spoon the butter mixture on the oysters.
4. Grill with the lid down until the tops are golden and the oysters are bubbling.

Savory Mussels in Packets

4 pounds fresh, live mussels
1 cup unsalted butter
1 cup dry white wine
4 cloves garlic, peeled and
    chopped
6 leaves fresh basil, shredded,
    or 2 teaspoons dried

1 teaspoon dried oregano or 2
    teaspoons fresh
Salt and pepper to taste
Red pepper flakes to taste

> **Serves 4 as a main course, 6 as an appetizer**
>
> Serve them plain, with their sauce for dipping, or in bowls over linguini, with plenty of crusty, toasted French or Italian bread.
>
>

1. To prepare the mussels, use a sharp knife to remove and discard the beards. Discard any mussels that are cracked or open or that make a hollow sound when tapped together.
2. To make the sauce: Melt the butter and mix it together with the wine, garlic, basil, and oregano. Add salt, pepper, and red pepper flakes to taste.
3. Set the grill on medium heat.
4. Tear off 4 large sheets of heavy-duty aluminum foil. Use twice the amount of foil that it looks like you need—mussels double in size as they open. Divide the mussels equally between the sheets of foil. Pull up the corners of the foil so the sauce does not run out.
5. Pour the sauce over the mussels and close the packets loosely, leaving a chimney for the steam to escape.
6. Place on grill. The mussels are done as soon as they open. This is obvious as they start to bulge the packets of aluminum foil.

Mussel Message

Buy your mussels only from a trusted fishmonger. They must be absolutely fresh or they will taste bad. And be sure to tap them for liveliness before cooking. Most mussels sold commercially are farm raised, which means they are not sandy and the beards are minimal. If you are buying wild mussels, give them a soaking in fresh water with a half cup of cornmeal thrown in. This will force them to expel any sand.

Grilled Oysters with Creamy Spinach

**Serves 4
as an appetizer**

This is really easy and elegant. Have your fishmonger open the oysters, or do it yourself.

1 dozen large oysters, freshly opened
¼ cup fresh lemon juice
4 slices bacon
1 package frozen creamed spinach, defrosted
Ground nutmeg to taste

Freshly ground black pepper to taste
1 cup breadcrumbs
½ cup freshly grated Parmesan cheese
2 tablespoons unsalted butter, cut into pieces

1. Place the oysters on a metal tray. Sprinkle each oyster with lemon juice.
2. Fry the bacon until crisp; drain and crumble. Mix the bacon bits with the defrosted spinach in a bowl and add nutmeg. Spoon some spinach on each oyster, add black pepper, breadcrumbs, and Parmesan cheese.
3. Set grill to high heat. Dot each oyster with butter. Grill until the oysters sizzle and the topping is golden.

Deep-Sea Diver Scallops with Dill Butter

Serves 4

Diver scallops (2 or more inches across and weighing 2 ounces each), also called jumbo scallops, are much bigger than sea scallops (1–1½ inches across).

12 2-ounce diver scallops
2 sticks sweet butter, softened
½ cup fresh dill weed, chopped
1 tablespoon lemon zest, freshly grated

1 teaspoon anise seed
1 tablespoon Pernod
¾ cup soft breadcrumbs
Salt and pepper to taste

1. Rinse the scallops. Spray 4 large scallop shells with nonstick spray.
2. Beat together the butter, dill weed, lemon zest, anise seed, Pernod, and breadcrumbs.
3. Set grill to medium.
4. Place 3 scallops in each shell or ramekin and spread the butter mixture on top of each scallop. Season with salt and pepper.
5. Grill until the butter mixture browns and the scallops are just hot. Serve on a bed of baby spinach.

Diver Scallops with Sesame and Lime

12 2-ounce scallops
½ cup soy sauce
Juice of 1 lime

2 tablespoons sesame seed oil
½ teaspoon Tabasco sauce, or
   to taste

1. Rinse the scallops and pat dry with paper towels.
2. Mix the rest of the ingredients in a bowl, and toss the scallops in the marinade. Cover and refrigerate for 20 minutes.
3. Set the grill to medium-high heat.
4. Drain the scallops; then on the grill, brown the scallops quickly on both sides and serve.

Serves 4

Don't marinate the scallops for more than 30 minutes or the lime juice will "cook" them. This is very nice served over baby greens.

Shrimp Marinated in Pernod Sauce

1½ pounds jumbo shrimp or
   prawns
⅔ cup Pernod

3 tablespoons olive oil
Salt and freshly ground white
   pepper to taste

1. Place the shrimp in a bowl. Pour the Pernod and olive oil over it and sprinkle with salt and pepper. Marinate for 1–2 hours in the refrigerator, covered.
2. Set grill on high heat.
3. Grill shrimp for about 20 seconds per side, and serve.

Serves 4

Pernod is an anise-flavored French aperitif. It is delightful with shellfish and fin fish.

Hearty Shrimp Wrapped in Bacon

1 slice bacon per shrimp
1½ pounds jumbo shrimp or
    prawns, cleaned
2 wooden toothpicks per
    shrimp, presoaked for 1 hour

Toasted rolls, chili sauce,
    lemon wedges, tartar sauce,
    lettuce, and tomatoes

1. Preset grill on medium heat.
2. Grill the bacon, keeping it limp.
3. Wrap a piece of bacon around each shrimp, making a packet, and
   secure with toothpicks.
4. Grill until the bacon is crisp and the shrimp pink. Serve on toasted
   rolls with condiments.

Spicy Grilled Shrimp with Curry Sauce

5 tablespoons Madras curry
    powder
2 teaspoons cayenne pepper
1½ pounds jumbo shrimp or
    prawns, peeled and cleaned
2 sticks butter

4 shallots, peeled and minced
2 cloves garlic, peeled and
    chopped
Juice of ½ lemon
2 teaspoons chopped cilantro

1. Mix 3 tablespoons of the curry powder and 1 teaspoon of the
   cayenne on a piece of waxed paper. Coat the shrimp with the curry-
   cayenne mixture. Cover with aluminum foil and chill for 1 hour.
2. To make the sauce, melt the butter, then add the shallots and garlic and
   sauté. Add the rest of the curry powder and cayenne pepper, the lemon
   juice, and the cilantro, and keep warm until ready to serve.
3. Set grill to medium-high. Grill the shrimp for about 20 seconds per
   side, until they turn pink. Mound the shrimp on a platter and drizzle
   the sauce over all. Serve with mango chutney.

CHAPTER 9

Wild Things—Game and Exotics

Western Bison Rib Eye Steaks

Serves 4

Serve with any favorite green vegetable and new potatoes roasted with parsley and butter.

4 bison rib eye steaks
½ teaspoon salt, or to taste
1 clove garlic
2 teaspoons freshly ground black pepper, or to taste

1 tablespoon chili sauce
1 teaspoon brown sugar
1 teaspoon A.1. sauce

1. Sprinkle the meat with salt.
2. Mix together the rest of the ingredients and spread mixture on both sides of the meat.
3. Set the grill to medium heat.
4. Grill the meat quickly, about 3 minutes per side. The sugar will caramelize quickly.
5. Let the steaks rest in a warm oven for 6–8 minutes.

Flavorful Wild Boar Fillet

Serves 4

Wild boar or javelina (wild pig) tends to be strong—it's an acquired taste. Many cooks stew it with aromatic vegetables, herbs, and spices.

2 pounds wild boar fillet
1 cup white wine vinegar
2 cups burgundy wine
2 tablespoons marmalade

½ cup orange juice
6 bay leaves
Salt and pepper to taste

1. Rinse the meat in cold water and dry with paper towels.
2. Mix the rest of the ingredients to make a marinade. Settle the pork in the liquid. Cover and refrigerate for 6–8 hours, turning once.
3. Set grill to medium heat. Grill, with rack set high above the coals, until medium, about 8–10 minutes per side. After cooking let the meat rest in a slightly warm oven for 15–20 minutes.

Quick Grilled Ostrich Steak

1½ pounds ostrich steaks,
    thick cut
¼ pound unsalted butter

1 teaspoon lemon rind, freshly
    grated
Salt and pepper to taste

1. Rinse the meat and dry it with paper towels.
2. Melt the butter and add the lemon rind.
3. Set the grill on medium.
4. Grill the ostrich as you would a fine steak, remembering not to over-cook, as it is very lean and will dry out and toughen. Baste the meat with the butter mixture. Season with salt and pepper.
5. Let the meat rest in a slightly warm oven for 5–8 minutes, depending on the thickness of the cut.

> **Serves 4**
>
> Grill as you would any piece of very, very lean meat. It's mild and easy to digest.
>
>

Old-Fashioned Roasted Pheasant

2 pheasants, split (about 1¾
    pounds each)
Salt and pepper to taste
1 cup flour, spread on waxed
    paper

4 ripe pears, quartered, peeled,
    and cored
2 cups heavy cream
4 springs fresh rosemary
4 grinds white pepper

1. Preheat grill to medium. Rinse the pheasants in cool water and dry on paper towels. Sprinkle the pheasants with salt and pepper, then roll the birds in the flour.
2. Place the half pheasants on large pieces of heavy-duty foil and draw up the sides to keep the juices and cream in the packet. Add the pears, cream, rosemary, and pepper. Then close the packets, leaving a "chimney" for the steam to escape. Roast over indirect heat for 30 minutes, or until a wing moves easily and when the bird is pricked, the juice is no longer pink. Spoon the sauce over the birds and serve.

> **Serves 4–6**
>
> Because pheasant is so lean, it's easy to dry it out and toughen it. Be sure you use heavy-duty aluminum foil, and serve with wild rice studded with toasted hazelnuts and dried cranberries.

Grandma's Pheasant with Currants

¼ cup currants
2 cups dry red wine
¼ teaspoon cinnamon
¼ teaspoon coriander seeds, ground

½ stick butter
¼ cup currant jelly
2 pheasants split lengthwise
Salt and pepper to taste

1. Soak the currants in the red wine for 1 hour or until plump.
2. Warm the wine and currant mixture, adding the cinnamon, coriander, butter, and jelly. Warm until the butter and jelly melt.
3. Rinse the pheasants and dry on paper towels. Sprinkle with salt and pepper.
4. Heat the grill to medium with rack high over coals or flames.
5. Place the pheasants on large squares of heavy-duty aluminum foil; draw up the sides to keep the sauce and juices from spilling. Divide the currant sauce among the packets. Close, leaving a "chimney" for the steam to escape.
6. Roast the packets for 35–40 minutes or until the juice is no longer pink. Serve with puréed chestnuts on the side.

Au "Currant"

Game and currant jelly seem to have a deep affinity for each other. For some reason, even though you may have bought farm-raised pheasants, this tastes as if you'd just come down from the hills with a brace of pheasants. Garnish with crumbled bacon and chopped parsley.

Pheasant Wrapped in Herbs and Bacon

2 pheasants, quartered
3 tablespoons butter, softened
Plenty of salt and pepper

8 large sage leaves
8 sprigs rosemary
8–12 slices bacon, stretched

1. Rinse the pheasant pieces and dry with paper towels. Smear the pheasant pieces with softened butter, then sprinkle with salt and pepper. Press the herbs to the pheasant pieces.
2. Set the rack high and the grill on medium.
3. Wrap the bacon around the pieces of pheasant and secure with small metal skewers. Grill until the bacon is very black.
4. Place the pheasants on a platter and remove the remains of the charred bacon. Leave the browned herbs. Serve with plenty of currant jelly, mustard, and French fries.

Serves 4

This works well when done quickly—don't worry if the bacon gets too black to eat. The important factor is that it keeps the birds moist.

Italian-Style Squab with Olive Oil and Herbs

8 squabs, bone in, butterflied
Salt and pepper to taste
¾ cup olive oil

Juice and zest of 1 lemon
½ cup fresh Italian parsley,
  chopped, for garnish

1. Rinse each squab and pat dry on paper towels. Sprinkle the birds on both sides with salt and pepper.
2. Set the grill on high.
3. Mix the oil, lemon juice, and lemon zest in a bowl. Spread on squabs and grill for 3 minutes.
4. Baste with the oil and turn. Grill for another 3–4 minutes or until nicely brown. Sprinkle with parsley and serve.

Serves 4

This is an easy and elegant recipe. It's fine to use frozen squab—thaw before using.

Quail Stuffed with Italian Mushrooms

Serves 4

Quail dry out easily but make a delicate morsel when boned and stuffed. If you don't know a hunter, you can buy boneless quail online.

8 boneless quail, rinsed
Salt and pepper to taste
1 package commercial chicken gravy
½ cup dry white wine
1 stick butter
1 cup porcini (Italian brown) mushrooms, brushed and sliced
½ cup sweet onion, finely chopped

1 cup wild rice, cooked to package directions
1 teaspoon dried sage leaves or 8 fresh ones, shredded
1 teaspoon fresh basil
¼ teaspoon ground nutmeg
Salt and pepper to taste
4 slices bacon

1. Rinse the quail and pat dry. Season with salt and pepper.
2. Make the gravy according to the package directions, adding the white wine. Set aside.
3. Melt the butter in a saucepan and sauté the mushrooms and onions until soft, about 8 minutes. Then add the cooked wild rice and stir in the rest of the ingredients (except the bacon).
4. Set the grill to medium and leave room for indirect heat.
5. Stuff the quail with the mushroom-and-rice mixture and close the opening with small metal skewers. Place in a metal or enameled roasting pan large enough to hold the quail without piling them up. Place them breast-side up.
6. Pour the gravy over the quail, then arrange half strips of bacon over the breast of the quail.
7. Place on the grill, over indirect heat, and close the lid. Roast for 20–30 minutes, depending on the heat of the grill. Grill until brown, or at least 150°F with a meat thermometer. Serve with fruit sauce and extra wild rice. Garnish with watercress.

Hunter-Style Rabbit Roasted with White Vermouth

*1 3–3½-pound rabbit, cut into
    serving pieces
1 cup flour, seasoned with salt
    and pepper
½ stick butter
1 cup white vermouth*

*6 bay leaves, dried
10 black peppercorns, bruised
    in a mortar and pestle
1 tablespoon rosemary leaves,
    dried, or 2 tablespoons
    fresh*

Serves 4

Rabbit is a delicious, light meat that goes well with winter vegetables such as beets, squash, and turnips.

1. Rinse the rabbit in cold water and pat dry on paper towels. Place the seasoned flour on a large piece of waxed paper and roll the rabbit pieces in the flour to coat.
2. Set the grill on low, or wait until the coals have died down.
3. Melt the butter in a large cast-iron frying pan. Add the rabbit and cook until browned. Then add the vermouth, bay leaves, peppercorns, and rosemary and remove from heat.
4. Place a piece of aluminum foil loosely over the frying pan and put the pan in the grill and close the lid.
5. Roast the rabbit for 40 minutes or until very tender. Remove bay leaves. Serve with wide egg noodles and a crisp salad.

Fresh Rabbit

If you know anyone who raises rabbits, one thing is for sure: They will always have too many! So, you may well benefit from fresh, ready-to-cook rabbits. There are dozens of recipes and all of them are fairly rich because rabbit is so lean.

Venison Medallions with
Wild Mushroom Sauce and Berries

1 pint fresh or frozen lingonberries or blueberries
Juice and zest of 1 large orange
½ cup sugar, or to taste
2 tablespoons honey
½ teaspoon ground cardamom
1 tablespoon cornstarch mixed with 3 tablespoons cold water
Pinch salt
3 tablespoons butter
4 shallots, peeled and minced
1 clove garlic, peeled and chopped
2 cups wild mushrooms such as morels, oysters, or chanterelles, peeled and chopped

2 tablespoons flour
2 cups beef broth, warmed
¼ teaspoon ground cloves
6 juniper berries, bruised in a mortar and pestle
¼ cup port wine
½ cup dry red wine
4 medallions of venison, about 6 ounces each
Salt and pepper to taste
4 tablespoons olive oil

1. Put lingonberries or blueberries, orange juice and zest, sugar, honey, cardamom, cornstarch-and-water mixture, and a pinch of salt in a saucepan and bring to a boil. Cook until thick, about 5 minutes. Set aside.
2. For the mushroom sauce, melt the butter in a large saucepan. Sauté the shallots, garlic, and mushrooms for about 8 minutes on low heat.
3. Blend in the flour, stirring and cooking for 3 minutes. Then stir in the warm beef broth. Bring to a boil and stir constantly for 2 minutes.
4. Add the cloves, juniper berries, port wine, and dry red wine. Reduce heat. Simmer for 20 minutes. Set aside for use with the venison.
5. Set the grill at medium-high (about 400°F).
6. Sprinkle the medallions with salt and pepper. Brush the meat with olive oil. Grill very quickly, about 4 minutes per side. Serve the medallions on a platter covered with warm mushroom sauce. Serve the berry condiment on the side.

Tender Marinated Venison Steaks

Salt and pepper to taste
1 2-pound boneless venison
steak or 4 8-ounce rib eye
steaks
4 tablespoons juniper berries
1 cup dry red wine such as
burgundy
½ cup olive oil
4 garlic cloves, peeled and
mashed

1 small onion, peeled and
sliced
10 black peppercorns, cracked
4 bay leaves
1 tablespoon Worcestershire
sauce
1 teaspoon sea salt

Serves 4

Both the Scandinavians and Native Americans cooked venison in similar ways—using wood fires, lots of smoke, and plenty of juniper berries.

1. Salt and pepper the steaks and stuff them with juniper berries, pressing them into the meat.
2. Mix the rest of the ingredients together to create a marinade. Place the steak(s) in the marinade, cover, and refrigerate for 1 hour.
3. Set the grill on medium-high.
4. Grill the steak(s) for 4 minutes per side, basting often. Serve with puréed chestnuts, mashed potatoes, or noodles.

The Taste of Venison

Though not "gamey," venison has a lot of flavor and can stand up to strong sauces and condiments. When overcooked, it dries out and gets tough and stringy. It is perfect when medium-rare. Although some deer are hunted for private consumption, the venison you buy is farm raised and very good indeed. It has no hormones added, is grass fed, and is tasty.

Creamy Puréed Chestnuts for Game

Makes 11½ cups

This is also excellent with chicken and turkey, duck and goose. It's a real holiday treat!

1 pound chestnuts
½ cup chicken broth
1 tablespoon butter

½ cup heavy cream
Salt and pepper to taste
Dash of nutmeg

1. Make X-shaped slits in the flat sides of the chestnuts.
2. Set the grill on high.
3. Grill the chestnuts until they pop open. Then cool and remove both shells and skins.
4. Place chestnuts in the blender with the rest of the ingredients at medium speed until puréed. Serve alongside any wild game.

Apple and Prune Sauce for Game

Makes 2 cups

These fruits are a natural with game but also go well with chicken, turkey, and pork. This simple sauce keeps in the refrigerator for at least a week.

12 pitted prunes, cut into pieces
Apple cider to cover the prunes, about 1 cup
3 Granny Smith or other tart apples, peeled and cored
Juice of 1 orange

¼-inch slice lemon, skin on
1 teaspoon cinnamon
½ teaspoon ground cloves
4 tablespoons brown sugar, or to taste
Pinch of salt

Soak the prunes in the cider for 2 hours or until they absorb all of the liquid. Cut the apples into chunks. Place all ingredients in a saucepan. Cover and simmer until soft, adding more cider if necessary. Serve over wild game.

Vegetables

Tuscan Baby Artichokes

½ cup extra-virgin olive oil
¼ cup aged balsamic vinegar
Juice of ½ lemon
½ teaspoon salt
½ teaspoon dry English mustard

Freshly ground black or white pepper
1 teaspoon salt
10 coriander seeds, bruised
12 baby artichokes, about the size of Ping-Pong balls

1. Whisk lemon, vinegar, olive oil, mustard, salt, and pepper together until emulsified, or whirl in a blender.
2. Bring a large pot of water to a boil. Add salt and coriander.
3. Trim stems off artichokes and remove outer leaves. Boil the artichokes for 15 minutes, or until barely tender.
4. Drain the artichokes and cool until they are comfortable to handle. Split the artichokes. Using a melon baller, scoop out the choke, the tiny inside leaves that are hair thin. Sprinkle the artichokes with the balsamic vinaigrette.
5. Set grill to medium.
6. Grill the artichokes until lightly browned, well above the coals or flame. Serve hot or cold with the rest of the vinaigrette as a dipping sauce.

Baby Your Artichokes

Baby artichokes are available in the spring. They are a traditional part of Italian Easter celebrations. You can easily double the recipe to serve as a green vegetable rather than as part of an antipasto. They must be parboiled before grilling or they will be inedible. Make extra artichokes and marinate them for use in salads.

Classic Asparagus with Lemon and Olive Oil

1 pound asparagus
½ cup olive oil

Juice of ½ lemon

1. Rinse the asparagus and pat dry on paper towels. Remove the tough, woody bottoms. Using a vegetable peeler, remove tough outer skin, starting halfway down the spears.
2. Set grill for medium-low and make room for indirect heat.
3. Using thin metal skewers of about 12 inches in length, skewer the asparagus across the bottom and again, halfway up. Sprinkle with oil and lemon juice.
4. Grill for about 8–10 minutes per side, depending on the heat of the grill and the thickness of the spears. Serve with lemon butter or Hollandaise sauce.

Serves 4

You need fairly thick asparagus spears for this recipe. Fast Perfect Hollandaise Sauce (page 240) is a nice addition, adding elegance to the dish.

Grill-Roasted Summer Corn

8–12 ears of corn

½ cup unsalted butter, melted

1. Set the grill on medium-high.
2. Remove the husks and silk from the corn. Presoak the corn in a bowl of water for 10 to 20 minutes. Paint the corn with butter.
3. Grill for about 4 minutes per side, turning often and adding butter. Serve with more butter, salt, and pepper.

How to Grill Corn

There is some disagreement on how to grill corn. Some people prefer to presoak it without disturbing the husks. Others do a delicate operation, folding back the husks, removing the silk, adding salt and butter, then tying the husks back over the corn. Still others peel the corn, spread butter on it, and put it directly on the grill.

Serves 4

The presoaked corn is more steamed than grilled. And, unless the corn is super young and tender, putting it directly on the grill can toughen it.

Nona's Baby Eggplant with Herbs

Serves 4
in an antipasto

Baby eggplants can be grilled and added to a vegetable mélange like ratatouille. Or they can be added to an antipasto with other grilled vegetables.

4 tablespoons sherry vinegar
4 tablespoons olive oil
½ teaspoon wasabi powder
Salt to taste

4–6 baby eggplants
½ cup Parmesan cheese, grated

1. Whisk together the vinegar, oil, wasabi, and salt.
2. Rinse the eggplants and trim off their stems. Cut the eggplants in half lengthwise. Score the eggplants crosswise, being careful to stay inside their skins.
3. Set grill to medium and place the rack 6 inches over the coals.
4. Paint the eggplant halves with the oil mixture and grill cut-side down for 4–5 minutes. Turn, sprinkle on the cheese, and grill for 2–3 minutes more.

French-Style Green Beans

Serves 4

This is a wonderful Italian-style dish. You need a two-sided grill rack with a long handle and close-together bars so the beans won't fall through.

1 pound green string beans
1 quart water with 1 teaspoon salt added
½ cup olive oil
6 fresh basil leaves, shredded, or 1 tablespoon dried basil

4 cloves garlic, smashed, peeled, and minced
Salt and pepper to taste

1. Rinse the beans and trim off the ends.
2. Bring the salted water to a boil and parboil the beans, about 5 minutes. Shock the beans in icy cold water to keep them green. Drain the beans. Set on paper towels to dry.
3. Set grill on medium. Mix the rest of the ingredients together.
4. Place the beans on the long-handled grilling utensil and brush the beans with oil mixture. Grill until lightly browned but not burned.

Milanese Cornmeal Cakes with Herbs and Bacon

6 strips bacon
3 cups water
1 teaspoon salt, or to taste
¾ cup cornmeal (or follow polenta directions on package)

½ cup fresh herbs of your choice, chopped (parsley, cilantro, rosemary, oregano, or mix it up)
½ cup Parmesan or Romano cheese, freshly grated
Salt and pepper to taste

Makes 6 cakes

You can use white or yellow cornmeal or you can spend some extra money and buy polenta. Serve with butter or, for breakfast, with maple syrup.

1. Fry the bacon until crisp, place on paper towels to drain, and set aside.
2. Bring the water to a boil and add salt. Stir in the cornmeal and keep stirring until thickened, about 10 minutes. Remove from the heat.
3. Crumble the bacon and stir it into the polenta/cornmeal. Add the herbs and cheese. Mix well and taste for seasonings.
4. Line a pie plate or small brownie pan with parchment paper or plastic wrap. Spread the cornmeal mixture in the pan. Cover and refrigerate for 2–3 hours. It will get very stiff.
5. Set grill to medium with the rack about 6 inches above the coals or low gas flame.
6. Remove the polenta from the baking pan or pie plate and cut in squares or triangles. Grill until nicely browned, about 3–4 minutes per side, turning frequently. Serve as a side or as a base for stew or grilled fish, meat, or chicken.

The Magic of Polenta

Most Europeans think of corn as animal fodder. They didn't have corn until well into the sixteenth century, when visitors to the colonies brought it back home. The resourceful Italians renamed cornmeal "polenta." Once cooked, it can be fried, sautéed, or grilled. It's very bland, so the more you add to it, the better. Using aromatic woods in your grill also adds to the flavor.

Cocktail Eggplant Slices

1 large eggplant	*Juice of 1 lemon*
Enough salt to cover both sides	*Pepper*
of each slice of eggplant	*8–10 slices white American*
²⁄₃ cup olive oil	*cheese*
2 cloves garlic, chopped	

Serves 4

The eggplants can be served as a side, dressed with tomato sauce, or included in a big hero sandwich.

1. Rinse the eggplant and trim off the stem. Cut crosswise into ½-inch slices.
2. Salt each slice of eggplant on both sides and place it on a dinner plate covered with a paper towel. Keep salting and stacking the eggplant. You may need to make a second stack if it gets too unstable. When all of the eggplant is stacked, invert a second plate on top. Place a weight on top of the inverted plate.
3. Heat the grill to medium-high.
4. After about 20 minutes, you will see brown liquid dripping onto the paper towel under the eggplant slices. Press down on the inverted plate and let more liquid drain out. Discard the liquid and pat the slices dry.
5. Mix together the oil, garlic, lemon juice, and pepper. Paint the oil mixture on both sides of the eggplant.
6. Grill for about 4 minutes per side, or until nicely brown. Then place a slice of cheese on each piece of eggplant and grill for another few minutes, or until the cheese melts.

Melting Cheese

Here's a secret. When you want a delicious melting cheese, use the best-quality white American—it really works. It's a blend of cheeses, which makes it easier to melt than others.

Yukon Gold Potatoes with Oregano

4 Yukon Gold potatoes,
scrubbed
4 tablespoons olive oil

4 teaspoons dried oregano
Salt and pepper to taste

1. Set the grill to medium.
2. Cut the potatoes in quarters, lengthwise, and place on a piece of heavy-duty aluminum foil.
3. Drizzle with olive oil and sprinkle with oregano, salt, and pepper.
4. Place on grill, lid closed, and let bake for 20 minutes; check often. They're done when the outside is brown and crunchy and the inside is soft.

> **Serves 4**
>
> Yukon Gold potatoes stand up to frying and grilling. They are very good and readily available. This recipe comes out crisp and tasty.
>
>

Roasted Garlic

2 heads unpeeled garlic
2 tablespoons olive oil

2 tablespoons water

1. Cut ¼ inch off the very top part of the garlic heads crosswise and place on large sheets of heavy-duty aluminum foil. Drizzle with olive oil and water.
2. Close the aluminum foil to make a packet, leaving a little "chimney" for the steam to escape.
3. Heat grill to low heat. Roast garlic for 20 minutes. When cool, you can squeeze garlic cloves out, as you need them for recipes. Store in plastic bags in the refrigerator for future use.

> **Makes 2 heads roasted garlic**
>
> Roasted garlic is an invaluable flavoring that can be used in many dishes or served on its own as a spread. Just don't let it burn.
>
>

Roasted Garlic Spread for Crostini

1 long, thin loaf French bread
5 ounces butter, softened
2–4 cloves Roasted Garlic (page 133), mashed
1 teaspoon capers

1 tablespoon mixed fresh herbs, your choice (parsley, sage, rosemary, oregano), chopped
1 teaspoon anchovy paste
1 teaspoon minced onion

1. Cut the bread in ¼-inch rounds.
2. Mix all of the ingredients for the spread together using a hand-held mixer.
3. Toast the bread on one side on the grill. Turn and toast on the other side, just a few seconds. Spread the bread and serve.

Roasted Garlic Salad Dressing

2 cloves Roasted Garlic (page 133), squeezed from their paper
¾ cup olive oil
½ teaspoon dry mustard
¼-inch slice fresh lemon with peel, seeds removed

½ teaspoon sugar
½ teaspoon salt
¼ cup red wine vinegar
1 tablespoon herbs de Provence

Mix all ingredients in the blender. Store in refrigerator for future use. This should keep for up to a week.

Roasted Garlic Stuffing for Meat

4 cloves Roasted Garlic (page
    133), mashed
6 ounces butter
¼ cup soft breadcrumbs
4 teaspoons fresh rosemary
    spikes, chopped

1 teaspoon fresh lemon zest
½ teaspoon fennel or anise
    seeds, bruised
Freshly ground black pepper to
    taste

Mix all of the ingredients together. Stuff into pockets cut into lamb or pork chops or place on chicken breasts that will be rolled and then grilled.

Makes 4–6 tablespoons

This recipe makes enough stuffing for 4 pork or lamb chops or 4 rolled chicken breasts.

Meaty Portobello Mushrooms

1 cup balsamic vinaigrette
    (page 128)

2 large portobello mushrooms,
    4–6 inches across

1. Marinate the mushrooms for 1–2 hours in the balsamic vinaigrette.
2. Heat grill to medium.
3. Grill well above the coals for 3 minutes, turn, and grill for 3–4 more minutes. Give larger mushrooms an extra minute or two.

Protein in Mushrooms

Mushrooms are rich in protein as well as vital minerals. And the deliciousness of these big brown mushrooms makes them a meal or an asset to a meal. They are great baked and stuffed. Just use commercial stuffing and toss some pieces of chopped bacon on top before baking.

Serves 2

These mushrooms are wonderful warm sliced over salads, in sandwiches, and as part of an antipasto. They go well with roasted peppers and Gorgonzola cheese.

Versatile Grilled Onions

*2 large Vidalia or Bermuda
   onions
Salt and pepper to taste
1 tablespoon cider vinegar
1 stick butter*

*1 tablespoon honey
1 tablespoon spicy brown
   mustard
1 teaspoon Worcestershire
   sauce*

1. Remove the skins and ends from the onions and cut them crosswise
   in thick wedges. Sprinkle sparingly with the salt and pepper.
2. Mix the rest of the ingredients in a small saucepan and warm until
   the butter melts.
3. Set the grill to medium, or place rack 6 inches over coals.
4. Paint the onions with the sauce and grill for 3 minutes. Then turn and
   grill for 3 minutes more. The onions should be golden brown, not burned.

Wisconsin Peppers with Gorgonzola Spread

*2 large red bell peppers,
   halved, cored, and seeded
4 tablespoons butter, softened
2 tablespoons Gorgonzola
   cheese, softened*

*½ teaspoon celery salt
1 teaspoon red pepper flakes,
   or to taste*

1. Heat grill to high.
2. Place peppers on the grill skin-side down. Grill until charred.
3. Remove the peppers with tongs and place in a paper or heavy plastic
   bag. When the peppers are cool, peel off the skin. If saving for future
   use, place in a bowl or jar with a few tablespoons of olive oil.
4. To make the spread, blend the rest of the ingredients together.
5. Toast the bread, and spread a thin covering of the butter mixture on
   each piece of toast. Place a small strip of roasted pepper on each
   crostini.

Summer Squash Boats

4 medium squashes
½ cup olive oil
½ cup onion, chopped
2 cloves Roasted Garlic (page 133), mashed
8 tablespoons breadcrumbs
2 sprigs fresh mint, chopped, or two teaspoons dried

1 teaspoon paprika
Salt and lots of freshly ground pepper
4 tablespoons Parmesan cheese
4 slices bacon, optional

Serves 4

Freshly picked zucchinis or yellow squashes taste best. Squashes from your local grocery will also work.

1. Rinse the zucchinis or squashes and dry them with paper towels. Cut the top third off, horizontally. Using a melon baller, scoop out the centers of the squashes, reserving the pulp.
2. Set the gas grill on medium or make a bed of hot coals.
3. Heat the olive oil and sauté the onion and reserved squash pulp until soft. Take off the grill and stir in the garlic, breadcrumbs, and mint, then add the paprika, salt and pepper, and cheese.
4. Place the "boats" on pieces of heavy-duty aluminum foil and add the bacon.
5. Roast on the grill for 20 minutes or until the bacon is crisp and the tops brown.

Dry versus Fresh Breadcrumbs

Dry breadcrumbs are usually the commercial variety that comes in a box, seasoned or unseasoned. They are also referred to in recipes as fine breadcrumbs. Making fresh breadcrumbs is very simple. Just take some stale or lightly toasted French or Italian bread and put it in the food processor until it forms crumbs of the consistency your recipe requires.

Herb-Stuffed North Carolina Tomatoes

Serves 4

This is delectable, a fine side dish with any entrée. You can stuff the tomatoes a day in advance and keep them in the refrigerator.

4 large beefsteak tomatoes
4 cloves Roasted Garlic (page 133), mashed
2 tablespoons fresh basil, shredded
8 tablespoons fresh breadcrumbs

Salt and pepper to taste
4 tablespoons olive oil
4 teaspoons Gruyère cheese, freshly grated
4 tablespoons fresh parsley, chopped, for garnish

1. Rinse the tomatoes and pat them dry on paper towels. Cut the very tops off the tomatoes. Using a melon baller, remove some of the juice and seeds from inside the tomatoes.
2. Mix together the garlic, basil, breadcrumbs, salt, and pepper. Add shredded cheese.
3. Get the grill going or wait until the coals are ashen.
4. Stuff the tomatoes, pressing the breadcrumb-and-herb meal down into the fruit. Place each tomato on a piece of heavy-duty aluminum foil and sprinkle top with extra olive oil.
5. Roast with lid closed for about 10 minutes, or until the tomatoes are soft and the tops browned. Sprinkle chopped parsley over the tops of the tomatoes.

Parboiling Vegetables

Many vegetables do not do well on the grill unless they are parboiled in advance. These vegetables will dry out and toughen before they are cooked. Some crisp or soft, pulpy vegetables, such as eggplant, do not need to be parboiled. Adding spice to the boiling water will enhance the flavor of the vegetables. You can also add lemon juice, lemon zest, or peppercorns, and always add some salt.

French-Style Fillet of Beef

¼ cup dry red wine
¼ cup red wine vinegar
1 cup olive oil
2 cloves Roasted Garlic (page 133), peeled
½ teaspoon sugar
½ teaspoon salt
½ teaspoon Worcestershire sauce
1 teaspoon green peppercorns, bruised
Freshly ground black pepper to taste
1½ pounds filet mignon

1. Blend all of the ingredients except the meat in a food processor or blender to make the marinade.
2. Cut the beef into bite-sized pieces and place in the marinade. Marinate the meat for 1–2 hours.
3. Set the grill to high temperature.
4. Thread the pieces onto 8 presoaked wooden skewers. Grill for about 2 minutes per side. Serve hot or cold.

About Skewers

Most supermarkets and all specialty food stores sell wooden skewers of about 10 to 12 inches in length. These will burn if they have not been presoaked for at least an hour, the longer the better. Also available are miniature swords, which are nice and thin and made of stainless steel. Some have very decorative handles. Whatever you choose, food on skewers is appetizing and can be very attractive.

Old-Fashioned Steak and Onions with Cheese Sauce

1 tablespoon butter
1 tablespoon flour
¼ cup chicken broth
½ cup rich milk or cream
⅛ teaspoon nutmeg
Salt and pepper to taste
½ cup sharp cheddar cheese, grated
½ cup white American cheese, grated

1½ pounds sirloin steak
16 pearl onions, about ¾–1 inch in diameter
½ cup butter
1 tablespoon Worcestershire sauce
1 tablespoon tomato paste
1 teaspoon sherry (optional)

Serves 4

You can make the sauce in advance, heating it at the last minute to melt the cheese. Do not over-heat the sauce or it will curdle.

1. Melt 1 tablespoon of butter over low heat and whisk in 1 tablespoon flour, letting the mixture cook for 3–4 minutes to get rid of "floury" taste. Slowly stir in the chicken broth, milk, nutmeg, salt, and pepper, giving the sauce time to "digest" each new addition. Add the cheeses and set aside. Keep warm (or reheat when meat is ready).
2. Cut the beef into bite-sized pieces. Cut off the ends of the onions and peel.
3. Prepare the gas grill or coals to medium-high.
4. Whisk the butter, Worcestershire, and tomato paste in a small pot and let the butter melt. Set aside.
5. Thread the meat and onions onto skewers (if wood, presoak them). Paint the meat and onions with the butter mixture.
6. Grill the skewers, basting with more sauce when you turn them.
7. Reheat the cheese sauce and stir in the sherry. Slather the finished meat and onions with cheese sauce and serve as is or on toasted rolls or bread.

Spicy Mustard Chicken

Serves 4

The mixture of two types of mustard, vinegar, and butter makes this delicious. Serve over baby greens with a light dressing on the side.

½ cup butter, softened
2 tablespoons Dijon-style
    mustard
2 tablespoons coarsely ground
    brown mustard
2 teaspoons white wine
    vinegar
1 teaspoon dried sage leaves

½ teaspoon celery salt
½ teaspoon freshly ground
    black pepper, or to taste
1½ pounds boneless, skinless
    chicken breasts
Flour for dredging
Vegetables of your choice—
    peppers, onions, etc.

1. Mix butter, mustards, vinegar, sage leaves, celery salt, and pepper together until well blended.
2. Cut the chicken into chunks and dredge with flour.
3. Place the mustard-butter mixture on a piece of waxed paper and roll the chicken in it until evenly coated. At this point, you can wrap the chicken in plastic and refrigerate if you want to cook and serve it later.
4. Set the grill to medium or let the coals die to ashes.
5. Thread the chicken and vegetables onto skewers. Grill until the chicken is nicely browned, about 3 minutes, and then turn and grill for 3 more minutes.

Teriyaki!

Don't be afraid to add other seasonings—you really can't mess up this one. It's very good with a teriyaki dipping sauce.

Chicken Breasts à la Indienne

1½ pounds boneless, skinless
  chicken breasts
1½ cups plain yogurt
Juice of ½ lime
1 tablespoon curry powder, or
  to taste
2 cloves garlic, peeled and
  minced

2 teaspoons Tabasco sauce,
  or to taste
Salt to taste
⅛ teaspoon ground coriander
  seeds
1 tablespoon fresh gingerroot,
  minced

Serves 4

This is a takeoff on an Indian recipe. Serve it with rice and Tamarind Glaze (page 62).

1. Cut the chicken into pieces. Mix the rest of the ingredients together in a bowl. Then add the chicken, turning to coat. Cover and refrigerate for 4–6 hours, turning occasionally.
2. Set the grill to medium.
3. Thread the chicken onto skewers (presoaked if wooden). Grill until nicely browned. Serve with rice and chutney.

Tangy Scallops with Bacon

12–16 of the largest scallops
  you can find
Juice of ½ lemon

Salt and pepper to taste
6–8 pieces bacon

Serves 4

The trick in this recipe is to cook the bacon partially, just on one side, so that you'll have soft scallops and crisp bacon.

1. Rinse the scallops in cold water and dry on paper towels. Sprinkle the scallops with lemon juice, salt, and pepper.
2. Fry the bacon on one side.
3. Wrap the scallops in bacon with the cooked side in (the raw side will get cooked on the grill). Put 2–3 scallops on each skewer. If the bacon is not tightly wrapped, secure it with toothpicks.
4. Set the gas grill to medium or wait until the coals have plenty of ash.
5. Grill until the bacon is crisp, turning once. This should take no more than 3–4 minutes per side.

Chicken Sate

For the sate:
1 cup peanut butter
½ cup canned, unsweetened coconut milk
2 tablespoons toasted sesame seed oil
¼ cup white wine vinegar or rice vinegar
2–4 cloves garlic, peeled and minced
1-inch piece gingerroot, peeled and minced, or to taste
½ teaspoon chili paste
1 tablespoon hoisin sauce
Juice of 1 fresh lime
1 tablespoon Asian fish sauce

For the chicken:
½ cup soy sauce
Juice of ½ lime
1 clove garlic, minced
1-inch piece fresh gingerroot, peeled and minced
¼ cup dry sherry
1¼ pounds boneless chicken breast, cut into bite-sized pieces

1. Place all sate ingredients in a food processor and whirl until very well blended. Store in a tightly closed container in the refrigerator. Remove from the refrigerator 1 hour before using so that it isn't cold.
3. Mix the soy sauce, lime juice, garlic, gingerroot, and sherry together in a nonreactive (ceramic or glass) bowl. Add the chicken and mix to coat well. Marinate for 1–2 hours.
4. Drain the marinade and discard. Put 1 or 2 pieces of chicken on each presoaked wooden skewer. (The number of sticks you need depends on how small you've cut the chicken—at least 16 to 24 skewers.)
5. Prepare the grill to medium.
6. Grill until nicely browned on both sides, turning as necessary. Serve on a large platter with a bowl of sate dipping sauce in the center.

Duck Breasts Marinated in Calvados

*1½ pounds boneless, skinless
    duck breast*
Salt and pepper to taste
*1 cup Calvados (apple
    brandy), divided*
½ cup apple cider
*1 tablespoon maple syrup or
    honey*

*A thin slice of orange with skin
    on, seeds removed, twisted
    to release orange oils*
*Juice of ½ lemon with lemon
    rind added in strips*
Salt and pepper to taste

Serves 4

Serve with wild rice
studded with dried
cranberries, and a
crisp salad on the side.

1. Rinse the duck breasts and pat them dry on paper towels. Cut them into 1½-inch chunks. Sprinkle the duck with salt and pepper.
2. Mix half of the Calvados with the rest of the ingredients in a large bowl. Cover and marinate duck, refrigerated, for 2 hours.
3. Prepare the grill to medium temperature.
4. Thread the chunks of duck onto skewers, and sprinkle with the remaining half cup of Calvados. Put on the grill and stand back—it will probably flare up, which is fine. Most gourmets recommend that you serve duck medium-rare, at least pink. Grill for 3–4 minutes, turn, and then grill for 2–3 minutes more.

Oranges, Limes, and Lemons

Whereas orange and lemon peel (zest) are very good when used in cooking, lime peel grows very bitter when heated. However, lime juice is delicious in many recipes and can be substituted for lemon juice. Also available in many Latino markets are "sour" oranges. These add a great flavor to many Cuban, Mexican, and other South and Central American dishes.

Cajun-Style Skewered Shrimp

Serves 4

Cajun "red or black" style comes from pepper, pepper, and more pepper.

1 teaspoon cayenne pepper
1 teaspoon black pepper, freshly ground
1 teaspoon white peppercorns, freshly ground
1 teaspoon pink peppercorns, freshly ground
1 tablespoon garlic powder
1 tablespoon onion powder
1/2 teaspoon dark brown sugar
1 teaspoon salt
1 teaspoon dried thyme
1 1/4 pounds jumbo shrimp, peeled and deveined
1/2 cup unsalted butter, melted

1. Mix all dry ingredients until well blended. (This will keep in a closed jar for months at a time.)
2. Preheat the grill to high.
3. Rub some of the pepper mixture into the shrimp (use rubber gloves if you have sensitive hands). Then thread the shrimp onto skewers.
4. Grill, basting with melted butter, for about 2 minutes per side, or until the shrimp are pink.

Cajun Spice!

Black peppercorns, red peppers, pink peppercorns, and white ones, too! Lots of pepper, mixed with garlic and onion powder, holds the secrets of the South. The true secrets are in the quantities of which peppers are employed. Some are heavier on the black, others on the red. It's said that some of the most successful Cajun cooks add a touch of brown sugar to the rub!

Chinese-Style Sweet and Sour Shrimp

*1¼ pounds jumbo shrimp,
   peeled and deveined
¼ cup black bean sauce
Juice of ½ lime*

*1 teaspoon white wine vinegar
2 teaspoons sugar
1-inch piece fresh gingerroot,
   minced*

1. Rinse the shrimp and pat dry on paper towels. Thread the shrimp onto wooden skewers that you have presoaked in water for 1 hour.
2. Mix the rest of the ingredients together and brush on the shrimp.
3. Set grill to high heat.
4. Grill the shrimp for 2 minutes per side.

Serves 4

This is so simple and delicious. You can get black bean sauce at Asian markets.

Mushroom Medley

*16 medium-sized mushrooms—
   mix them up (shiitake,
   Italian brown, and/or white)
⅓ cup balsamic vinegar
½ cup olive oil*

*2 tablespoons fresh rosemary,
   or one tablespoon dried
Salt and pepper to taste*

1. Brush the dirt off the mushrooms and remove the stems.
2. Prepare the grill to medium.
3. Just before grilling, mix the vinegar, oil, rosemary, salt, and pepper, and coat the mushrooms.
4. Thread the mushrooms onto skewers and grill for 3–5 minutes, turning and grilling for another 3 minutes.

Serves 4 as a side dish

This is fine as a side dish with any meat or poultry entrée. The grilled mushrooms can also be added to sandwiches— especially good with cheese.

Middle Eastern Lamb and Apricot Kebabs

16 whole dried apricots
2 tablespoons fresh mint, chopped
Juice and zest of 1 lemon, minced
4 cloves garlic, peeled and minced
1 tablespoon cumin

1 tablespoon ground coriander seeds
4 whole cloves
⅔ cup olive oil
1 teaspoon salt
Cayenne pepper to taste
1½ pounds lamb, from the leg, cut into 1½-inch chunks

1. Place the apricots in a bowl with water to cover and soak until they are plump.
2. Mix the mint, lemon juice and zest, garlic, cumin, coriander seeds, cloves, olive oil, salt, and cayenne pepper together in a large bowl. Add the lamb, turning to coat each piece.
3. Cover tightly and refrigerate for 4 hours, turning once.
4. Preheat the gas grill to medium or start the coals, waiting until they are covered with ash.
5. Thread the lamb, alternating with apricots, onto skewers. Grill to the desired degree of doneness (about 4 minutes per side for medium-rare).

The Garlic Capital

Every year thousands flock to the tiny town of Gilroy, California, to celebrate the town's annual garlic festival. Gilroy has been hosting the world's best food festival for twenty-five years, since 1979.

East Indian Shrimp with Curry Rub

1 cup whole mayonnaise
1 teaspoon lime juice
1 teaspoon lemon juice
1 teaspoon Dijon-style mustard
1 teaspoon high-quality curry
  powder
1¼ pounds raw shrimp, tails
  on, peeled and deveined

1 cup fresh orange juice
1 tablespoon orange rind,
  grated
4 tablespoons curry powder
Salt and pepper to taste

> **Serves 6–8 as an appetizer, 4 as an entrée for a summer lunch**
>
> This simple recipe works well with cocktails at a party. Make the sauce in advance and refrigerate it until you are ready to serve.

1. For the sauce, mix mayonnaise, lime juice, lemon juice, mustard, and curry powder together and store in the refrigerator until ready to serve.
2. Set grill to medium.
3. Rinse shrimp and sprinkle with orange juice and orange rind. Sprinkle the shrimp with curry powder, salt, and pepper.
4. Thread onto skewers and grill until just pink, about 2 minutes per side. Serve hot or at room temperature, with the sauce on the side. Remove from the skewers and use tails to hold the shrimp if the occasion is casual, or provide toothpicks.

Shrimp Is Great When Dipped

Try a dip that's a little different for cocktail shrimp by adding some lime juice and soy sauce to mayonnaise for a fine flavor. You can also mince some fresh gingerroot and add it. Adding some Japanese wasabi will heat things up for shrimp or crabs.

Cherry Tomatoes and Fennel

2 medium fennel bulbs, trimmed and cut into quarters
16 cherry tomatoes

½ cup any good French dressing
2 tablespoons olive oil
10 fresh basil leaves

1. Parboil the fennel chunks in salted water for 10 minutes. Drain the fennel on paper towels. Thread the tomatoes and fennel onto separate skewers. Brush them with dressing.
2. Heat grill to medium, place the fennel over indirect flame and cook for 4 minutes per side, or until browned. Put the tomatoes on when you turn the fennel. The tomatoes will cook quicker than the fennel.
3. Place the vegetables on a platter, sprinkle with olive oil and basil, and serve warm or cool.

Classic Italian Hot Sausage and Peppers

1½ pounds Italian sausage
4 green or red Italian frying peppers (thin-skinned)

2 red onions, peeled
2 tablespoons olive oil

1. Parboil the sausages for 10 minutes, then drain them on paper towels and cut into 2-inch chunks.
2. Rinse the peppers and dry on paper towels. Remove the cores and seeds from the peppers. Cut the peppers into large pieces.
3. Cut the onions into quarters, vertically.
4. Thread the sausage, peppers, and onions onto skewers.
5. Preheat the grill to medium or wait until the coals are ash covered.
6. Brush the onions and peppers with oil. Grill until the sausages are brown and the vegetables soft.

Baby Vegetables

*4 tiny eggplants, cut into
   chunks*
8 cherry tomatoes
8 small onions, cut in half
*4 Italian frying peppers, cored,
   seeded, and cut into pieces*
*12 medium-sized mushrooms,
   cleaned and stemmed*
*2 medium zucchini, cut into
   chunks*

Juice of 1 lemon
½ cup olive oil
*1 tablespoon fresh thyme or
   1 teaspoon dried*
Salt and pepper to taste
1 teaspoon hoisin sauce
12 sage leaves

Serves 4

You can mix this up
and have a very col-
orful side dish or use
the veggies in salads
or grilled sandwiches.

1. Rinse the vegetables, except the mushrooms, and dry on paper towels.
2. Make sure the grill is not overly hot but set on medium if gas and
   well ashed if you are cooking over coals.
3. Mix the lemon juice, olive oil, thyme, salt, pepper, and hoisin sauce in
   a small bowl.
4. Thread the vegetables and sage leaves onto skewers. Brush the vegetables with the sauce and grill until softened.

Asian Shopping

*Many supermarkets now have extensive Asian sections, and there are
excellent Asian markets in most towns and all cities. Mix up your
vegetable choices with exciting alternatives from the Far East, such
as napa cabbage or baby bok choy.*

CHAPTER 12
Calzones, Pizzas, and Paninis

Tomato, Basil, and Cheese Calzones

Serves 4

A calzone is a folded, stuffed piece of pizza dough that is baked until the crust is brown.

Cornmeal to sprinkle under the crusts
1½ pounds pizza dough
8 ounces pizza sauce
1 cup mozzarella cheese, shredded
½ cup Parmesan cheese, grated
1 cup ricotta cheese

1 cup loosely packed fresh basil leaves, shredded
2 tablespoons fresh oregano leaves or 2 teaspoons dried
Red pepper flakes to taste
Salt and freshly ground black pepper to taste
1 egg yolk, beaten

1. Spread cornmeal on a board. Roll out the pizza dough into 4 rounds, each 6 inches in diameter.
2. Mix the sauce, cheeses, herbs, and red pepper flakes. Season with salt and pepper. Spread ¼ of the filling on each calzone, covering only half of the dough. Fold the halves that are not sauced over the filling and crimp the edges with a fork.
3. Heat grill to high.
4. Place rounds on a heavy baking pan or pizza stone. Brush the calzones with egg and use a fork to prick the top in two places. Bake in a covered grill for 8–10 minutes, or until brown and bubbly.

Dough-Making Basics

Dough for pizza and calzones is readily available at supermarkets and bakeries. If you buy your dough you will save a great deal of time—aside from the original process of mixing and kneading, dough has to rise for an hour, then after rolling, rise for another 15–20 minutes. Give yourself and your family a break and buy it. You can also use fresh or frozen bread dough, which is pretty much like pizza dough.

Filet Mignon Calzones

1½ pounds pizza dough
2 tablespoons olive oil
½ cup onion, minced
1 tablespoon flour

½ cup beef broth
¾ pound filet mignon, sliced
  thinly
4 slices white American cheese

Serves 4

This is great with a side salad and perhaps a hot black bean casserole.

1. Roll the dough into 4 rounds, each 6–7 inches across.
2. Heat the olive oil in a saucepan, then add the minced onion and sauté. Blend in the flour, then stir in the beef broth and cook until smooth.
3. Add the filet and cook for 1 minute. Spoon the filling onto the bottom half of each calzone, adding one slice of cheese to each. Fold the top over and seal with a fork.
4. Heat grill to high.
5. Bake the calzones on a pizza stone in a covered grill for about 6 minutes or until very hot and golden brown.

Calzones as Fast Food

If you don't mind dribbling down your front, you can eat them on the run—street food. The fillings vary in terms of cheeses, stews, sauces, and veggies. Some may be messier than others!

Pepperoni, Mushroom, and Goat Cheese Calzones

Serves 4

This is savory and goes well with a cold drink, such as beer.

½ cup cornmeal
1½ pounds pizza dough
1 cup mushrooms, stemmed and chopped
2 tablespoons olive oil

8 slices pepperoni, chopped
4 fresh sage leaves, shredded
4 ounces goat cheese, at room temperature

1. Sprinkle the cornmeal on the board and roll the dough into 4 rounds of 6–7 inches across.
2. Sauté the mushrooms in the olive oil, then add pepperoni and sage. Cook for five minutes.
3. Spread goat cheese on bottom half of each calzone and add mushroom mixture. Fold the top half of each calzone over the bottom and crimp shut with a fork.
4. Heat grill to high. Warm pizza stone in grill before placing calzones on it.
5. Bake calzones in a covered grill until sizzling and golden brown.

Fresh Tomato Sauce

Makes 2 cups

Really good pizza sauce is not cooked before it goes on the pizza. You can also use this sauce over pasta.

2 cloves garlic, minced
¼ cup olive oil
16 ounces fresh cherry or plum tomatoes, washed
½ bunch fresh parsley leaves
12 fresh basil leaves

1 teaspoon dried or 2 teaspoons fresh oregano
1 teaspoon salt
Black pepper and/or red pepper flakes to taste

Sauté the garlic in olive oil for 4 minutes, over low flame. Place the garlic and the rest of the ingredients in a blender and purée until very smooth. Don't worry about seeds or stems, they just become added fiber. Use on pizza or pasta.

Florida-Style Calzones

½ cup cornmeal
1½ pounds pizza dough
1 cup of your favorite barbecue sauce
1 pound boneless, skinless
  chicken breasts

1 red onion, thinly sliced
1 cup iceberg lettuce, washed
  and shredded

Serves 4

Kids love these if they
aren't too highly
spiced. You can also
substitute barbecued
pork or beef.

1. Spread the cornmeal on a rolling board and roll out 4 rounds of dough about 6–7 inches in diameter.
2. Prepare grill for indirect heat.
3. Spread sauce on the chicken breasts and barbecue over indirect heat until done, about 5 minutes on each side (depending on the heat of the grill).
4. Place the chicken on a platter and cut it in pieces. Add extra barbecue sauce. Divide the chicken between the 4 rounds of dough, mounding it on the bottom half of each calzone. Add the onion and lettuce. Fold the tops of the calzones over the filled halves and crimp shut with a fork.
5. Grill calzones on a pizza stone until they are brown and crispy.

Egg Washes

An egg wash gives the dough a pleasant yellow color and helps to crisp it. You can use a whole egg, egg yolks, or egg whites. Some egg washes call for the addition of a little water or milk. Using an egg wash is a nice touch but not absolutely necessary. The only time you must have an egg wash is when you are sticking fruit, sprinkles, or nuts to coffee cakes or buns.

Calzones with
Mega Vegetables and Cheese

½ cup cornmeal
1½ pounds pizza dough
4 tablespoons olive oil
1 medium zucchini, sliced thinly
1 roasted red pepper, cut into strips
4 scallions, outside paper removed from bottoms, chopped

8 cherry tomatoes, halved
1 teaspoon dried rosemary
1 teaspoon dried oregano
1 teaspoon red pepper flakes, or to taste
Salt to taste
4 ounces Gorgonzola cheese, crumbled

1. Spread the cornmeal on a rolling board and roll out 4 rounds of dough about 6–7 inches in diameter.
2. Heat the olive oil in a large frying pan and add the vegetables, herbs, and red pepper flakes. Season with salt to taste. Sauté for five minutes, leaving the vegetables crisp.
3. Spread the vegetables on the bottom half of each calzone. Crumble the cheese on top of the vegetables. Close and crimp shut with a fork.
4. Heat grill to high.
5. Bake calzones in a covered grill for 5–8 minutes or until golden brown and very hot.

It's All in the Pan

Pizza pans are generally made from heavy black cast iron and tend to heat evenly and hold the heat. It's important to keep your pizza and calzone crusts nice and crisp. Soggy crusts are not good. Both stones and pans for pizza are quite inexpensive, ranging from $12 to $30, and from 13 inches to 24 inches in size. Buy according to the size of your family and its appetite for pizza and calzones.

Panini with Cheese, Tomatoes, and Mortadella

8 slices Tuscan bread (these should be very large ovals and ¼ inch thick)
¼ cup olive oil
1 teaspoon oregano leaves
2 cloves garlic, or to taste, minced
1 teaspoon freshly ground black pepper, or to taste

16 thin slices fresh, ripe tomato
Provolone cheese sliced to cover the tomatoes
16–24 thin slices mortadella sausage (or salami)
Extra olive oil for the outside of the sandwiches

> **Makes 4 very large sandwiches**
>
> Panini make wonderful, filling lunches or are great cut up as a sports snack, say, while watching a game on TV.
>
>

1. Lay the bread on a cutting board.
2. Mix the oil, oregano, garlic, and pepper and brush it on the bread.
3. Stack up the tomato, cheese, and mortadella. Close the sandwiches and brush with extra olive oil.
4. Arrange the sandwiches on a heavy cast-iron grill pan or in a large cast-iron skillet. Cover with a second pan and add a brick for weight.
5. Set grill to medium.
6. Grill the sandwiches for about 4 minutes on one side, then turn and grill again, using the weight on the other side for a few minutes, until the bread is browned and the cheese is melted.

Other Fillings for Panini

Try some Brie and leftover ham in a panini. Or some cheddar and onion with sliced apple. You may find a raw egg adds some protein to the sandwich. Of course, it will cook when the panini cooks. Try various relishes and meats, too, for exciting changes.

Four-Cheese Panini

Makes 4 extra-large sandwiches

This toasty sandwich is a favorite for any season.

8 slices Tuscan bread (these should be very large ovals and ¼ inch thick)

¼ cup olive oil

1 teaspoon thyme leaves

2 cloves garlic, or to taste, minced

20 Kalamata or Sicilian olives, pitted and chopped

1 teaspoon freshly ground black pepper, or to taste

8 slices provolone cheese

8 slices mozzarella cheese

8 sweet red peppers, roasted

8 slices tomato, to cover surface of sandwich

½ cup Gorgonzola cheese, crumbled

½ cup Parmesan cheese, grated

1. Lay the bread on a cutting board.
2. Mix the oil, thyme, garlic, olives, and black pepper, and brush the bread slices with the mixture. Stack up the provolone and mozzarella cheeses, red peppers, and tomato slices, alternately ending up with tomato or pepper.
3. Sprinkle with the crumbled Gorgonzola and Parmesan cheeses. Close sandwiches and brush with extra olive oil.
4. Arrange the sandwiches on a heavy cast-iron grill pan or in a large cast-iron skillet. Cover with a second pan and add a brick for weight.
5. Set grill to high heat.
6. Grill the sandwiches in a heavy pan, under a weight, on a hot grill until the cheeses are melted and the bread is browned. Turn and finish.

Panini, Pressed, Not Puffed

Panini, being pressed, seems to meld and intensify the flavors within. These sandwiches can be cut in halves, quarters, even eighths, depending on the size of the bread. Buy the big rounds of Tuscan bread. If you have to use regular Italian bread, slice it lengthwise. The bread must have body rather than puff.

Santa Barbara–Style Panini

8 thick slices Tuscan bread
6 ounces cream cheese, at
room temperature
2 teaspoons freshly ground
black pepper
1 teaspoon red pepper flakes

4 tart apples, peeled, cored,
and thinly sliced
¼ pound prosciutto ham, sliced
paper thin
Extra olive oil to brush on the
outside of the sandwiches

> **Makes 4 extra-large sandwiches**
>
> You can cut these up into small wedges and serve them with cocktails. The flavor combination is tantalizing.
>
>

1. Lay out the bread on a cutting board.
2. Whip together the cream cheese, black pepper, and red pepper flakes. Spread the cheese on both sides of the bread; arrange the apple slices on one side and the prosciutto over them. Close the sandwiches and brush with oil.
3. Arrange the sandwiches on a heavy cast-iron grill pan or in a large cast-iron skillet. Cover with a second pan and add a brick for weight.
4. Set grill to high heat.
5. Grill the sandwiches in a heavy pan, under a weight, on a hot grill until golden brown and hot. Turn and bake the other side under a weight.

Complementing Panini!

Serve sprigs of fresh parsley or arugula with panini. Small gherkin pickles, Sicilian or Greek olives, or cherry tomatoes are also nice.

Santa Fe–Style Panini on Sourdough

Makes 4 sandwiches

A great thing about American cooking is the ability to combine ingredients in a variety of ways. Try anything!

8 slices, ¼-to ⅓-inch thick, cut from a large, round loaf of sourdough bread
1 stick butter, at room temperature
4 teaspoons Dijon-style mustard

½ jicama, peeled and thinly sliced (about 16 slices)
8 slices Virginia ham
4–6 ounces sharp cheddar cheese, thinly sliced
Olive oil

1. Lay out the bread on a cutting board.
2. Whip the butter and mustard together and spread it on both sides of the bread. Stack the jicama, ham, and cheese. Close sandwiches and brush with olive oil.
3. Set grill to high heat.
4. Place sandwiches on heavy skillet or pan with a weighted pan on top and grill until the bread is golden brown and the cheese melts.

Panini with Smoked Turkey and Baby Spinach

Makes 4 sandwiches

This makes an excellent light supper or lunch served with a cup of soup and a salad.

8 slices Tuscan or sourdough bread
¾ cup whole mayonnaise
1 teaspoon Tabasco sauce, or to taste

2 teaspoons fresh lime juice
24 leaves baby spinach, washed, dried, and stemmed
16 slices smoked turkey
Olive oil

1. Lay out the bread on a cutting board.
2. In a bowl, mix together the mayonnaise, Tabasco, and lime juice. Spread it on the bread.
3. Arrange the spinach leaves on the bread with the smoked turkey covering them. Close sandwiches and brush with the olive oil.
4. Set grill to high heat.
5. Place on a skillet or heavy cast-iron griddle and grill until brown and heated through.

Flavored Oils for Pizza

1 cup olive oil
1 clove garlic, sliced

*¼ cup of your favorite herb
or a combination of herbs,
such as basil, rosemary,
and oregano*

Place the oil, garlic, and herbs in a saucepan over high heat. Scald the oil, cool, and store for future use. This will keep for up to three weeks, longer if refrigerated. Oil may be strained before storing, but it is not necessary.

> **Makes 1 cup**
>
> Flavored oils can be spread on pizza and used in salads and soups.
>
>

Kids' Favorite Pizza

¼ cup cornmeal
1 pound fresh pizza dough
*1 cup Fresh Tomato Sauce
    (page 156)*
*8 slices bacon, cooked and
    crumbled*

12 fresh basil leaves, shredded
*8 ounces fresh mozzarella,
    coarsely grated*
*4 ounces Parmesan cheese,
    grated*

1. Sprinkle the cornmeal on a board and roll the dough over it.
2. Spread the tomato sauce evenly on the dough; then sprinkle the crumbled bacon, the shredded basil, and first the mozzarella, then the Parmesan cheese over the top.
3. Heat grill to 450°–500°F.
4. Place dough on a pizza stone and place in grill. Bake until the crust is brown and the topping bubbles.

> **Makes one 22-inch pizza or two 12-inch pizzas**
>
> This is as basic as you can get it; however, it's very popular and just great!
>
>

Tuscan Caponata Pizza

Makes one 22-inch pizza or two 12-inch pizzas

This tastes and smells of summer. It's adult in flavoring and makes a fine lunch or supper.

4 ounces cornmeal

1¼ pounds pizza dough

¼ cup flavored olive oil (page 163)

1 medium eggplant, peeled and cut into small cubes

1 medium zucchini, diced

½ small red onion, peeled and chopped

½ cup Sicilian green olives, pitted and chopped

¼ cup small capers

Salt and pepper to taste

1 cup Fresh Tomato Sauce (page 156)

8 ounces mozzarella cheese, shredded

4 ounces Parmesan cheese, grated

1. Sprinkle the cornmeal on a board and roll the dough over it.
2. Heat the herbed olive oil and add the eggplant, zucchini, onion, olives, capers, salt, and pepper. Sauté until the onion is soft. Add the tomato sauce.
3. Spread the sauced vegetables on the dough. Sprinkle with mozzarella and then with Parmesan.
4. Heat grill to high.
5. Bake the pizza on a preheated pizza stone for about 7 minutes.

Magical, Meltable Mozzarella

Like most good things, the richer the cheese, the smoother and tastier. Low-fat mozzarella tastes like nothing and acts like chewing gum. If you can find it, try imported buffalo's milk mozzarella—it's delectably creamy and melts beautifully. It's worth the extra calories and money it costs.

Mesquite-Smoked Chicken and Olive Pizza

4 ounces cornmeal
1¼ pounds pizza dough
¾ pound boneless, skinless cooked chicken breast, shredded
½ cup flavored olive oil (page 163)
⅔ cup green olives, chopped
1 tablespoon lemon juice
Salt and freshly ground black pepper to taste
¾ cup Parmesan cheese, grated

1. Sprinkle the cornmeal on a board and roll the dough over it.
2. In a bowl, mix chicken, oil, olives, lemon juice, salt, and pepper. Spread evenly on the dough. Sprinkle with Parmesan cheese.
3. Heat grill to high, adding two cups of soaked mesquite chips in the fire.
4. Transfer to a pizza stone in a preheated grill. Cover and bake for about 7–8 minutes.

> **Serves 4 with two 12-inch pizzas or one 22-inch pizza**
>
> This is a hearty pizza and good for a supper or lunch.
>
>

Pizza Casa Nostra

4 ounces cornmeal
1¼ pounds pizza dough
½ cup extra-virgin olive oil
1 inch anchovy paste, or to taste
1 teaspoon dried oregano
1 teaspoon red pepper flakes, or to taste
½ pound mozzarella cheese, coarsely grated
4 ounces Parmesan cheese

1. Sprinkle the cornmeal on a board and roll the dough over it.
2. Mix together the olive oil, anchovy paste, oregano, and pepper flakes. Spread on the dough. Cover with mozzarella cheese and sprinkle with Parmesan.
3. Heat grill to high.
4. Bake on a pizza stone in a covered grill for 7 minutes.

> **Serves 4 with two 12-inch pizzas or one 22-inch pizza**
>
> Anchovies can be an overwhelming flavor. This recipe calls for a hint, not a dose, of those fun little fish.
>
>

Shrimp and Scallops Fra Diavolo Pizza

Makes two 12-inch pizzas or one 22-inch pizza

Fra Diavolo, literally translated, means "Brother Devil." When it's on a menu, the dish is usually very peppery. You can adjust the heat as your taste buds dictate.

½ cup cornmeal
1¼ pounds pizza dough
1 cup Fresh Tomato Sauce (page 156)
2 tablespoons red pepper flakes, or to taste
¼ cup Italian flat-leaf parsley, chopped
2 tablespoons fresh lemon juice
1 tablespoon lemon zest
½ pound raw shrimp, shelled and deveined, sliced lengthwise
½ pound bay scallops, rinsed and patted dry
1 cup breadcrumbs
¼ cup butter, softened

1. Sprinkle the cornmeal on a board and roll the dough over it.
2. In a large bowl, mix together the tomato sauce, pepper flakes, parsley, lemon juice, and lemon zest. Add the shrimp and scallops, coat evenly, and spread on the pizza.
3. Make breadcrumbs by mixing the crumbs and softened butter. Sprinkle over the pizza.
4. Heat grill to high.
5. Bake on a pizza stone on the grill, covered, for 6–7 minutes.

Flavored Oils Have Many Uses

You can use flavored oils for sautéing and in salad dressings. Try them also as additions to marinades, such as rosemary oil for veal or chicken. An oregano oil brushed on a sizzling steak is wonderful. And a garlic oil with some dill is great on seafood. Also, if you have grilled a bunch of sweet red peppers, store them in the refrigerator soaking in infused oil.

New Haven–Style Pizza with Clams and Bacon

½ cup cornmeal

1½ pounds pizza dough

2 dozen littleneck clams, freshly opened, drained, and chopped

2 strips cooked bacon, chopped

½ cup olive oil

4 cloves garlic, chopped

1 teaspoon dried oregano

½ cup fresh Italian flat-leaf parsley, washed and chopped

1 teaspoon freshly ground black pepper or to taste

1 cup Parmesan cheese

> **Serves 4—two 12-inch pizzas or one 22-inch pizza**
>
> Seafood is tricky to cook under the easiest of circumstances. It's very easy to overcook it and thus turn it to leather while destroying the flavor.

1. Sprinkle the cornmeal on a board and roll the dough over it.
2. In a bowl, mix together the bacon, clams, olive oil, garlic, oregano, parsley, and pepper. Spread the mixture evenly on the dough. Sprinkle the pizza with Parmesan cheese.
3. Heat grill to high.
4. Bake on a pizza stone in the grill, covered, for 6–7 minutes.

Clamming Up

If you steam the clams open, then use them on pizza, they will get very tough and rubbery, so go the old-fashioned way and open them with a clam knife. Also, reserve the clam juice for chowder!

Chapter 13
Texas/Southwest BBQ Cuisine

Preparing a Grill for Barbecuing or Smoking

You can use a kettle grill to barbecue and smoke your food (meats up to 10 pounds), replicating the good old-fashioned flavor derived from barbecuing in a pit. Barbecue is slow cooked over low, indirect heat with lots of smoke. Sauces are used later for basting and dipping the meat.

Many of the recipes in this chapter call for you to prepare your grill with wood. Here's what you need to know about getting the grill ready. To prepare your grill for barbecuing, you need the following:

- *A large kettle grill with metal side holders for charcoal, to keep it out of the middle of the kettle. The middle of the kettle is where you will have the pan of water and where you will cook the food.*
- *Natural wood charcoal.*
- *½ cup wood chips (hickory, apple, mesquite, etc.), soaked in water, for every 30 minutes of cooking. These chips must be the same kind of wood as the charcoal.*

1. Bank the charcoal to one side of the grill, or around the water pan. Make sure there is an inch of water in the pan at all times.
2. Set the charcoal on fire using newspaper or twigs. Make sure that the heat in the kettle is a constant 200°F. (Double the amount of charcoal for a lengthier cook time, and give it extra time to go "white hot." Cook time, covered, will be at least 2–3 hours. If coals burn off, you may have to add more.)
3. After putting the meat on the rack, set the bottom vents at half open and the cover vents at a quarter open.
4. Add water to the pan in the grill whenever necessary to keep it an inch deep. Otherwise, the meat will dry out. Add ½ cup of wet chips every half hour.

Old-Fashioned Barbecued Beef Brisket

5 cups wood chips, soaked
Plenty of salt and freshly
  ground pepper

10 pounds brisket of beef, fat
  left on one side
1 quart barbecue sauce

1. Prepare the fire with water pan and presoaked wood chips (see "Preparing a Grill for Barbecuing or Smoking," page 170). Salt and pepper the brisket.
2. Put the meat on the rack, fat-side down, and "mop" the top with the barbecue sauce.
3. Mop the meat every 30 minutes and check the water pan. Add chips every 30 minutes or when smoke stops coming out of the vents. Add hot coals when necessary.
4. Carve in thin slices across the grain before serving.

Serves 15–20

Thick pieces of meat such as brisket make excellent candidates for long, slow cooking. Use any of your favorite barbecue sauces—from the store or homemade.

Big, Big Barbecued Buffalo Ribs

5 pounds buffalo ribs
1 quart of your favorite bar-
  becue sauce
1 lemon, sliced thinly

4 bay leaves
Mesquite charcoal briquettes
  and 3 cups presoaked
  mesquite wood chips

1. Place the ribs in a large plastic bag. Add the sauce, lemon, and bay leaves to the bag and shake to cover. Marinate overnight.
2. Prepare grill with banked mesquite coals (see sidebar on page 170), a water pan, and presoaked chips.
3. Barbecue the ribs for 5–6 hours. Add sauce each time you turn the ribs, and wood chips every half hour. Serve with extra barbecue sauce.

Serves 5–6

Grass-fed buffalo is lighter than beef and very easy to digest.

Tender Barbecued Loin of Pork

4 cups presoaked maple wood chips and maple wood briquettes
1 5–6-pound pork loin roast, bone in

Salt and pepper to taste
3 cups Citrus Barbecue Sauce (page 181)

1. Prepare a kettle grill (see page 170) with natural wood coals and a pan of water.
2. Sprinkle the roast with salt and pepper.
3. Barbecue over low heat for 5 hours, mopping with barbecue sauce every half hour. Add chips every 30 minutes and water to pan as needed.

Texas Gulf Shrimp Roast

2 pounds jumbo shrimp, heads and shells on
2 tablespoons kosher salt

2 cups Citrus Barbecue Sauce (page 181) plus 2 cups for dipping

1. Set the gas or ready the coals to medium heat.
2. Dip the shrimp into the sauce. Sprinkle with salt.
3. Grill for 2 minutes per side. Serve outdoors, on paper plates, with wedges of lemon and lots of paper napkins. Diners remove the heads and shells of the shrimp themselves, then dip!

Shrimping on the Gulf
Shrimp netted from the Gulf of Mexico is world famous—large and luscious. All along the Gulf shores, from Galveston to other lovely beach resorts, excellent shrimp is plentiful.

Chuck Wagon Kidney Beans and Chili

½ cup olive oil

1 red onion, chopped

4 cloves garlic, minced

1 sweet red pepper, cored, seeded, and chopped

2 serrano chilies, or to taste, cored, seeded, and minced

2 Scotch bonnet chilies, or to taste, cored, seeded, and minced

1 pound dried kidney beans in water to cover, soaked overnight

1 pound ground beef

1 29-ounce can crushed tomatoes

1 can low-salt beef broth

1 tablespoon instant coffee dissolved in ¼ cup hot water

2 tablespoons cocoa powder dissolved in ¼ cup cold water

1 bottle beer (not dark or light, use regular)

1 tablespoon Worcestershire sauce

1 teaspoon ground cinnamon

1 teaspoon ground cumin

1 teaspoon dried thyme

2 tablespoons chili powder

½ cup red wine

Salt and freshly ground black pepper to taste

Serves 6–8

Combining the beans with tomatoes and chilies and spices and herbs changes them into more than a chuck wagon staple.

1. Heat the olive oil in a large, heavy-bottomed soup pot. Add the onion, garlic, and peppers; sauté over low heat, stirring for 5 minutes.
2. Blend in the rest of the ingredients, cover, and simmer for 5–6 hours.
3. Serve in bowls garnished with sour cream, chopped scallions, and grated cheddar cheese. A bowl of taco chips on the side is a classic accompaniment.

Café au Chili

Chocolate is an indigenous Central and South American product. It enhances flavors and adds a very nice richness to chili. Coffee is also indigenous to the same area and adds a depth of flavor to the chili. Wine has a chemical in it with the property of bringing out flavors in tomatoes that are otherwise undetectable. Southwestern cooking has developed under the influences of Spanish and native Mexican cuisines.

Chuck Wagon Corn Bread

4 slices bacon, fried and drained
   on paper towel, fat reserved
2–4 jalapeño peppers, cored,
   seeded, and minced
4 scallions, chopped
1 tablespoon butter
¾ cup yellow or white
   cornmeal
1½ cups all-purpose flour
2 teaspoons double-action
   baking powder
½ teaspoon salt
1 cup buttermilk
2 tablespoons molasses or
   brown sugar
2 whole eggs

1. Fry the bacon, then drain and reserve the fat. After the bacon has
   been removed from the pan, sauté the peppers and scallions in the
   reserved fat, adding a tablespoon of butter if the pan gets dry. Remove
   from the heat. Crumble the bacon and mix it with the peppers and
   scallions.
2. Measure the cornmeal, flour, baking powder, and salt into the bowl of
   an electric mixer. With the motor on low, blend in the buttermilk. Then
   add the rest of the ingredients, scraping the bowl from time to time.
3. Preheat the oven to 400°F. Prepare an 8" square pan with nonstick
   spray.
4. Pour half of the batter into the pan. Spread with the bacon, pepper,
   and scallion mixture. Pour the rest of the batter on top.
5. Bake for about 25 minutes or until golden brown.

King Corn

*There are two kinds of corn: sweet corn for eating and field corn
for feeding animals and making corn oil and cornmeal. Some vari-
eties of corn have become extinct, but botanists are trying to bring
them back for historical reasons. Cowboys ate their beans with
hardtack, thin bread made with cornmeal.*

Native American Squash Soup

2 pounds butternut squash or
a 3-pound pumpkin
½ onion, peeled and chopped
2 cloves garlic, peeled and
minced
2 poblano peppers, or to
taste, cored and seeded
½ cup butter
1 tablespoon red pepper flakes
1 quart chicken broth (canned,
low-salt is fine)

2 tablespoons rum, sherry, or
bourbon
4 fresh sage leaves, shredded,
or 1 teaspoon dried
Salt and freshly ground pepper
to taste
¼ teaspoon ground nutmeg
1 teaspoon chili powder
1 cup heavy cream

**Serves 8–10
as a first course**

This soup can be
made with pumpkin,
butternut, or any
other winter squash.
It's delicious hot and
excellent chilled on a
warm fall day.

1. Cut squash or pumpkin in half, remove seeds, and wrap in aluminum foil, making a "chimney" for the smoke to escape.
2. Smoke-roast for 2 hours or until tender in a 250°F barbecue/smoker.
3. When the squash or pumpkin is soft, spoon the pulp into the bowl of a food processor and discard skin.
4. Sauté the onion, garlic, and peppers in the butter until soft. Add to the squash in the processor. Whirl until smooth. Add the rest of the ingredients and purée.
5. Pour into a bowl and put it over low heat on the stove. Bring to a simmer but do not boil or the soup may curdle. (You can also chill until ready to serve.) Serve garnished with crumbled bacon, sour cream, paprika, or chopped chives.

American Heritage

Squash has been a mainstay of American cuisine since prehistory. It is nourishing and full of vitamins. Founding Fathers Thomas Jefferson and George Washington were among America's foremost squash growers.

Navajo Southwestern Pulled Pork Sandwiches

Makes 4 sandwiches

This is a great way to use up extra barbecued pork—make it into pulled pork sandwiches.

1 pound leftover barbecued
  pork loin
1 cup cider vinegar
½ cup brown sugar

1 cup of your favorite tomato-
  based barbecue sauce
4 hard rolls, Portuguese rolls,
  or hero rolls, toasted

Place the pork with the rest of the ingredients (except the rolls) in a pot and bring to a boil. Simmer for 4 hours. Remove the meat, and using two forks, pull it apart. Pile the meat on the rolls and spoon any extra sauce over the top.

Spanish-Style Spit-Roasted Rabbit

Serves 4

A young, not-too-large rabbit is preferable to an old, huge one. Look for a rabbit of about 3 pounds.

1 cup mayonnaise
2 cloves garlic, peeled
2 ripe tomatoes
1 teaspoon salt

1 3-pound rabbit, cut into
  serving pieces
½ cup white wine
Salt and pepper

1. Place the mayonnaise, garlic, tomatoes, and salt in the blender and whirl until smooth to make a basting sauce.
2. Sprinkle the rabbit pieces with white wine, salt, and pepper.
3. Place on a rotating spit over hot coals and baste often with the sauce. Spit-roast slowly for about 1 hour (depending on the size of the rabbit). You'll know it is done when it is well browned and a meat thermometer inserted into the thickest part of the rabbit reads at least 155°F.

Juicy Hens on the Spit

4 game hens or young pullets
½ pound butter
2 tablespoons Worcestershire
  sauce
1 teaspoon Tabasco sauce
  (or to taste)
1 teaspoon dried thyme leaves

1 teaspoon dried rosemary
  leaves
1 teaspoon onion powder
1 teaspoon garlic powder
1 teaspoon lemon zest
¼ cup dry white wine or
  white vermouth

Serves 4–8

Grills equipped with
spits that rotate are
an excellent feature.
They can be adjusted
to be farther from or
closer to the flame.

1. Rinse the hens and pat them dry.
2. Set the grill to low heat and place the hens on the spit.
3. Melt the butter over low heat and add the rest of the ingredients to make a sauce. Remove from heat and place on trivet.
4. Brush the hens with the sauce and start the rotisserie. Place the hens inside and cover the grill. The hens will need at least an hour. Add chips every 30 minutes to keep the smoke going.

The Art of the Roasting Spit

Roasting whole or parts of animals on spits is an ancient, primitive form of cooking. It probably began soon after the advent of fire. Today, you don't have to assign a member of your tribe to turn the spit—electricity is the appointed spit turner. An interesting and delicious aspect to spit roasting is that the juices and the sauces stay in and on the bird. However, after the roasting process is over, it is important to let the food rest on a tray for 10 minutes to ensure its juiciness.

Barbecued Short Ribs of Beef

Serves 4

This is the fastest way to produce a barbecue without spending many hours leaning over the grill/barbecue/smoker. It works for pork spare ribs, too.

4 cloves garlic, unpeeled
4–5 pounds meaty short ribs of beef
½ cup cider vinegar
1 cup apple cider
2 onions, unpeeled and quartered
2 tablespoons red pepper flakes

2 tablespoons juniper berries, bruised in a mortar and pestle
Apple wood briquettes and 2 cups presoaked apple wood chips
1½ cups Hot Barbecue Sauce (page 180)

1. Smash the garlic cloves under a wide blade or frying pan. In a large container, cover the short ribs with water and add the vinegar, cider, onions, garlic, and spices. Soak, refrigerated, overnight.
2. In a large pot with a cover, add enough water to the marinade to cover the ribs. Simmer on stove for 2 hours.
3. Prepare the grill with the wood chips and briquettes.
4. Grill or smoke the ribs over barbecue about 1 hour, or until brown and juicy, brushing often with sauce. When glossy brown but not burned, serve on a platter.

Saucy Selections

There must be a hundred "barbecue" sauces in any large supermarket. However, you can make your own with very little trouble. And, there's nothing better than having a guest say, "Where did you find this sauce?" and you reply, "I made it!"

Restaurant-Style Barbecued Spareribs

Hickory briquettes
1 cup presoaked hickory wood
  chips
5 pounds pork spareribs
1 cup cider vinegar
4 bay leaves
2 cloves garlic, peeled and
  crushed

6 whole cloves, bruised
1 teaspoon sea salt
1 tablespoon red pepper flakes
2 cups of your favorite bar-
  becue sauce

Serves 4

You can use a kettle grill to barbecue and smoke your food, replicating the good old-fashioned flavor derived from barbecuing in a pit.

1. Prepare grill with banked mesquite coals (see page 170), a water pan, and presoaked chips.
2. Place the spareribs in a pot with the vinegar, bay leaves, garlic, cloves, salt, and red pepper flakes. Add water to cover. Simmer for 1 hour over low heat, then drain on paper towels.
3. Place ribs on grill and brush with barbecue sauce. Close the lid to let smoke infuse ribs. Grill for about 1 hour. Turn and baste with sauce every 20 minutes, adding a handful of chips.

Trade Secrets

Did you ever wonder, when a restaurant doesn't have a smoker or barbecue pit, how it gets the ribs out so fast? Well the secret is that they parboil them, then slap on the sauce and put them on a smoky grill. They may also use a product called liquid smoke, which works quite well. Many sauces have smoke flavor in their ingredients.

Hot Barbecue Sauce

Makes 1 quart

Somehow, when you put your own imprimatur on a sauce, it tastes better and people appreciate it so much. And, the fresher the ingredients, the better.

½ cup olive oil

2 onions, peeled and chopped

4–5 cloves garlic, peeled and chopped

4 jalapeño peppers, cored, deribbed, seeded, and chopped

2 canned chipotle peppers, chopped

1 red Scotch bonnet pepper, cored, seeded, and chopped

1 quart fresh or canned tomatoes

2 cups chili sauce

1 teaspoon ground cloves

½ teaspoon ground cinnamon

2 tablespoons dark brown sugar

½ cup cider vinegar

2 teaspoon salt

1 tablespoon prepared brown mustard

1 ounce bittersweet chocolate

1 tablespoon liquid smoke (optional)

¼ cup bourbon, rum, or tequila (optional)

1. Heat the oil in a large soup kettle. Add the onions, garlic, three kinds of peppers, and tomatoes. Sauté until soft.
2. Add the rest of the ingredients and stir. Cover and simmer for 2 hours, reducing to 1 quart.
3. Remove bay leaves and whirl in blender until smooth. Cool and place in a jar. This will keep for at least a week.

According to Taste

You can vary ingredients according to taste. Some people do not like really sweet food, others like it so sweet it'll make your teeth hurt. Try it with more or less sugar, or more or less vinegar. And vary the intensity and quantity of peppers as well.

Citrus Barbecue Sauce

1 clove garlic, peeled and chopped
1 onion, peeled and chopped
1 sweet red pepper, cored, seeded, and chopped
2 poblano peppers, cored, seeded, and chopped
2 jalapeño peppers, cored, seeded, and chopped
½ cup olive oil
1 teaspoon curry powder
4 whole cloves, bruised
3½ cups fresh orange juice

Juice of 2 limes
Juice of 1 lemon
1 lemon, sliced thinly, seeds removed
2 bay leaves
½ cup dry white wine
¼ cup dry English mustard, mixed with ¼ cup water to blend
1 tablespoon salt, or to taste
2 tablespoons dark brown sugar, or to taste

> **Makes 1 quart**
>
> This is great with all kinds of poultry, seafood, and game, especially squab, game hens, shrimp, oceangoing white fish, and rabbit.
>
>

1. In a large soup kettle, sauté the garlic, onion, and all the peppers in olive oil until soft.
2. Blend in the curry powder, then slowly add the rest of the ingredients.
3. Cover and simmer for 1 hour or until reduced to 1 quart. Cool and place in a jar; refrigerate until ready to use. You may leave bay leaves, lemon slices, and cloves whole in the sauce; strain sauce before using. The sauce will keep for at least a week.

The Science of Hot Sauce

The pungency of chili peppers is measured in multiples of 100 Scoville units, from the bell pepper at zero Scoville units to the habanero at 300,000 Scoville units! One part of chili "heat" per 1,000,000 drops of water rates as only 1.5 Scoville units, a measurement that gauges the capsaicin (the substance that makes a chili pepper hot) level in a particular pepper or variety. Pure capsaicin rates approximately 16,000,000 Scoville units!

CHAPTER 14

International Dishes

Chinese-Style Beef Tenderloin

Serves 4

This is a fine way to serve tenderloin. If tangerines are not available, you can substitute orange zest.

2 tablespoons rice wine vinegar or white wine vinegar
1/4 cup soy sauce
1 teaspoon fresh ginger, minced
1 1/2 pounds filet mignon, cut into four thick steaks

1 tablespoon tangerine zest, freshly grated
1/4 cup fresh parsley or cilantro, finely minced
2 cloves garlic, chopped

1. Mix together the vinegar, soy sauce, and ginger. Brush it on the steaks and marinate for 30 minutes.
2. While the steaks are marinating, mix the zest, parsley, and garlic together and set aside.
3. Set the grill to high.
4. Grill the steaks for 4 minutes per side for rare; 6 minutes for medium. Just before serving, sprinkle with the tangerine, herb, and garlic mixture.

Beefsteak with Garlic and Pickled Red Ginger

Serves 4

This is tangy and fun to eat!

3 cloves garlic, minced
1/2 cup soy sauce
1 tablespoon Asian toasted sesame seed oil
1/2 teaspoon ground coriander seed

1 teaspoon cayenne pepper
1 1/2 pounds boneless sirloin steak, cut into 16 chunks
16 slices pickled red ginger
8 large shiitake mushrooms, cut in half

1. Mix together the garlic, soy, oil, coriander, and pepper.
2. Thread the meat, ginger, and mushrooms onto 8 presoaked wooden skewers.
3. Set the grill to high heat.
4. Grill the meat for about 8 minutes, turning often.

Thai-Inspired Beefsteak

2 tablespoons honey
1 teaspoon five-spice powder
1 teaspoon mirin
1 tablespoon lime or lemon juice

1 tablespoon hot chili oil or
  Thai chili paste
1½ pounds boneless beefsteak
¼ cup sesame seeds

1. Mix together the honey, five-spice powder, mirin, lime or lemon juice, and chili oil or paste to make a marinade. Brush the marinade on the steak and let rest, refrigerated and covered, for 2 hours.
2. Sprinkle with sesame seeds and press into the meat with the back of a spoon.
3. Set grill to high heat.
4. Grill 4 minutes per side for rare, 6 for medium, and 8 for well done. Timing depends on the thickness of the steak and whether there is a bone or not.

> **Serves 4**
>
> Sirloin works great in this recipe. You can use bone-in steak with this recipe as well. If you do, get 2 pounds.
>
>

Japanese-Style Marinated Beef

1½ pounds boneless steak, cut
  into 16 chunks
2 cups teriyaki sauce
A variety of mushrooms

Pieces of sweet pepper and/or
  hot pepper, cored and
  seeded

1. Marinate the steak in 1 cup of the sauce for 2 hours.
2. Thread the meat, mushrooms, and peppers onto 8 presoaked wooden skewers.
3. Set grill to high.
4. Grill for 4 minutes per side, turning often. Serve over rice or noodles.

> **Serves 4**
>
> The Japanese love beef cooked on their traditional, wrought-iron hibachi grills.
>
>

Vietnamese-Style Chicken Patties Wrapped in Lettuce

Serves 4

This is very spicy but the wrap cools it off a bit. Many Asian cuisines wrap food in leaves, adding herbs to the outside of the cooked meat.

1½ pounds ground chicken
  (dark meat is tastier)
1 egg
2 tablespoons fresh mint
  leaves, minced
2 jalapeño peppers, cored,
  seeded, and minced
2 tablespoons fresh gingerroot,
  minced

1 teaspoon ground coriander
½ teaspoon ground cardamom
¼ teaspoon ground cloves
1 teaspoon salt
16 lettuce or spinach leaves,
  rinsed

1. In a bowl, mix all of the ingredients except the lettuce or spinach together. Form 16 patties.
2. Set grill to medium.
3. Grill until nicely brown and done through, about 5 minutes per side with the lid of the grill closed.
4. Wrap in spinach or lettuce leaves and eat out of hand.

Creating Fusion from "Con-fusion"

The true origin of Asian-fusion cooking as we know it today began when the French occupied Vietnam. Vietnamese chefs learned from the imported French chefs and vice versa. The Portuguese trade with Japan added much to that country's cuisine. And, as we all are told, Marco Polo brought pasta to Italy. Today, any mixture of Eastern and Western qualifies as "fusion," and certainly some of the most delicious recipes and dishes are fused!

Asian Sesame Chicken

*1½ pounds boneless, skinless
  chicken breasts
1 cup yogurt
2 teaspoons sesame seed oil
4 cloves garlic, minced
½ cup lime juice*

*Zest of ½ lemon
1 teaspoon Madras curry
  powder
1 teaspoon salt
1 teaspoon cayenne pepper
½ cup sesame seeds*

Serves 4

Sesame adds a nutty
flavor to the chicken,
as does the spicing in
the marinade.

1. Rinse the chicken breasts and pat them dry. In a glass baking dish
   large enough to hold the chicken, mix all but the sesame seeds and
   chicken together, then add the chicken. Turn to coat, cover, and marinate, refrigerated, for 2 hours.
2. Spread the sesame seeds on waxed paper and turn the chicken in the
   seeds to coat.
3. Heat grill to medium.
4. Grill the chicken for 10 minutes per side or until the seeds are toasty
   brown and the chicken is no longer pink inside.

Favorite Old-Style Lemon Chicken

2 lemons

*1 teaspoon cayenne pepper,
    or to taste*

*½ cup parsley or cilantro,
    chopped*

*2 tablespoons fresh rosemary
    leaves, chopped*

½ cup olive oil

1 teaspoon salt

1 teaspoon onion salt

*1½ pounds skinless, boneless
    chicken breasts, cut into 16
    pieces*

1. Zest and juice the first lemon into a large bowl. Slice the second
   lemon thinly and set aside.
2. Mix in the rest of the ingredients, tossing the chicken to coat. Don't
   marinate for too long or the acid in the lemon will cook the chicken.
3. Place chicken pieces on 8 presoaked wooden skewers, with slices of
   lemon interspersed between them.
4. Heat grill to medium.
5. Grill for about 10 minutes per side or until the chicken is browned
   and the lemons are crispy. You can eat or discard the lemon slices.

How to Use Citric Acid

*When you use any citric acid (lemon, lime, orange, or grapefruit), it
will "cook" meat, seafood, or fish. The Latin American ceviche is
made with fish and seafood "cooked" in acid. That's why you must
limit the amount of marinating time. Also, because acid reacts with
metal, it's best to use a glass bowl or pan for marinating. You
don't want your food to taste like old aluminum!*

Hawaiian Coconut Chicken

½ cup canned, unsweetened
  coconut milk
¼ cup lime juice
¼ cup fresh cilantro or
  parsley, chopped
1 teaspoon Thai chili paste or
  Tabasco sauce
½ teaspoon ground white
  peppercorns

1 teaspoon sea salt
1½ pounds boneless, skinless
  chicken breasts, cut into 16
  pieces
Pieces of fruit such as
  pineapple, orange slices,
  or apple

> **Serves 4**
>
> Hawaiian cuisine melds Japanese and Chinese cuisines with the rich array of fruits, vegetables, birds, and flowers native to Hawaii.
>
>

1. Mix the coconut milk, lime juice, cilantro, chili paste, pepper, and salt in a large bowl and add the cut-up chicken. Cover and refrigerate for 2 hours.
2. Thread the pieces of chicken and chunks of fruit onto the skewers.
3. Set grill to medium.
4. Grill for about 10–15 minutes, or until the chicken has browned and is no longer pink inside. The time will vary according to the heat of the grill and the thickness of the chicken.

Cilantro: Love It or Leave It?

Cilantro is one of those herbs that people either love or hate. The people who hate it say it tastes like soap or medicine. But those who love it, really love it. Just don't overdo it!

Latino-Style Grilled Fish in Banana Leaves

2 teaspoons Asian fish sauce (nam pla)
Juice of ½ lime
1 tablespoon peanut oil
1 tablespoon cilantro or parsley, chopped
1 clove garlic, mashed
4 fish fillets or steaks, about ½ to ¾ inch thick (a firm white fish is best)
2 banana leaves

1. Mix the fish sauce, lime juice, peanut oil, cilantro, and garlic together and add the fish. Turn to coat the fish. Marinate for 20 minutes.
2. Blanch the banana leaves in boiling water for 30 seconds or until soft and pliable. Shock them in cold water and drain on paper towels.
3. Lay the banana leaves on a cutting board and cut into 4 pieces, each 8" x 12". (Banana leaves are about 24" x 12" when purchased.) Place a piece of marinated fish on each cut leaf. Fold into neat packets and secure with toothpicks.
4. Heat grill to medium.
5. Place packets on grill and grill for about 12 minutes. If the leaves start to burn, move to indirect heat. To serve, snip the packets open with scissors and sprinkle with fresh herbs such as dill or basil.

Making Grill Cleanup Easier

Peanut oil works great for oiling your grill. If you don't oil the grill, your food is likely to stick. Another good tip for a quick grill cleanup between courses is to make a ball out of a piece of aluminum foil, stick it on a long-handled fork, and use it as an improvised Chore Boy. This is good in a pinch when you are grilling several courses.

Japanese Seafood Grill

³⁄₄ cup chili sauce
2 tablespoons Worcestershire
sauce
Juice of 1 lemon
¹⁄₄ teaspoon wasabi or hot
chili oil
12 oysters

12 littleneck clams
12–16 mussels, tightly closed,
scrubbed
12 prawns, shelled and cleaned
Plenty of lemon and lime
wedges

1. Mix the chili sauce, Worcestershire sauce, lemon juice, and wasabi together to make sauce and set aside.
2. Heat grill to high.
3. Start with the oysters—put them right on the grill in the shell. The shells will pop open. Grill until bubbling. Then paint the meat with sauce and serve. Repeat with the clams in the shell, directly on the grill. Put the mussels on a metal pan. Grill until they open. The prawns should come last, directly on the grill, and grill them only until pink, or about 45 seconds per side. Serve with lemon and lime wedges.

The Asian Grill

Pots of charcoal of all sizes are found all over Asia. These can hold racks for meats, a pot of stew, or a metal plate for small vegetable pieces. Skewers are very useful and used a great deal. Vegetables are an excellent way to stretch meat. And, tofu is given a meaty flavor with the use of soy sauce.

Tuna with Hot Chili Peppers

1 pound fresh tuna
2 habanero peppers, cored and seeded, minced
Juice of ½ lime
1 tablespoon Worcestershire sauce
1 teaspoon salt, or to taste
Pickled ginger, cucumber, chives or scallions, for garnish

1. Grind the tuna in a food processor, adding bits of the peppers as you go along.
2. Add the rest of the ingredients to the tuna and form patties, from 8 to 16, depending on whether you want appetizers or canapés.
3. Set heat at medium for medium or well-done tuna. For rare, set to high.
4. Grill until barely warm or well done—that's up to you and your guests. Garnish with pickled ginger, thinly sliced cucumber, or chopped chives or scallions.

Where to Find It

Banana leaves and Asian fish sauce are available at Asian markets and many supermarkets. If you're lucky enough to live in an urban setting or with a diverse population, you should be able to find a specialty grocer. There will always be hard-to-find items, but the Internet can help you in your search.

Sweet and Spicy Ham

½ cup dark brown sugar
¼ cup cider vinegar
*1 tablespoon dry English
  mustard*
½ teaspoon ground cloves
¼ teaspoon ground cinnamon

½ cup butter, melted
*1 pound smoked ham, cut
  ½-inch thick, cubed*
*1 fresh pineapple, cut into
  chunks*

1. Mix together the sugar, vinegar, mustard, spices, and butter.
2. Thread the ham and pineapple on skewers. Brush with the sugar mixture.
3. Set grill to medium.
4. Grill for a few minutes, or until the fruit starts to caramelize.

**Serves 4 as a lunch and
8–12 as an appetizer**

This is popular and very satisfying, so if it's a first course, be sure to make a bit less. It's also delightful cold.

Indian-Style Grilled Lamb Steaks

*4 cloves garlic, peeled and
  chopped*
1 teaspoon cumin
1 teaspoon turmeric
1 teaspoon Madras curry powder
Juice and zest of 1 lemon
*2 teaspoons fresh cilantro or
  parsley, minced*

*2 tablespoons fresh mint, finely
  minced*
Salt to taste
*1 teaspoon red pepper flakes,
  or to taste*
*4 lamb steaks, from the leg,
  bone in, about 6 ounces
  each*

1. Using a mortar and pestle, make a paste of the garlic, spices, lemon, herbs, salt, and red pepper flakes. Spread the mixture on both sides of the lamb steaks, cover, and refrigerate overnight.
2. Set grill to high heat. Grill hot and fast, giving the steaks 4 minutes per side for rare, 6 for medium, and 8 for well done.

Serves 4

This is a fine entrée and goes with many fruits, vegetables, and relishes on the side. Serve it with mango salsa, rice, and braised celery.

Vietnamese Grilled Pork Patties

1½ pounds lean ground pork

2 cloves garlic, peeled and mashed

1½-inch piece fresh gingerroot, peeled and minced

4 teaspoons dry sherry, Chinese rice wine, or sake

1 tablespoon soy sauce

1 tablespoon Asian sesame seed oil

1 teaspoon salt, or to taste

1 teaspoon red pepper flakes or Tabasco sauce

12 Boston lettuce leaves, washed and dried

12 mint sprigs, washed and dried

12 sprigs cilantro, washed and dried

1 cup Oriental dipping sauce

1. In a large bowl, mix the pork, garlic, gingerroot, sherry, soy sauce, oil, salt, and red pepper flakes and combine thoroughly. Refrigerate for at least 1 hour, or overnight.
2. On a serving platter, lay out the lettuce leaves individually and place a sprig of mint and cilantro on each.
3. Set grill to medium.
4. Remove the chilled meat mixture from the refrigerator and form the patties into ovals. Wrap them in lettuce leaves and grill until very brown and done through. Serve with dipping sauce.

Fruit Relish/Salsa

Sausages go very well with fresh fruit. Mix apples, mangoes, pears, or pineapple chunks with mustard, chili peppers, curry, lemon juice, or vinegar and add to your sausages for a delicious treat. Work on great combinations that will give your palate a nice zing! You can also add brown sugar to give it some zip.

Hawaiian Tenderloin of Pork with Macadamia Nut Stuffing

2½ cups pineapple juice
¼ cup soy sauce
1 tablespoon fresh gingerroot, minced
¼ cup dry white wine
1 tablespoon Madras curry powder
1 teaspoon Thai chili paste or Tabasco sauce, or to taste
1 teaspoon sugar

2 pork tenderloins, about 1½ pounds each
Salt and freshly ground black pepper
1 cup macadamia nuts, coarsely chopped
Fresh parsley, mint, cilantro, and whole macadamia nuts, for garnish

---

Serves 6

Grilled sweet potato slices make a nice, colorful accompaniment. The glaze can be divided between the pork and a sauceboat to serve on the side.

---

1. In a medium saucepan, mix together the pineapple juice, soy sauce, ginger, wine, curry powder, chili paste, and sugar. Bring to a boil and simmer until reduced to 1½ cups.
2. Make holes in the ends of the tenderloins using the handle of a knife or a fat knitting needle. The pork tenderloins will become tubes. Salt and pepper the pork, inside and out, pressing into the tube.
3. Stuff in the chopped macadamia nuts and close ends with small metal skewers. Marinate the pork for 1 hour in ½ cup of the pineapple sauce.
4. Set grill to medium.
5. Place pork on grill over indirect heat until the pork is slightly pink inside and brown on the outside. Carve crosswise so that each piece has some nuts in it. Serve with the extra pineapple sauce on the side. (Never reuse sauce that has been placed on raw meat.) Garnish with sprigs of fresh parsley, mint, cilantro, and whole macadamia nuts.

Spanish-Style Chicken Breasts

*4 boneless, skinless chicken
  breast halves (about 1½
  pounds)*
*⅔ cup olives—chopped, green,
  black, mixed*
¼ cup scallions, minced
2 tablespoons parsley, minced

*1 teaspoon fresh tarragon,
  minced, or ½ teaspoon
  dried*
2 tablespoons olive oil
Salt and pepper to taste
Paprika

1. Rinse the chicken and dry on paper towels. Carefully cut a pocket into each half breast.
2. Mix together the olives, scallions, parsley, and tarragon. Stuff into the pockets in the chicken breasts and close with small metal skewers.
3. Brush the chicken with olive oil and sprinkle liberally with salt, pepper, and paprika.
4. Set grill to medium.
5. Grill for 5–6 minutes per side and serve.

The Olive Garden

Spanish olives vary from region to region, town to town. Some are lemony, others vinegary, others smoky or herbal in flavor. Try a selection.

Italian-Style Squabs

4 squabs, butterflied
2 tablespoons olive oil
1 clove garlic, or to taste
*2 tablespoons fresh lemon
   juice*
Zest of ½ lemon
*2 plum tomatoes (fresh or
   canned)*

*2 tablespoons fresh oregano
   leaves or 2 teaspoons dried*
½ teaspoon red pepper flakes
⅛ teaspoon ground cinnamon
½ teaspoon sugar
Salt and black pepper to taste

Serves 4

Fresh squabs can be purchased at specialty stores or online. Frozen squabs work equally well. Just be sure to have them butterflied for easy grilling.

---

1. Rinse the squabs and pat dry with paper towels. Whirl the rest of the ingredients in a blender until smooth to make a marinade.
2. Marinate the squabs, covered and refrigerated, for 4 hours, turning occasionally.
3. Set grill to medium-high.
4. Grill for about 6–8 minutes per side, using the marinade to baste the squab. Garnish with fresh Italian parsley.

Freshly Ground Pepper

Pepper originally came from Asia and Southeast Asia. When brought to Europe and the Americas, it became as valuable as the coin of the realm. Today it's also grown in Africa and South America.

Squab Dijonnaise

Serves 4

This requires real Dijon mustard for the best flavor. It's got a spicy, crusty coating with soft, moist meat inside. It's very nice with risotto with added mushrooms.

4 squabs, butterflied
1 stick unsalted butter, at
   room temperature

2 tablespoons Dijon mustard
2 tablespoons flour
Salt and pepper to taste

1. Rinse the squabs in cold water and dry on paper towels.
2. In a small bowl, mix the butter, mustard, flour, salt, and pepper. Mix into a paste. Paint the butter mixture on the squabs.
3. Set grill to medium-high.
4. Grill quickly for about 8 minutes per side. They should be golden brown.

French-Style Lamb Chops

Serves 4

Grill some asparagus (see page 129) and make a nice salad of spring greens with French dressing to serve with the lamb.

12–16 baby rib lamb chops,
   well trimmed
Salt and pepper to taste
1/4 cup fresh mint leaves,
   chopped

2 tablespoons fresh rosemary
   leaves, chopped
4 tablespoons butter, softened
4 cloves garlic, minced
Juice and zest of 1/2 lemon

1. Sprinkle both sides of the chops with salt and pepper.
2. In a small bowl, mix the rest of the ingredients together and brush on the chops.
3. Set grill to medium-high.
4. Grill the chops for about 4 minutes per side. They should be served pink. Garnish with extra sprigs of fresh rosemary.

Greek-Style Lamb Roast

1 5–6-pound leg of spring
   lamb, all fat removed
4 garlic cloves, slivered
1 cup dry red wine
1 cup olive oil
1 onion, sliced
1 carrot, peeled and sliced
2 fresh tomatoes, sliced
½ cup parsley sprigs

¼ cup mint leaves, crushed
4 sprigs rosemary leaves
1 tablespoon dried oregano or
   3 tablespoons fresh
Plenty of salt and freshly
   ground pepper
4 whole anchovy fillets
2 slices bacon

Serves 8

This is so springy—the younger the lamb the better. Lamb fat is very strong, so remove all of it before marinating.

1. Make slits all over the lamb and insert garlic slivers.
2. In a nonreactive (glass) pan large enough to hold the lamb, mix together all the rest of the ingredients except the bacon.
3. Place the lamb in the pan, making sure the lamb is well coated with the marinade. Turn it every hour or two and marinate it overnight.
4. Just before roasting, wrap the bacon around the meat and skewer in place with toothpicks or small metal skewers. Reserve the marinade liquid but discard the vegetables.
5. Set grill to medium.
6. Roast for 15 minutes per pound over indirect heat. Baste with the marinade. Let rest for 15 minutes after it's done.

Getting a "Reaction"

When you marinate meat, fish, or shellfish, you generally have some kind of acid in the mix. These acids include wines and citrus fruit juices. These will react with any kind of metal except for stainless steel. That reaction will give your food a bad taste. It's best to marinate in glass or porcelain-covered metal.

Savory Italian-Style Veal Chops

4 thick veal rib chops
Salt and pepper to taste
2 teaspoons oregano

2 tablespoons olive oil
1 cup tomato sauce, your own or jarred

1. Place the chops, one at a time, between sheets of waxed paper. Using a mallet or a 5-pound weight, pound the chops until they have doubled or, even better, tripled in size.
2. Sprinkle the chops with olive oil, salt, pepper, and oregano. Paint with tomato sauce.
3. Set grill to high.
4. Grill over high heat, browning quickly. Turn and brush with more sauce. Grill for about 5 minutes per side. Let the chops rest for 10 minutes on a warm platter before serving.

Rolled Italian-Style Veal Scallops

4 slices veal, cut from the leg, about 4 ounces each
Salt and pepper
1/2 cup cooked spinach, moisture squeezed out

1/2 cup ricotta cheese
2 tablespoons Parmesan cheese
1/4 teaspoon ground nutmeg
Flour
Olive oil

1. Pound the veal thin between two sheets of waxed paper. Sprinkle with salt and pepper on both sides.
2. Mix together the spinach, cheeses, and nutmeg. Divide between each piece of veal.
3. Roll the veal and fasten it with small metal skewers. Dust with flour and drizzle with olive oil.
4. Heat grill to medium. Grill over indirect heat for 10 minutes, turning often. The stuffing should be hissing or bubbling.

Pacific-Style Pork Tenderloin

1 mango, peeled and chopped
1 teaspoon white wine vinegar
Juice of ½ lemon
1 teaspoon curry powder
2 cloves garlic, mashed
Salt and pepper to taste

2 tablespoons honey
1¼ pounds pork tenderloin
1 cup peanuts, chopped
Extra peanuts and cilantro
*   sprigs for garnish*

Serves 4

Pork goes well with tropical fruits and can be delicious. Slice the meat crosswise so that each piece gets some peanuts.

1. In a glass pan large enough to hold the tenderloin, mix together the mango, vinegar, lemon juice, curry powder, garlic, salt and pepper, and the honey.
2. Using a large knitting needle or the handle of a butter knife, pierce the tenderloin from end to end, making it into a tube. Fill with the chopped peanuts. Place the pork in the mixture and let marinate for 2–4 hours.
3. Set grill to medium.
4. Grill the pork over medium heat for about 8 minutes per side, or until brown. Baste frequently with the mango mixture. (Discard any remaining marinade, and do not use the platter until it has been washed.) Let rest on a warm platter for 10 minutes. Carve crosswise. Garnish with extra peanuts and sprigs of cilantro and serve.

Go Tropical

Where mangoes are plentiful, other tropical and subtropical fruits are available. Palm leaves are also easy to get in the United States, either at Latino stores or on the Web. A rice dish with some chopped nuts added would be excellent with this.

Mexican-Style Shrimp

Serves 4

For a fast meal, "doctor" a jar of commercial salsa with extra lime juice, garlic, and either parsley or cilantro. Sour oranges are available at Latin markets.

1½ pounds (24 extra large or jumbo) shrimp, peeled, deveined, and rinsed
8-ounce jar commercial salsa
3 ounces sour orange juice
Juice of ½ lime
2 ounces tequila
2 tablespoons honey
Salt and red pepper flakes to taste

1. Thread the shrimp onto skewers.
2. Mix together the rest of the ingredients and brush on the shrimp.
3. Set grill to high.
4. Depending on the size of the shrimp, grill for about 2–3 minutes per side or just until the shrimp turn pink.

Scandinavian-Style Anchovies

Serves 4

Any really fresh small fish will do. You will need a rack with small perforations so the fish won't fall into the fire.

⅓ to ½ pound fish per person, cleaned, heads and tails left on
½ cup flour
½ cup unsalted butter, softened
½ cup fresh dill weed, finely minced
½ teaspoon freshly ground black pepper, or to taste
4 lemon wedges, for garnish

1. Rinse the fish and pat them dry with paper towels.
2. Make a paste with the flour, butter, dill, and pepper. Rub it on the fish inside and out.
3. Set grill to high heat.
4. Grill over hot fire, just a few minutes per side, or until well browned. Serve with lemon wedges, coleslaw, and potatoes. Be careful of the bones; however, the fillets should just slip right off the bones.

Asian-Style Seafood Combo

8 extra-large shrimp, peeled
   and deveined
8 sea scallops
½ pound monkfish, rinsed and
   cut into 8 chunks
½ cup soy sauce
2 tablespoons dry white wine
   or sake

1 teaspoon fresh gingerroot,
   peeled and minced
1 tablespoon fresh lime juice
1 tablespoon Asian sesame
   seed oil
½ teaspoon (or less) wasabi

> **Serves 4**
>
> Small hibachi grills, so popular with the Japanese and their neighbors for hundreds of years, provide intense, concentrated heat.
>
>

1. Rinse the seafood and pat dry with paper towels.
2. In a large, nonreactive bowl, mix the rest of the ingredients together. Add the seafood and marinate, covered and in the refrigerator, for 1 hour.
3. Set grill to medium-high.
4. Thread seafood onto presoaked skewers and grill for about 3 minutes per side, or until the shrimp turn pink.

Hibachi Cooking

Hibachis can be very large or tiny, and much of Japanese cooking is oriented toward the hibachi. They are perfect for camping or cooking on a patio.

Spanish-Style Grilled Salmon

2 teaspoons prepared Dijon-style mustard
1¼ pounds salmon fillet, skin on, rinsed and patted dry
1 tablespoon dry Spanish sherry

2 tablespoons chicken broth
¼ cup sour orange juice
Minced fresh parsley and lemon wedges, for garnish

1. Spread mustard on the salmon. Sprinkle with sherry, broth, and juice.
2. Set grill to medium heat.
3. Grill salmon skin-side down for about 8 minutes or until the fish flakes when tested with a fork. Garnish with minced fresh parsley and lemon wedges. Serve with rice and lots of vegetables. You can put a few things alongside the fish, such as mushrooms, eggplant, or peppers.

Japanese Grilled Squid

1 pound very small squid, cleaned
½ cup peanut oil
½ cup soy sauce
1 tablespoon fresh gingerroot, peeled and minced

1 jalapeño pepper, cored, seeded, and minced
2 tablespoons fresh garlic, peeled and minced
1 teaspoon dark Asian vinegar

1. Rinse the squid and dry on paper towels.
2. Heat grill to high heat.
3. Dip the squid in the peanut oil and sear on the grill, 90 seconds per side.
4. Mix the rest of the ingredients together and use as a dipping sauce. This can be done ahead. Serve the squid piping hot.

Caribbean-Style Swordfish Steaks

Juice of 1 lime
1 tablespoon cooking oil
½ teaspoon ground clove
1 teaspoon cayenne pepper, or to taste
1 teaspoon black pepper, or to taste

1 teaspoon coarse salt
2 cloves garlic, or to taste, minced
4 swordfish steaks, about 1 inch thick, 6–7 ounces each, rinsed and patted dry

1. Make a paste by mixing together the lime juice, cooking oil, clove, cayenne pepper, black pepper, salt, and garlic.
2. Spread the paste on both sides of the fish and marinate for 1 hour.
3. Set grill to high heat.
4. Place steaks on grill, browning quickly but not overcooking, about 4 minutes per side.

Serves 4

This can be very hot and tasty or just very tasty. Just be sure not to use the lime zest for cooking as it will turn bitter.

Follow Your Nose, and Look at the Eyes

The best-smelling seafood has almost no smell at all. If it smells at all sour or strong, don't buy it! Try to make friends with the local fishmonger and ask when a fish was caught and when it came into the store. Never buy a fish with dull scales; they should be shiny and bright. Dull eyes are another tip-off that the fish is not fresh—the eyes should look alive. Be sure, too, to rinse any fish before cooking it.

Adirondack Grilled Trout

½ cup butter
2 tablespoons parsley, minced
Juice of ½ lemon
Salt and pepper to taste

4 trout, cleaned, heads removed
4 strips smoky bacon

1. Melt the butter and add parsley, lemon, salt, and pepper. Brush the fish with the butter mixture, inside and out.
2. Heat grill to medium.
3. Grill the bacon and set aside.
4. Grill the fish until brown on the outside and just beginning to flake, about 5 minutes per side. Serve the fish with a strip of crisp bacon on top and extra lemon wedges.

Down on the Farm

Farmed trout is very good and much easier to get than wild trout. It's sweet and mild—a lot of seasoning or garlic will mask the natural delicacy of the fish. Thus, the simpler the preparation, the better.

CHAPTER 15

Smoking and Aromatic Woods

Sweet Pecan Wood Grilled Striped Bass

Serves 4

Striped bass is firm, mild, and delicate. Chunks of pecan wood, or pecan charcoal, give food a buttery flavor.

1½ pounds striped bass fillets, skin on
Plenty of salt and freshly ground pepper
4 ounces butter
10 sage leaves, shredded

2 lemons, thinly sliced
½ cup fresh parsley, rinsed and chopped
Extra sage for garnish

1. Prepare your grill (see page 170) with chunks of pecan wood or pecan charcoal and presoaked pecan chips. Prepare a hot zone and cool zone fire, accomplished by banking the hot coals to one side of the grill.
2. Rinse the fillets and pat dry. Sprinkle the fish with salt and pepper.
3. Melt the butter and add the shredded sage leaves to it. Brush the fish with the sage butter. Place lemon slices over the fish and put it on the grill when the wood and chips are smoky but not flaring.
4. Sprinkle the coals or embers with a bunch of fresh sage. Grill the fish over a smoky fire with the lid closed. Check every few minutes or until the fish flakes easily at its thickest. Sprinkle the fish with the parsley and some fresh sage.

Smoking and Grilling over Smoky Fires

Traditional smoking is a long and arduous process. However, even with a modern gas or charcoal grill, you can produce pretty much the same effect. You will need plenty of wood chunks or wood charcoal and presoaked chips of the same wood. You will need to replenish the wood and chips every 15–20 minutes. A simple chimney starter, or three or four if you're doing a huge piece of meat, will keep your smoke going. However, smoke can be overdone and many cooks prefer to finish the food in the oven.

Southwestern Mesquite Grilled Sirloin Steaks

2 cups mesquite chips, pre-soaked, or mesquite wood chunks
4 pounds sirloin steak, bone in, about 2–inches thick, some fat on

Salt and pepper
Steak sauce (your own or A.1. or BBQ)

Serves 6

Mesquite and beef-steak seem to have been created for each other, a match made of necessity in the old Texas country, ending up divine.

1. Make a fire with 3 zones: hot, medium, and barely warm. Use pre-soaked mesquite wood chips (see page 170).
2. Sprinkle the steak liberally with salt and pepper.
3. Grill when you see plenty of smoke rising from the bed of coals. Add chips every 5 minutes. Sear on hot zone, about 10–15 minutes per side for medium to well done, 8–10 per side for rare. When the steak reaches desired level of doneness, place it on your medium-hot zone to finish inside. Let it rest on the barely warm side for 10 minutes.
4. Serve with steak sauce or BBQ sauce on the side. You can garnish with fried or sautéed onions or chopped parsley.

Keep the Fire Going

You don't want your fire to go out, or to get so high it burns your food. The two- and three-zone fires are excellent for grilling and smoking in stages. The first zone is very hot, so be careful of the flames. The second zone is for indirect heat, and when you get to that, and half-close the vents, your grill can become a smoker. The third zone is simply for keeping food warm.

Old West Wood Grilled Bison Burgers

Makes a 6–7-ounce burger per person

Be sure to use mesquite chips or wood chunks with this to make one of the most wonderful burgers you'll ever eat.

1 6–7-ounce burger per person
Salt and pepper
A.1. sauce
1 teaspoon butter per burger
A loaf of sourdough bread, cut in thick slices, or rolls, cut in half

Ketchup, chili sauce, hot sauce, BBQ sauce, relish, fresh onions, lettuce, and tomato

1. Make your fire according to the number of burgers you will be cooking. Mesquite or hickory are fine with bison.
2. Sprinkle the meat with salt, pepper, and A.1. sauce and form into patties.
3. Sear on each side; then cook over medium until done to perfection. Ranchers recommend that you eat it rare because the meat is so lean.
4. When you turn the burgers, put a pat of butter on top of each patty. Grill the bread or rolls. Serve with garnishes.

Buying Bison and Venison Online

Most recipe ingredients, even some exotics, are available online. Shipped directly from the ranch or farm where they are grown, you get them the next day, well packed and chilled. You can also get prime beef, free-range poultry, and ostrich and other exotic meat online.

New England–Style Wood Grilled Chicken

*Hickory or apple wood chunks
    and/or wood chips*
1½ cups cider
½ stick sweet butter

1 teaspoon dried thyme
1 4–5-pound chicken, whole
Salt and pepper

> **Serves 4–6**
>
> Young chickens, up to 4 pounds, tend to be sweeter and juicer than big ones, and have less fat.
>
>

1. Prepare the grill with the wood chunks (see page 170).
2. Bring the cider to a boil and reduce to 1 cup. Add the butter and thyme. Remove from heat.
3. Sprinkle the chicken inside and out with salt and pepper. Sear over hot embers. Move to indirect heat for up to 2 hours. Baste every 10 minutes with the cider/butter mixture.
4. Let the chicken rest on a warm platter for 15 minutes. Carve and serve.

Delicate Peach Wood Grilled Sea Trout

Peach wood chunks or chips
*1 tablespoon lemon rind, finely
    grated*
*1 tablespoon orange rind,
    finely grated*

1 teaspoon dried oregano
3 tablespoons olive oil
Salt and pepper
*1 1½-pound sea trout fillet,
    skin on*

> **Serves 4**
>
> Sea trout is a firm, white, mild seagoing fish. There are many, many ways of cooking it. This is one of the best!
>
>

1. Prepare grill with wood chips (see page 170), making it very hot.
2. Mix the lemon and orange rinds together with the oregano and olive oil. Rinse, dry, and liberally salt and pepper the fish. Spread the citrus mixture onto it.
3. Put the fish on a medium grill, skin-side down, with a small fire of peach wood underneath. You can put a piece of heavy-duty aluminum foil under the fish. The fish is done when it flakes at the thickest part.

Kentucky's Best Bourbon and Hickory Grilled Turkey

1 cup bourbon
1 cup maple syrup
½ cup salt
½ cup apple cider vinegar
Water to cover

1 10–12-pound turkey
Salt and pepper to season the
    turkey
4 cups presoaked wood chips
5 pounds wood chunks

1. Mix the bourbon, maple syrup, salt, and cider vinegar together. Add the turkey and then cover with water. Keep cool for 8 hours or overnight.
2. Drain the turkey and discard all but 1 quart of the marinade. Put the quart of marinade in a saucepan on the stove and simmer to reduce to 2 cups for use as a basting liquid.
3. Prepare grill with wood chips (see page 170).
4. Smoke the turkey for 3 hours in a smoker or covered grill with plenty of wood. After smoking, place in a 350°F oven, basting frequently, for an additional 2 hours or until internal temperature reaches 165°F at the thickest part of the bird.

Kosher Salt

Kosher salt has large, coarse grains and sticks to the food better than regular table salt. There are salt connoisseurs just as there are wine and beer connoisseurs—some like French sea salt, others like Adriatic or Dead Sea salt. The coarseness of the salt is what is most important. Coarse salt has many facets, sides that will stick to the food.

Vermont Maple Wood Smoked Pheasant

*2 pheasants, cleaned and split
from neck to tail
Salt and pepper
1 cup Hot Currant Sauce for
Game (page 220)*

*8 thick slices bacon
Apple wood chips and either
apple briquettes or pre-
soaked wood chunks*

> **Serves 6**
>
> Pheasant is a very lean, dry meat, so be sure to wrap it in bacon to keep it from drying out. Serve with Hot Currant Sauce (page 220) and Creamy Chestnut Purée (page 218).
>
>

1. Rinse the birds in cold water and dry with paper towels. Sprinkle them liberally with salt and pepper.
2. Divide the currant sauce in half and separate it. Reserve half for serving with the cooked pheasant (you want to make sure that what you serve on the table hasn't come in contact with what you brush on the birds). Brush each half bird with some of the currant sauce. Using small metal skewers, affix strips of bacon to each half bird.
3. Prepare the grill with wood chips (see page 170).
4. Smoke/grill the birds for 1 hour, or until they reach at least 150°F inside. If the wood runs out and the birds are not done, put them in a 325°F oven for an extra 30 minutes.
5. Cut the browned halves in two, and you may want to discard the bacon.

Other Wild Birds

It's nice to know that if you suddenly are gifted with some wild grouse or partridge, you can grill them as you would pheasant. Both are light in flavor and very good on the grill; however, make sure they do not dry out or get overcooked. That will make them tough and stringy.

Northwest Oak Grilled Salmon Fillets

Oak chips
1 1½-pound salmon fillet, rinsed and dried on paper towels
10 juniper berries, bruised
Salt and pepper to taste
2 tablespoons butter, melted
1 ounce anise-flavored liqueur
¼ cup fresh rosemary spikes, plus several stalks to add to the fire
1 lemon, cut into wedges, for garnish

1. Prepare the grill with wood (see page 170).
2. Stud the fish with juniper berries and sprinkle with salt and pepper. Mix the butter, liqueur, and rosemary together and brush the fish with the mixture.
3. Grill over an oak fire, adding stalks of rosemary every 10 minutes. Depending on the thickness of the fish, it will take 15–20 minutes. The fish flakes easily when done, or it can be served medium. Serve on a warm platter with lemon wedges.

Experimenting with Wood

When you are cooking delicately flavored foods such as fish, chicken, or pheasant, it's best not to overpower their natural flavors with heavy wood smoke. You may want to experiment with different wood and wood chips for smoking and grilling your favorites.

Long Island Apple Wood Grilled Duckling

Apple wood chunks or chips
1 5-pound duckling
Salt and pepper

1 tart apple, peeled, cored,
  and cut into pieces
½ orange, sliced thinly

1. Prepare the grill with wood (see page 170).
2. Rinse the duck and pat it dry. Salt and pepper the duck inside and out. Stuff the inside of the duckling with the apple and orange pieces. Prick the duck all over with a fork.
3. Sear the duck over a hot fire for just a few minutes, turning constantly. When brown, put the duck on indirect heat and turn it on its side. After 20 minutes, turn it on the other side. Roast it until it reaches at least 150°F internal temperature. Every 10–15 minutes, put the duck on a metal platter and prick it with a fork to drain the fat. Dispose of the fat or it will flame up.
4. Serve the duck with currant sauce or with a bowl of raspberry jelly. You may eat the apple and orange or discard. The duckling will be perfumed by the fruit.

Smokers and Grills

Smokers are available in hardware stores, and for rent when you are having a big party. However, it's not difficult to turn your gas or charcoal grill into a smoker by damping down the vents and adding presoaked wood chips every 15 minutes. You can also use chunks of wood with charcoal from the same wood. The thing to do is watch, watch, watch!

Hickory Grilled Pork Chops with Apples

Serves 4

The "other white meat" has lost much of its rich flavor and tenderness, so get the fattiest pork chops you can find. The fat in the meat liquefies and burns off in the cooking.

Hickory wood chips or chunks of wood
1 tablespoon kosher salt
1 tablespoon red pepper flakes
1 tablespoon dried thyme

4 thick rib pork chops, a pocket made in each
1 tart apple, peeled, cored, and cut into 8 thin slices
2 tablespoons olive oil

1. Prepare the grill with wood (see page 170).
2. Mix together the salt, red pepper flakes, and thyme. Sprinkle ½ of it in the pork pockets. Slide in the apple slices.
3. Close the pockets and fasten them securely with small metal skewers. Brush the chops with olive oil. Sprinkle with the rest of the thyme, salt, and red pepper mixture, pressing it into the meat with the back of a teaspoon.
4. Grill the chops with the lid closed for 15 minutes. Turn and grill until done, about 8–10 minutes more, depending on the heat of your fire and the thickness of the chops.

Hickory Grilled Veal Chops

Serves 4

Serve this with a side dish of boiled artichokes and some orzo laced with butter, fresh parsley, and Parmesan cheese.

Hickory wood chunks or chips
4 thick rib or loin veal chops, about 7–8 ounces each, bone in
2 tablespoons dried rosemary leaves

2 teaspoons dried oregano
1 tablespoon kosher salt
1 teaspoon freshly ground black pepper, or to taste
2 tablespoons dry mustard
¼ cup olive oil or butter

1. Prepare the grill with wood (see page 170).
2. Putting the chops between layers of waxed paper, pound them with a mallet or a 5-pound weight until they are almost double in size.
3. Mix the herbs, salt and pepper, mustard, and oil together and spread on the chops, pressing into the meat with the back of a spoon.
4. Grill quickly to brown, then place on indirect heat to smoke for 10–15 minutes. Serve medium-rare.

Old English Spit-Roasted Leg of Venison

*2 quarts dry red wine, such
   as burgundy*
4–6 bay leaves
4 whole cloves, bruised
10 black peppercorns, cracked
*1 lemon, cut in half and
   squeezed into the marinade,
   peel added*

½ cup Worcestershire sauce
1 teaspoon salt
*1 6-pound boneless leg of
   venison*

Serves 10–12

Farms selling fresh
venison are listed on
the Web, or you can
order through a spe-
cialty butcher.
Get a big piece and
have a party.

1. Mix together all the ingredients except the meat to create a marinade.
   Soak the venison in the marinade, refrigerated, for 8 hours. Reserve
   the marinade to use as a basting sauce.
2. Prepare your grill with a lot of charcoal, a pan of water, and have 3
   cups of presoaked chips ready. Set the spit 12 inches above the coals.
3. Spit roast the venison, adding wood chips and basting every 20–40
   minutes. Roast the meat for 20 minutes per pound, or 10 minutes per
   pound if you like it rare, as do the deer farmers.
4. Boil the leftover marinade and serve on the side. Also, serve with
   bowls of warm currant jelly and puréed chestnuts on the side. Roasted
   potatoes are excellent with venison.

Jimmy Crack Corns

*Some recipes may tell you to bang a mallet or hammer on the
peppercorns. Of course, your kitchen floor will crunch with pepper.
Don't do that! Try this—place the peppercorns between two layers
of waxed paper. Using a good old-fashioned cast-iron pan, gently
crack and crush the pepper until it reaches the desired consistency.
Use the bottom piece of waxed paper to funnel the pepper into the
pot or dish.*

Old-Fashioned Maple Wood
Grilled Venison Steak

Serves 4–5

Try serving this with
Creamy Chestnut
Purée (below) and
Hot Currant Sauce
(page 220). Classical
side dishes are
braised Brussels
sprouts and wild rice.

*1 2-pound venison steak, thick
    cut, or 4 strip steaks*
2 tablespoons fresh parsley, minced
1 cup red wine
1 tablespoon garlic, minced

10 juniper berries, bruised
½ cup olive oil
Kosher salt and pepper to taste
*Hickory wood chunks and
    chips for smoking/grilling*

1. Mix the wine, garlic, juniper berries, and olive oil together. Place in a
   nonreactive pan and marinate the venison, covered and refrigerated,
   for 4 hours, turning the meat after 2 hours.
2. Drain the meat and add the salt and pepper. Grill quickly over a hot
   fire, then let it rest and smoke over indirect heat. Venison should be
   rare to medium-rare to be good. Timing depends on the thickness of
   the meat and the heat of your fire; however, it will be done when it
   reaches at least 145°F.

Creamy Chestnut Purée for Venison

Makes 1½ cups

You can buy roasted,
peeled, and skinned
chestnuts ready to
use, in a jar. Just
don't buy the ones
packed in sugar syrup
for this recipe!

*1 jar or 8 ounces roasted
    chestnuts, peeled and skinned*
¾ cup heavy cream
Nutmeg to taste

*Salt and cayenne pepper to
    taste*
2 tablespoons butter

1. Place the chestnuts in a food processor and whirl, slowly adding
   cream and seasonings. Don't overprocess or the cream will turn to
   butter!
2. Heat the butter in a saucepan and add the chestnut purée. Warm over
   low heat and serve in a small bowl.

Orange-Sage Jam for Veal and Poultry

*1 whole, fresh, thick-skinned
   orange
Juice of 1 fresh orange
¾ cup sugar, or to taste*

*Pinch salt
½ teaspoon Tabasco sauce
¼ cup sage leaves, shredded*

1. Peel orange, cut into very small pieces, and remove seeds.
2. Place all ingredients in a small, nonreactive pot—such as a glass or an enamel-covered pot.
3. Bring to a boil and stir until the sugar is melted and the jam has thickened. Serve hot, cold, or at room temperature, whichever you prefer.

Makes 1½ cups

This will keep in the refrigerator for at least 2 weeks. You can vary this by adding some lemon zest and/or chopped and toasted walnuts or pecans.

Cranberry-Walnut Sauce for Turkey

*1 cup walnut pieces
2 cups cranberries, washed,
   stems picked off
1 cup claret
1 cup sugar, or to taste*

*1 cinnamon stick
10 peppercorns, cracked
Pinch salt
1 cinnamon stick*

1. Toast the walnut pieces under the broiler until brown and crunchy.
2. Place all but the walnuts in a saucepan and bring to a boil. The cranberries will pop, so cover the pot! Reduce heat and cook until thickened. Remove cinnamon stick before serving.
3. Add the nuts and stir gently. Serve in a sauceboat.

Makes 3 cups

Try this delicious sauce with other game and pork. Enjoy it with all your holiday dishes.

Hot Currant Sauce for Game

Makes 1½ cups

Sauces made with currants and currant jelly are heavenly with game. The sweet/tart combinations with mild or even full-bodied meats and poultry are perfect.

½ cup dried currants
½ cup dry red wine
8 ounces currant jelly
4 fresh or 2 dried bay leaves

2 coriander seeds, bruised
4 juniper berries, bruised
Salt and pepper to taste

Soak the currants in the wine for 45 minutes. Then, place the currants in a nonreactive saucepan and bring to a boil. Add currant jelly, bay leaves, coriander seeds, juniper berries, and salt and pepper. Cook for 30 minutes, until reduced to 1½ cups. Set aside until just warm. Remove bay leaves before serving. You can add 1 tablespoon butter if you want a richer sauce.

Currants and Gooseberries
Currants are divided into red and white currants, and the European black currant is a third member of the same family. Currants and gooseberries are closely related berry-producing shrubs well suited to home gardens throughout most of the upper Midwest. Hardy and productive, they provide fruit useful in jams and desserts. A mature gooseberry or currant shrub can produce up to four quarts of fruit annually.

CHAPTER 16

Fruit and Desserts

Tangy Apple, Pear, and Cranberry Crisp

Serves 4

This is a great fall dessert. Perfect after a dinner of chicken or game.

2 tart apples, peeled, cored, and chopped
2 ripe pears, peeled, cored, and chopped
½ cup fresh cranberries, rinsed and stemmed
2 tablespoons flour
1 teaspoon orange peel, minced
6–8 tablespoons golden brown sugar

½ teaspoon salt
1 tablespoon lemon juice
½ teaspoon ground cinnamon
½ teaspoon ground allspice
¼ teaspoon ground nutmeg
2 tablespoons cold butter
½ cup brown sugar
⅔ cup oatmeal
4 tablespoons butter, melted

1. Prepare a heavy cast-iron skillet with nonstick spray.
2. Mix the apples, pears, and cranberries with flour, orange peel, sugar, salt, lemon juice, cinnamon, allspice, and nutmeg. Put fruit in the pan. Dot with cold butter.
3. Mix the brown sugar, oatmeal, and melted butter together and spread over the fruit.
4. Set grill to very low heat.
5. Bake on indirect heat in a covered grill for 20 minutes or until topping is crisp and the fruit bubbling.

Parsley, Sage, Rosemary, and Thyme

Fruit can be both sweet and, when mixed with herbs and lemon juice, savory. Parsley, sage, rosemary, and thyme go well with fruit such as apples, pears, or grapes in stuffing. Put some ham or turkey salad in a grilled peach and you've created a terrific lunch.

Spicy and Sweet Baked Apples

4 large Granny Smith apples
¼ cup dark brown sugar
1 teaspoon ground cinnamon

¼ teaspoon ground nutmeg
4 teaspoons walnuts, chopped
4 teaspoons butter

1. Wash and dry the apples. Remove the cores, making sure not to cut all the way through to the bottom or the stuffing will fall out.
2. Mix the sugar, cinnamon, nutmeg, and walnuts together and fill the apples.
3. Make cups for the apple bases with heavy-duty aluminum foil. Dot the tops of the filling with butter.
4. Set the grill to low.
5. Place on indirect heat, cover the grill, and bake the apples for 20 minutes.

Makes 4 baked apples

These are delicious served for breakfast or as dessert with whipped cream or ice cream.

Apple and Ham Kebabs

2 thick slices smoked ham,
  about ½ pound, cubed
1 large apple, cored and sliced

2 teaspoons Dijon-style or
  American brown mustard
4 teaspoons maple syrup

1. Thread the ham cubes and apple slices onto four presoaked wooden skewers. Brush mustard on the ham, and drizzle syrup on both ham and apples.
2. Set grill to high heat.
3. Place on a hot grill and turn every 20 seconds.

Serves 4

After grilling the kebabs, you can either eat them off the stick or put them on buns for sandwiches.

Apple and Dried Fruit Roasted Chicken

Serves 4

You can also use game hens in this recipe. They are just wonderful when stuffed with fruit and savory herbs.

1 3-pound chicken
1 cup seedless green or red grapes
½ Granny Smith apple, peeled, cored, and chopped
6 dried apricots, cut into quarters and soaked in water to cover
¼ cup dried cranberries

4 ounces butter, melted
2 tablespoons fresh thyme or 2 teaspoons dried
6 scallions, chopped
Salt and lots of freshly ground black pepper
1½ cups soft breadcrumbs
2 tablespoons butter, melted to brush the bird

1. Remove the packet of neck, gizzard, heart, and liver. Rinse the chicken and pat dry. Set aside.
2. Mix together the fruit, butter, thyme, scallions, salt and pepper, and breadcrumbs. Stuff the bird(s) and close the cavities with small metal skewers.
3. Prepare the grill for indirect heat.
4. Brush the chicken with more melted butter and roast over indirect heat for 35 minutes or until the internal temperature is 160°F at the thickest part.

Apple Substitutes

Try substituting quinces or guavas for the apples in this sauce. Or, you can remove the zest and juice a tangerine for a great mixture with currants. You can also reduce port to a sauce. Concentrated cranberry juice is also fine with apples and currants.

Apricots with Berry Sauce

1 pint strawberries, washed
and hulled
½ cup claret or red wine

½ cup sugar
8 medium fresh apricots
1 tablespoon butter, melted

1. Put the berries, wine, and sugar in a blender and whirl until puréed. Strain and then heat over low flame for 10 minutes.
2. Rinse the apricots and cut them in half; remove pits. Brush them with butter.
3. Set grill to medium heat.
4. Place the apricots cut-side down on the grill for 1 minute. Turn and grill for another 45–60 seconds. Serve hot with the berry sauce. You can also add ice cream or whipped cream.

> **Serves 4**
>
> This is a very refreshing end to a big meal. The sauce is a cinch to make and the apricots take but a few minutes.
>
>

A South African Specialty

In South Africa, grilled meat is flavored with apricots. The term sosaties *comes from the Malay words* sate, *which means "spiced sauce," and* sesaste, *which translates as "skewered meat." There are many variations on sosaties, but all of them involve apricots!*

Avocados with Rémoulade Sauce

Serves 4 as a side; if stuffed, a good lunch
The small, pebbly skinned avocados hold up best on the grill. This makes a good side dish.

1 hard-boiled egg yolk
1 raw egg yolk
1 teaspoon Dijon mustard
Salt and pepper to taste
3 drops Tabasco sauce

1 teaspoon tarragon vinegar
⅔ cup olive oil, very well chilled
4 avocados, halved and pitted

1. Put the eggs, mustard, salt, pepper, Tabasco, and vinegar in a blender or food processor. Whirl until puréed. Slowly add the olive oil, blending until thickened.
2. Set grill to low.
3. Grill the avocados for 45–50 seconds, cut-side down. Turn and grill for 30 seconds. Drizzle with sauce and serve. You can add cooked shrimp at this point to make a heartier dish.

Grilled Bananas with Ice Cream

Serves 4
If banana splits were part of your youth, you'll love this recipe. These could be called "fairly grown-up sundaes."

4 bananas
4 scoops vanilla, strawberry, or chocolate ice cream

1 cup chocolate sauce, heated
½ cup walnuts, chopped

1. Set grill to low.
2. Peel the bananas and place them on the grill, whole. Grill for a minute on each side. Remove to plates and split.
3. Add ice cream, chocolate sauce, and nuts. Serve!

Grilled Bananas Are Versatile
Try flaming your grilled bananas with orange liqueur or even raspberry liqueur. All of the alcohol cooks away, leaving a delightful flavor. You can also melt jam or jelly to brush on grilled bananas.

Roasted Grapefruit with Honey and Rum

2 large grapefruit, halved
4 tablespoons honey

4 teaspoons unsalted butter
4 tablespoons rich, golden rum

1. Arrange a large piece of heavy-duty aluminum foil on the grill. Spray foil with nonstick spray. Set grill to low.
2. Cut the grapefruit in half and place on the foil, cut-side down. Close the lid and roast for 3–4 minutes.
3. Turn the grapefruit to the noncut side, add honey, and roast for 3 more minutes. Then remove the grapefruit to a flameproof platter.
4. Run a knife around the sections without cutting through the skin. Add butter and rum. Light with a wooden kitchen match and serve flaming.

Serves 4 (½ grapefruit per person)

This is a great side at brunch. You must be careful not to under- or overcook. Watch the grapefruit carefully. Bring them to the table flaming!

Hot and Cold Grilled Nectarines

½ cup heavy cream
2 tablespoons sugar
½ teaspoon pure vanilla extract

8 teaspoons slivered almonds, toasted
4 firm nectarines, halved and pitted

1. Whip the cream, gradually adding the sugar and vanilla. Set aside.
2. Toast the almonds under the broiler until golden.
3. Set grill to low.
4. Grill the nectarines for 1 minute on the cut side and 30 seconds on the skin side. Place on plates and fill the centers with cream; spike with almonds.

Serves 4

This recipe tastes like a whole lot of work, but it's very quick, easy, and delicious.

Grilled Peaches with Cream Cheese and Bacon

Serves 4

This is a super brunch dish. It combines sweet and savory.

8–ounce block of cream cheese, not low fat, at room temperature
½ cup heavy cream
½ teaspoon Tabasco sauce

4 slices bacon, fried until crisp and crumbled
4 firm peaches, halved and pitted

1. Whip the cream cheese, cream, and Tabasco sauce together until soft.
2. Fry the bacon, drain on a paper towel, and crumble.
3. Set grill to low.
4. Put the peaches, cut-side down, on a hot grill and turn after 1 minute. Grill for another half minute. Spoon the cheese-and-cream mixture into each peach half. Sprinkle with bacon and serve immediately.

Grilled Peaches with Lemon Vinaigrette

Serves 4

This is an excellent hot and cold salad that is refreshing with meat or poultry.

Juice of ½ lemon
½ cup olive oil
Salt and pepper to taste

4 peaches, halved and pitted
1 bunch watercress, washed and spun dry

1. Whisk the lemon juice, oil, salt, and pepper together.
2. Set grill to low.
3. Grill the peaches cut-side down for 1 minute and skin-side down for 30 seconds. Place the watercress on salad plates, add the peaches, and drizzle with lemon dressing.

Grilled Pears with Claret Sauce

1 cup claret
2 whole cloves, bruised
¼ cup sugar (optional)

¼ cup heavy cream
4 unpeeled pears, halved and
*   cored*

1. Bring the claret, cloves, and sugar to a boil and reduce to half. Add the cream and keep warm.
2. Set grill to high heat.
3. Grill the pears over a hot fire for 1 minute, cut-side down. Turn and grill for 30 seconds. Remove pears to serving plates, spoon sauce over all, and serve immediately.

Serves 4
This is a takeoff on an old, complicated, and elegant dessert.

Grilled Pineapple with Caramel Coating

¼ cup dark corn syrup
2 tablespoons butter

1 tablespoon rum
4 thick slices fresh pineapple

1. Bring the syrup and butter to a boil. Add the rum.
2. Brush the pineapple rounds with the syrup mixture.
3. Set grill to low.
4. Grill the pineapple rounds until they start to get golden brown. Turn and grill for another few seconds. Serve immediately with ice cream or sorbet.

Serves 4
Use only fresh pineapple. When served, the pineapple can be garnished with shredded coconut, ice cream, sorbet, or any fruit sauce.

Spicy Pineapple Kebabs

16 chunks fresh pineapple
4 teaspoons brown or white sugar

1 teaspoon ground cloves
1 teaspoon lemon juice

1. Mix sugar, cloves, and lemon juice in a bowl.
2. Thread the pineapple onto the skewers and sprinkle with sugar mixture.
3. Set grill to high heat.
4. Grill over hot fire until slightly brown and very hot. Serve immediately.

Why Grill Fruit?

By grilling fruit, you concentrate its natural sweetness without adding sugar or syrup. You get a lot of goodness with your sweet, not a lot of empty calories and fat, as you would with more traditional kinds of desserts. Also, grilled fruit is a fine way to introduce your children to eating fruit on a regular basis, and you can use fruit that is not so ripe for grilling.

CHAPTER 17
Grilling Sauces, Marinades, and Rubs

Hill Country Barbecue Sauce

Makes 3 cups

Adding whiskey to your sauce changes it radically. This sauce is especially good with chicken and sturdy fish such as bluefish and swordfish.

1 large yellow onion, peeled and chopped
2 cloves garlic, peeled and chopped
½ cup peanut oil
½ cup yellow mustard
1 tablespoon Worcestershire sauce
1 tablespoon Tabasco sauce
1 cup blended whiskey

1 cup chicken broth
1 tablespoon fresh parsley, chopped
1 teaspoon salt, or to taste
1 teaspoon dried sage leaves, crumbled
Freshly ground black pepper to taste
1 tablespoon cold butter

1. In a large pot, sauté the onion and garlic in peanut oil until they are soft.
2. Add all ingredients except the butter and simmer until reduced to 3 cups. When ready to use, add the butter to finish.
3. Just before grilling, spread the sauce on the chicken or fish and inhale the wonderful aroma as it cooks.

Where Did Worcestershire Come From?

Worcestershire Sauce makes a great addition to many grilling specialties. The sauce came from an Indian recipe, in which the governor of Bengal prepared a concoction that sat too long at a chemist's. Lo and behold, the mixture had mellowed, and was brought to Great Britain in 1838.

Old-Fashioned Barbecue Sauce

½ cup olive oil

4 cloves garlic, peeled, smashed, and chopped

1 onion, peeled and chopped

2 serrano peppers, cored, seeded, and chopped

1 sweet red pepper, roasted, cored, seeded, and chopped

½ cup flat beer

1 quart fresh plum tomatoes, blanched, skins removed

¼ teaspoon cinnamon

½ cup strong coffee

2 tablespoon dark brown sugar

2 ounces tequila

Salt and freshly ground black pepper to taste

1. Using a large soup pot, heat the olive oil and add the garlic, onion, and peppers. Sauté until very soft.
2. Add the rest of the ingredients and remove the lid. Simmer until reduced to 1 quart, 2–3 hours.
3. Place in bowl or jar, covered, in the refrigerator. When ready to serve, spoon or brush onto food.

> **Makes 1 quart**
>
> It's a fact that you ingest no alcohol when you add liquor or wine to a sauce; all you get is flavor.
>
>

Flavoring with Alcohol

You will note that a famous bourbon distiller has produced a sauce with bourbon in it for supermarket sales. Most people enjoy the increasingly popular pasta sauce à la vodka with just a hint of vodka, which enhances the flavor.

Asian Ginger Sauce

1½ cups soy sauce
1 clove garlic, peeled and
    mashed to a paste
½-inch piece gingerroot, peeled
    and minced

1 tablespoon lemon juice
2 ounces dry sherry
1 teaspoon hot sauce

Mix all ingredients together and let stand for 1 hour before using. It can also be refrigerated for up to a week.

Spicy Indian Curry Yogurt Marinade

1 cup plain yogurt (not low fat)
Juice of ½ lime
½ teaspoon red pepper flakes
¼ teaspoon ground black
    pepper

1 tablespoon curry powder
½ teaspoon garlic powder
½ teaspoon salt

Mix all ingredients together and brush on meat, fish, or seafood. Marinate for 1 hour. Grill and serve. Be sure to discard the remaining marinade. You may add cilantro, parsley, and/or other herbs to the marinade.

Hot Thai Dipping Sauce

1 cup canned, unsweetened
    coconut milk
½ cup peanut butter or tahini
    (sesame seed paste)
1 teaspoon Asian fish sauce
½ teaspoon Thai red pepper
    paste or Tabasco

Juice of ½ lime
1 teaspoon garlic, minced
2 teaspoons fresh gingerroot,
    peeled and minced
10 chives or 5 scallions,
    minced

Whirl all ingredients in your blender. Taste for heat and season accordingly. Serve with skewered chicken, meats, fish, and seafood.

> **Makes 2 cups**
>
> This recipe makes enough for a party and is wonderful with chicken, shrimp, or beef on skewers. You can adjust the heat to your taste.
>
>

Hawaiian Citrus Marinade and Dipping Sauce

1 cup canned, unsweetened
    coconut milk
2 tablespoons frozen pineapple
    juice concentrate
Juice and finely grated zest of
    ½ lemon

¼ cup sour orange juice
1 teaspoon Asian fish sauce
1 teaspoon dark soy sauce
1 teaspoon cayenne pepper
Salt to taste

Whirl all ingredients in a blender, bring to a boil, and serve at room temperature or chilled. This can be made a week in advance. Store in refrigerator.

> **Makes 1½ cups**
>
> This sauce is perfect with poultry and pork. Divide in half and use half as a marinade and the other half for dipping.
>
>

Old English Marinade for Game

Makes 2 quarts

A large piece of elk or venison, or a couple of rabbits or pheasants will benefit by marinating in this concoction for 6–8 hours.

$1\frac{1}{2}$ quarts dry red wine such as burgundy

4 bay leaves

1 onion, peeled and sliced

4–6 cloves garlic, smashed, unpeeled

2 ounces Worcestershire sauce

$\frac{1}{2}$ cup parsley, rinsed and minced

2–3 whole sage leaves, torn

1 whole lemon, sliced thinly

10 black peppercorns, bruised

5 green peppercorns, pickled

$\frac{1}{2}$ cup spicy brown mustard

10 juniper berries, bruised

Mix all ingredients in a large nonreactive container or bowl. Marinate 6–8 hours in this sauce. After using, discard the marinade or, if you intend to use the marinade in your sauce, boil it for 10 minutes.

Vermouth versus Wine

Vermouth has flavorings that wine does not. The recipes are secret, kept in families for hundreds of years. Legend has it that the original recipes for French and Italian vermouth are locked up in the Vatican. The important thing to know about vermouth is that the French is white and not sweet. Italian vermouth is sweet and spicy, too. Both are good for cooking.

French Marinade for Poultry

½ cup onion, peeled and
chopped

1 clove garlic, peeled and
chopped

½ cup fresh fennel bulb,
chopped

1 cup olive oil

2 teaspoons dry English mustard

½ cup white vermouth or wine

1 teaspoon Worcestershire
sauce

2 ounces white wine vinegar

1 tablespoon honey

¼ cup fresh basil leaves or
2 teaspoons dried

1 teaspoon salt and plenty of
freshly ground black pepper

> **Makes 2 cups**
>
> This is delightfully tart/sweet and savory with vermouth, herbs, and aromatic vegetables.
>
>

1. In a medium-sized, nonreactive saucepan, sauté the onion, garlic, and fennel in olive oil.
2. Mix the mustard and vermouth together in a small bowl until smooth.
3. Place the vegetables, mustard mixture, and the rest of the ingredients in the bowl of a blender and whirl until smooth. Place in a cruet or jar. Will keep for a week.

How Fennel Changes Its Flavor

Fennel is delicious in salads and cooked as a hot vegetable. However, when fennel is cooked, its sweetness comes out through the magic of heat! Fennel tastes delicious when grilled. When you are grilling fish or chicken, take some of the stalks and leaves, put them on the rack of your grill, and put a piece of fish or chicken on top. The fennel will char, giving you delicious smoke. You can also throw a teaspoon of aniseeds or fennel seeds on the fire for a similar effect.

Tenderizing Marinade for Beef

Makes 2 cups

Marinate a piece of shoulder steak or not-so-great sirloin in this for a tender and flavorful grilled steak.

1½ cups dry red wine
¼ cup olive oil
4 garlic cloves, smashed and peeled

6 juniper berries, bruised in a mortar and pestle
1 lemon, thinly sliced
Salt and pepper to taste

Mix all of the ingredients together and place, with the meat, in a non-reactive pan. Marinate beef or lamb, covered and refrigerated, for 3–8 hours, turning occasionally.

Spicy Cajun Rub

Makes about ½ cup

This is delicious— a dry mixture of spices to rub on poultry, fish, or meat to add flavor and heat!

1 tablespoon cayenne pepper
1 teaspoon sweet paprika
1 teaspoon hot paprika
2 tablespoons freshly ground black pepper
2 teaspoons garlic powder
2 teaspoons onion powder

¼ teaspoon ground cloves
1 teaspoon dry English mustard
1 teaspoon aniseeds, bruised in a mortar and pestle
1 teaspoon salt, or to taste

Mix all ingredients together and spread on meat, poultry, or fish, pressing the rub into the meat. Let stand for 1 hour before grilling. This Cajun rub is more than open for variations in spices and heat. Have fun with it!

Caribbean Jerk Rub

1 tablespoon freshly ground
   black pepper
1 tablespoon cayenne pepper
1 teaspoon ground coriander
1 teaspoon ground cardamom
1 tablespoon garlic powder
¼ teaspoon ground cinnamon

½ teaspoon ground nutmeg
1 tablespoon dark brown
   sugar
1 teaspoon fresh lemon zest
1 tablespoon fresh orange zest
¼ cup Jamaican rum
   (optional)

Mix all ingredients thoroughly. Rub on meat, fish, shellfish, or poultry.
Let soak in for 1 hour and grill.

Makes ½ cup

This is piquant, hot,
and sweet, all at
once. Adding the rum
will turn the rub into
a paste.

Garlicky Aioli

6 cloves garlic, peeled, coarsely
   chopped
1 cup olive oil, at room
   temperature
1 teaspoon lemon juice

Pinch salt
Grinding of white pepper or
   a few grains of cayenne

1. Place the garlic in the bowl of your blender.
2. Very slowly drizzle in the oil while blending.
3. When thickened, add the lemon juice, salt, and pepper. Refrigerate,
   and when ready, use as a sauce or dressing on the side.

Makes 1 cup

One of the mothers of
all sauces, aioli was
devised by the
Egyptians, then
spread to Europe by
conquering Romans. It
is marvelous on fish,
shellfish, and chicken.

Mayonnaise Piquant

Makes 2 cups

You can vary this recipe by adding or subtracting mustard, chilies, tomatoes, and garlic.

2 whole eggs and 1 egg yolk, at room temperature
1 clove garlic, peeled and chopped
1½ cups olive oil, at room temperature

½ teaspoon dry mustard
2 teaspoons chipotle chilies, chopped
2 plum tomatoes, chopped
1 teaspoon salt
¼ teaspoon cayenne pepper

Put the eggs and garlic in the bowl of your blender. Slowly drizzle in the olive oil until you get a very thick mayonnaise. Then add the rest of the ingredients. Refrigerated, it will last 1 week. Other optional ingredients are curry powder, Tabasco sauce, dried dill, and tarragon or oregano leaves. You can use vinegar instead of lemon juice. Store until ready to use. Serve on the side.

Fast Perfect Hollandaise Sauce

Makes 1¼ cups

This classic sauce is perfect with vegetables, fish, and poultry. It's rich, velvety, and delightful. Just keep it warm; don't cook it or it will curdle.

½ pound unsalted butter
2 egg yolks and 1 whole egg, at room temperature
1 tablespoon lemon juice

2 tablespoons heavy cream
½ teaspoon salt
A grinding of white pepper or a few grains of cayenne

1. Place the butter in a small, heavy-bottomed saucepan to melt.
2. Put the eggs and the lemon juice in the bowl of a blender or food processor. With the motor running on low, slowly drizzle in the melted butter. Add the rest of the ingredients.
3. Return the sauce to the pan and whisk vigorously until thickened. Immediately pour the sauce into a warm sauceboat. (If you don't do this immediately, you will end up with scrambled eggs.) Serve alongside vegetables, meat, or fish.

Classic Béarnaise Sauce

1 stick unsalted butter, melted
1 whole egg and 1 yolk
1 teaspoon tarragon vinegar or
  white vinegar

½ teaspoon dried tarragon
Pinch salt and drop of
  Tabasco

1. While the butter is melting in a small saucepan, whirl the rest of the ingredients in the blender or food processor.
2. Very slowly, with the motor running, drizzle in the hot butter.
3. Return to the saucepan and beat until thickened. Immediately pour into a sauceboat and ladle over meat, vegetables, or fish.

Makes 6 servings

This sauce is classically served on filets mignon. It is also very delicious on chicken breasts and fish. Do not cook the finished sauce.

Hudson Valley Steak Sauce

1 stick butter
3 tablespoons Worcestershire
  sauce
½ cup chili sauce

2 drops Tabasco sauce,
  or to taste
Juice of ½ lemon

Melt the butter and stir in the rest of the ingredients. Baste the food with the sauce as it grills, preferably over a wood fire.

Makes 1 cup

Born in a camp on a bank of the Hudson River, this sauce does wonders for steaks. It can also be used on fish, lobster, clams, and shrimp.

CHAPTER 18

Best Side Dishes and Salads

Mexican Black Bean Casserole

Serves 6

This is an excellent side dish. To create a delicious main course, add ground beef, pork, or goat.

4 strips bacon

½ pound ground turkey, beef, or pork (optional)

1 onion, peeled and minced

2–4 cloves garlic, or to taste, peeled and minced

1 sweet red bell pepper, rinsed, cored, seeded, and chopped

2 jalapeño peppers, or to taste, cored, seeded and minced

Juice of 1 lime

Juice of ½ lemon

1 cup crushed tomatoes

Salt and freshly ground black pepper to taste

1 teaspoon coriander seeds, ground

¼ teaspoon cinnamon, ground

½ cup fresh cilantro, rinsed and chopped

2 ounces rum

2–3 cans black beans

1. Fry the bacon, place on paper towels, and crumble.
2. To the same pan, add the meat, onion, garlic, and peppers and sauté until soft. Add the cooked bacon; then add the rest of the ingredients and simmer slowly, covered, over low flame for 1 hour.
3. Serve with sour cream and some grated cheddar cheese on the side.

Taking Sides

The nice thing about having lots of side dishes is that there will be something for each person's taste. It's easy to omit the meat from the Mexican Black Bean Casserole if you are having a lot of vege-tarians to your home. You can also make extra salads with dressing on the side for the dieters. So, the more sides you make, the better for your party.

Smoky Applesauce

4 large tart apples, peeled,
    halved, and cored
2 tablespoons butter
½ cup cider
¼ teaspoon ground cinnamon

⅛ teaspoon ground nutmeg
2 teaspoons dark brown sugar
½ teaspoon salt
Juice of ½ lemon
Rind of ½ lemon, minced

1. Set the grill to high heat.
2. Peel and core the apples with a melon baller. Place them on the grill over a hot fire for 1 minute per side.
3. Put the rest of the ingredients in a saucepan and heat. Add the grilled apples to the sauce. If the applesauce is too dry, add more cider. Mix, breaking the apples up with a fork. Serve hot, cold, or at room temperature.

Serves 4–6

If you add some wood chips to your fire, this will be even more delicious.

Red Salad

4 medium-sized beets, cleaned
10 radishes, rinsed, stems
    removed, and thinly sliced
1 large red apple, cored and
    sliced
Juice of ½ lemon

1 red onion, peeled and sliced
¼ cup cider vinegar
¾ cup olive oil
Salt and pepper to taste
1 teaspoon fennel seeds,
    bruised

1. Set grill on low, about 250°F.
2. Package beets in aluminum foil and place them over indirect heat for 30 minutes. Cool, unwrap, and pop the beets out of their skins. Slice and place in a bowl.
3. Add the radishes and apple to the beets in the bowl, sprinkle with lemon juice, toss, and add the onion.
4. Whisk the vinegar, olive oil, salt, pepper, and fennel seeds together and toss into the salad. Serve chilled.

Serves 4–6

This is really great with many different dishes. It's crunchy and tasty, sweet and sour.

Grilled Savory Herb Bread

Serves 8–10

This recipe is for the savory side and goes well with just about anything.

$\frac{1}{4}$ cup unsalted butter
1 teaspoon dried oregano, crumbled
1 teaspoon dried basil, crumbled

Freshly ground black pepper
Celery salt to taste
1 cup Parmesan cheese, grated
1 loaf Italian bread

1. Mix the butter, herbs, spices, and cheese in a small saucepan. Heat until the butter melts, mixing constantly.
2. Cut the bread in half lengthwise; then score crosswise so that guests can break off chunks. Don't cut all the way through. Brush the butter and herb mixture on the bread.
3. Preheat oven to 300°F.
4. Wrap the loaf in aluminum foil and bake for 10 minutes. Unwrap the bread and run it under the broiler until lightly browned.

Stuffed Celery

Serves 4–6

This is an old favorite with a new twist. Adding the hot, spicy peppers gives it a great new tang.

$\frac{1}{4}$ pound Gorgonzola cheese
$\frac{1}{4}$ pound cream cheese, at room temperature
$\frac{1}{2}$ cup sour cream

2 canned chipotle peppers, finely minced, or 2 teaspoons red pepper flakes
4 large stalks celery

1. Mix the cheeses, sour cream, and peppers together in a food processor.
2. Wash the celery, remove the strings, and cut into 2-inch pieces. Stuff the pieces of celery with the cheese mixture. Arrange on a platter, and keep chilled until ready to serve. Some variations include the addition of: 2 chopped scallions, 1 teaspoon celery seeds, $\frac{1}{2}$ teaspoon fennel seeds, or some green peppercorns packed in brine.

Colorful Coleslaw

½ red cabbage, tough outer
leaves removed

1 head Chinese cabbage,
tough outer leaves removed

3 carrots, peeled and grated

1 sweet onion, or to taste,
peeled and sliced paper thin

12 radishes, ends removed,
sliced thinly

1 cup mayonnaise

¼ cup white wine vinegar

1 teaspoon Dijon-style prepared
mustard

1 teaspoon caraway seeds

Salt and pepper to taste

> ### Serves 8–10
>
> This holds up well for
> a big group. Use the
> shredding blade of
> the food processor
> on the vegetables to
> make this very quickly.
>
>

1. Shred the cabbages in batches, using the food processor. Place in a large, chilled bowl. Toss in the rest of the vegetables.
2. Mix together the mayonnaise, vinegar, mustard, caraway seeds, salt, and pepper. Keep chilled until ready to serve.

Cool Cabbage

The name "coleslaw" comes from the Dutch term koolsla, *which means, "cool cabbage." The term was adapted in the United States in the late nineteenth century. Coleslaw salad is made with shredded cabbage mixed with mayonnaise as well as a variety of ingredients.*

Deviled Eggs with Garnishes

**Makes 10
stuffed halves**

Everybody loves dev-
iled eggs, and the
spicier the better. For
a party, double the
recipe and use a
variety of garnishes.

5 hard-boiled eggs
½ cup mayonnaise
1 tablespoon Dijon-style prepared mustard
1 teaspoon curry powder
1 teaspoon Tabasco sauce, or
   to taste

1 teaspoon garlic powder, or
   to taste
Salt and freshly ground black
   pepper to taste
Shrimp, chopped olives, capers,
   caviar, seafood salad,
   and/or chives, for garnish

1. Peel and halve the eggs. Arrange the whites on a platter.
2. Put the yolks in a food processor. Add the mayonnaise, mustard, curry
   powder, Tabasco, garlic powder, salt, and pepper. Whirl the yolk mixture in the food processor until smooth.
3. Fill eggs and decorate with any of the garnishes.

How to Boil an Egg

*There is a trick to hard-boiling eggs. Place the required number of
eggs in cold water to cover, leaving plenty of room. If they are
crowded, they are likely to break before they are cooked. Bring
them to a boil and turn the heat down to a simmer. Simmer the
eggs for 7 minutes. Remove them from the heat and run them
under cold water, hitting the shells against the pot. When they are
cool enough to have shrunk a bit, they will be easy to peel neatly.*

Hearty Cheese and Arugula Salad

2 bunches arugula, stemmed,
  rinsed, and spun dry
2 ounces imported Provolone
  cheese
2 ounces prosciutto ham,
  chopped

2 ounces red wine vinegar
5 ounces extra-virgin olive oil
½ teaspoon dry mustard
1 egg yolk
½ teaspoon anchovy paste

1. Arrange the arugula on salad plates and place the cheese and prosciutto on top.
2. Whirl the rest of the ingredients in your blender. Drizzle over the salads or serve on the side.

> **Serves 4**
>
> This is tangy and tasty, a fine side salad for pasta or any grilled meat, fish, or poultry.
>
>

Spanish Gazpacho

3 pints cherry tomatoes
6 ounces dry red wine
Juice of 1 lemon
2 garlic cloves, peeled, minced,
  and mashed to a pulp
1 teaspoon dried oregano leaves
2 tablespoons fresh basil
  leaves, shredded

1 tablespoon Tabasco sauce,
  or to taste
1 tablespoon Worcestershire
  sauce, or to taste
1 teaspoon salt, or to taste
1 teaspoon freshly ground pink
  peppercorns, or to taste

Rinse and purée the tomatoes in a blender. Place the blended tomatoes in a large soup pot with the rest of the ingredients. Bring to a boil and turn off the heat. Chill. Serve the soup chilled, with a variety of finely chopped vegetables such as sweet onions, celery, green peppers, and cucumbers.

> **Makes 4
> 6-ounce cups**
>
> You can let your guests help themselves to the various veggies that go into gazpacho. It's important to make a good base soup and then add the vegetables.
>
>

Mushrooms à la Grecque

1 cup olive oil
Juice of ½ lemon
1 tablespoon red wine vinegar
1 garlic clove, minced
½ cup sweet onion, chopped
1 tablespoon coriander seeds, cracked
1 teaspoon black peppercorns, cracked
1 teaspoon salt, or to taste
8 ounces tiny button mushrooms
1 head Romaine lettuce, outer leaves removed
1 bag baby field greens
1 bunch parsley, for garnish

1. In a saucepan, mix together the olive oil, lemon juice, vinegar, garlic, onion, spices, and salt.
2. If the mushrooms are not tiny, cut them in half. Add the mushrooms to the olive oil mixture. Heat until almost boiling.
3. Place in a nonreactive bowl and chill, covered, for at least 2 hours or overnight.
4. Shred the Romaine lettuce. Rinse and spin dry all the greens. Arrange the greens on chilled plates. Build the salad with mushrooms.
5. Rinse, dry, and chop the parsley, and sprinkle over salads. Spoon any extra oil mixture over the salads.

Cracking Peppercorns

Sometimes, you need very coarsely cracked pepper or coriander seeds. You can use a rolling pin or a really heavy cast-iron frying pan. Put the spices in a sturdy plastic bag and seal. (This keeps the cracked peppercorns or coriander seeds from shooting all over the kitchen.) Or you can get an extra coffee grinder, strictly for spices, and set it on coarse. This is fine for the Mushrooms à la Grecque recipe or for steak au poivre, just to name two.

Macaroni Salad with Shrimp

8 ounces commercial French
   dressing
Juice of ½ lemon
½ cup onion, minced
1 cup celery, minced
1 sweet red pepper, roasted
   and chopped
1 cup walnut pieces, toasted

2 tablespoons capers
1 cup fresh parsley, rinsed,
   dried, and chopped
2 tablespoons fresh chives,
   minced
1 pound elbow macaroni
1 pound small shrimp, peeled,
   deveined, and cooked

Serves 6–8

This is an old favorite with some delicious innovations. You can omit the shrimp and this will still taste great.

1. Mix together everything except the macaroni and shrimp in a large serving bowl.
2. Cook the macaroni according to package directions. When the macaroni is done, drain it thoroughly and add it to the ingredients in the bowl. Mix quickly to coat. Add the shrimp and mix well. Chill until ready to serve.

Tomato Basil Salad with Buffalo Mozzarella

1 tablespoon red wine vinegar
1 tablespoon lemon juice
½ teaspoon kosher salt
Plenty of freshly ground black
   pepper
½ cup extra-virgin olive oil

2 ripe beefsteak tomatoes,
   rinsed and sliced thinly
4 ounces buffalo mozzarella,
   sliced thinly
16 large, fresh basil leaves,
   rinsed, dried, and shredded

Serves 4

You may have to go to a specialty market for the buffalo mozzarella. It's richer and more expensive than regular mozzarella, but so worth it.

1. In a small bowl, mix together the vinegar, lemon juice, salt, pepper, and oil. Set aside.
2. Build the salad on individual plates: Start with the tomatoes, then arrange the mozzarella, and finally the basil on top. Sprinkle with the dressing and serve immediately.

Traditional Potato Salad with Egg

4 medium or 3 large potatoes
Cold water to cover with 1
   tablespoon salt added
¼ cup cider vinegar
1 cup mayonnaise
1 teaspoon dark honey mustard
10 sweet gherkin pickles,
   chopped

4 hard-boiled eggs, peeled and
   chopped
½ cup sweet onion, peeled
   and chopped
1 cup celery, rinsed and
   chopped
Small sprinkle celery salt

1. Peel the potatoes and cut into chunks. Put them in cold, salted water; bring to a boil. Boil potatoes until tender, about 20 minutes, depending on size. While the potatoes are cooking, prepare a large bowl for the salad by chilling it well.
2. Drain the potatoes, put them in the chilled bowl, and sprinkle them with the cider vinegar while they are still hot.
3. In a separate bowl, mix the rest of the ingredients together until very well combined to make the dressing.
4. Add the bowl of dressing and vegetables to the potatoes and mix to coat. Refrigerate until ready to serve.

Potatoes Are A-peeling

There are many types of potato peelers on the market today. There is the old-fashioned up-and-down peeler, the "cross bar" peeler, and a sleekly modern one with a curved aluminum handle. As it turns out, the sleek one is for left-handed cooks. The trouble with peelers is that they are difficult to sharpen, so they get dull. You may want to replace your peelers if you find yourself at war with a carrot or potato.

German Potato Salad

*1 pound red bliss, fingerling,
or creamery new potatoes
Cold water to cover with
1 tablespoon salt added
½ cup red wine vinegar
¾ cup olive oil
1 red onion, peeled and sliced
paper thin*

*1 teaspoon peppercorns,
cracked
1 teaspoon caraway seeds,
cracked
½ cup fresh parsley, rinsed
and chopped*

Serves 4–6
This salad is very good plain, or you can add some roasted beets for a pink salad. Try adding marinated herring for a wildly tasty salad.

1. Scrub the potatoes but do not peel. Cut into bite-sized pieces. Put them in cold, salted water and bring to a boil. Boil potatoes for about 20 minutes, depending on size, until soft.
2. While the potatoes are cooking, mix the rest of the ingredients in a large serving bowl to make the dressing.
3. Drain the potatoes and mix them with the dressing. Serve hot, cold, or at room temperature.

An Extra Something in Potato Salad

When you are making any kind of potato salad, add some cooked and crumbled bacon to it. This adds a bit more salt, some crunch, and a savory, smoky taste, which perks up the potatoes considerably.

Autumn Fennel and Orange Salad

½ cup fresh sour orange juice
½ cup extra-virgin olive oil
1 egg yolk
Salt and pepper to taste
½ cup cilantro or parsley, rinsed and chopped
1 large bunch watercress, rinsed and dried
1 large or 2 small fennel bulbs, sliced thinly
2 fresh oranges (such as temple or navel), peeled and sliced crosswise
Red pepper flakes

1. Put the juice, oil, egg yolk, salt and pepper, and either cilantro or parsley in a blender and mix until emulsified.
2. Divide the watercress between four serving plates. Layer the fennel and orange slices over the watercress. Sprinkle with dressing and red pepper flakes and serve chilled.

No Sour Oranges?

If you can't find sour oranges or don't have access to a good Latino market locally, you can make regular orange juice sour by adding a tablespoon of lemon juice to ½ cup orange juice.

CHAPTER 19

Cheers! Drinks to Go with Grilled Food

Pink Ladies' Ade

1 box frozen raspberries, defrosted
1 small can frozen lemonade, mixed with 2 cans water
1 bottle pink champagne

1 bottle regular brut champagne (or club soda)
1 pint fresh strawberries, washed, hulled, and halved
20 fresh mint leaves

Whirl the raspberries and lemonade in your blender until puréed. Place in a punch bowl. Add the rest of the ingredients and mix gently.

Making Creative Ice Blocks

This couldn't be simpler, or more attractive. Using a round freezer container, slice in fresh oranges, lemons, limes, or a combination and add water. Freeze and use in your punch bowl. You certainly can use other fruits such as fresh strawberries, blueberries, peaches, or whatever is in season. However, if you do use peaches or nectarines, add 2 tablespoons of lemon juice to a quart of water to make sure the fruit doesn't turn an unattractive brown. You can also freeze sprigs of mint and individual pieces of fruit in regular ice cube trays for a cooling and pretty effect.

Green Tropic Ade

1 large can frozen limeade
1 can ice water
Juice of 1 fresh lime
2 cups melon liqueur

1 cup Absolut Citron
2 bottles club soda, 7Up,
*   or Sprite*
½ pound green grapes, washed

Defrost the frozen limeade until slushy, then mix with 1 can of ice water. Mix all ingredients except grapes together in a chilled punch bowl. Float grapes on top and add a block of fruited ice.

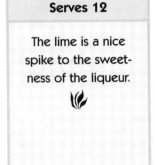

Serves 12

The lime is a nice spike to the sweetness of the liqueur.

Fourth of July Ade

2 cups pomegranate juice
12 ounces pink grapefruit juice

2 bottles of ginger ale

Mix all ingredients together and chill well.

Serves 12

This is for those who like very sweet drinks.

Prechilling
Always prechill your bowl and ingredients. Otherwise, your lovely cold drink will soon warm up to a lackluster tepid temperature. You can also freeze raspberries and strawberries in ice cube trays.

Cranberry Grey Goose Cocktail

Makes 4 drinks

This is an adaptation of one of today's most popular cocktails.

8 ounces cranberry juice
8 ounces vodka

4 ounces Cointreau or Grand Marnier

Shake all ingredients together in a large cocktail shaker with plenty of ice in it, until well chilled. Pour into chilled martini glasses.

Early American Cider

Serves 12

This tastes so wonderful in the fall on a slightly nippy day. If you can find a natural, unprocessed, local cider, so much the better.

2 quarts cider
1 small can frozen orange juice, slightly thawed
1 3-inch cinnamon stick
1 bottle sparkling cider

Juice of 1 lemon
1 orange, sliced crosswise thinly
12 red-hot candies

Mix all ingredients except the candies. Float the candies on top or freeze them into ice cubes.

Autumn Cider

3 quarts cider
3 tablespoons brown sugar
4 cinnamon sticks

15 whole cloves
¼ teaspoon nutmeg

Mix together and heat. Keep warm. Ladle liquid into cups to serve.

Alcoholic versus Nonalcoholic Drinks

When you figure quantities, it's important to assume that your guests will drink fewer alcoholic drinks than nonalcoholic drinks. Always have enough nonalcoholic drinks on hand.

> **Serves 12**
>
> Keep a pot of this bubbling on the grill and serve in mugs on chilly days or evenings.
>
>

Celebratory Sparkling Cider

1 bottle sparkling cider
  (nonalcoholic)
1 bottle brut champagne

8 ounces Calvados or other
  apple brandy
1 tart apple, cored and sliced,
  sprinkled with lemon juice

Make sure that the pitcher or bowl is well chilled and that all of the ingredients are also well chilled. Mix the liquids together and float the apple slices on top, serving a slice with each glass.

Dilute as Desired

You can further dilute the alcohol to make sure things do not get out of hand if your barbecue is taking much longer than planned. And, the drink will still taste good and be sociable, but be more thirst quenching.

> **Serves 8–10**
>
> Warning: this is very potent! But also very delicious. Make sure that everything is well chilled in advance.
>
>

Citron, Lemon, and Orange Float

Serves 10–12

This is really refreshing on a hot day. You can add more lemonade if it's really hot and people are beginning to flag.

12 ounces Absolut Citron
1 can frozen lemonade, mixed
*   with 2 cans water*
1 bottle orange soda

1 bottle champagne
*   or club soda*
1 orange and 1 lemon, sliced

Chill all ingredients before making. Mix, in a punch bowl, Absolut Citron and lemonade (this can be done in advance). At the last minute, add the soda and champagne, give a quick mix with a fork, add the orange and lemon slices, and pour.

Island Rum Punch

Serves 12–16

This requires a mixture of rums and a mixture of juices. It can be quite lethal, so be sure to dilute on hot days.

½ cup confectioners' sugar
*   mixed with 1 cup water*
1 bottle golden rum
1 bottle white rum
8 ounces freshly squeezed
*   lemon juice*
1 can frozen pineapple juice,
*   mixed with three cans water*

Juice of 1 lime
6 ounces peach brandy
Fresh pineapple chunks frozen
*   into ice cubes*
1 bottle ginger ale (optional)

Mix all ingredients together at the last minute and serve in chilled glasses or punch cups.

Spicy Glug—Hot Mulled Wine, Scandinavian Style

1 quart dry red wine
1 quart muscatel
8 ounces red vermouth
1 tablespoon orange or
    Angostura bitters
Zest of 1 orange, in strips
1 cup golden raisins (sultanas)
5 whole cardamom seeds,
    bruised

6 whole cloves
1-inch stick gingerroot, peeled
1 whole cinnamon stick
½ cup aquavit
½ cup confectioners' sugar
1 cup blanched almonds,
    toasted under the broiler
    until golden

Makes 2½ quarts

When you are outside grilling on a chilly night, try this and you'll have lots of company! It's very warming.

1. Mix everything except the aquavit, sugar, and almonds in a nonreactive container and let rest, covered, for 12 hours.
2. Just before serving, heat the wine mixture. When wine mixture is hot, add the aquavit and sugar. Float the almonds on top and serve.

Iced Margarita Slush

2 large cans frozen limeade,
    slightly defrosted to a slushy
    consistency
2 trays of ice cubes
Lime wedges and kosher salt

1 bottle tequila
Juice of 2 lemons
12 ounces triple sec (orange
    liqueur)

Serves 12

This is really terrific on a hot day, but do be careful. And, if your guests are getting a bit funny, just give them limeade.

1. Whirl the limeade and ice in a blender until frothy. Place in a large, chilled pitcher.
2. Prepare the glasses by freezing them, rubbing rims with lime, and dipping them into a saucer with kosher salt in it.
3. Add the rest of the ingredients to the pitcher and pour into prepared glasses.

Lime/Rum Slush

Serves 6

This is a fairly lethal drink—be careful!

2 large cans frozen limeade, partially defrosted
2 trays ice cubes

20 ounces Jamaican rum (such as Mount Gay)

Whirl the limeade and ice in the blender. When it becomes the consistency of slush, add the rum and keep blending.

Raspberry-Lemon Slush

Serves 10

This can have some vodka added or not; it's very good either way. If you choose to omit the vodka, use 7Up or club soda instead.

2 packages frozen raspberries, slightly thawed
1 can frozen lemonade, slightly thawed, mixed with 1 can water

1 tray ice cubes
20 ounces Absolut Citron vodka or 7Up

If you wish to remove the raspberry seeds, strain the raspberries through a fine sieve before using. Prechill all ingredients and whirl raspberries, lemonade, and ice. Mix in batches in the blender until very slushy. Add vodka or 7Up, and serve.

Spanish Sangria

1 cup water
½ cup confectioners' sugar
1 orange, sliced thin

1 lemon, sliced thin
Juice of 1 lime
1 quart dry red wine

1. In a medium, nonreactive saucepan, bring the water and sugar to a boil. Cook, stirring, until the sugar is dissolved. Add the fruit and lime juice and return to a boil. Take off the heat and let cool.
2. Put the sugared fruit in a pitcher with the wine and add ice. Serve in chilled glasses.

> **Makes 1 quart**
>
> This tasty and refreshing classic can be watered down with club soda. It's fine alone or with food because it is not too sweet.
>
>

Caipirinha—The Spirit of Brazil

1 lime, washed and rolled on
*   the countertop to bring out*
*   the juices*
1 teaspoon sugar, or to taste

2 ounces cachaca (you can
*   substitute white rum)*
Ice cubes

1. Cut the lime in pieces and put them in a glass, skin-side down; sprinkle with sugar.
2. Muddle the lime with a pestle to release the juice. Do not overdo this or the oil in the skin will make the drink bitter. Add the cachaca and ice cubes. Stir and serve.

Native Brazil
This drink is so representative of Brazil, using Brazil's native ingredients and ingenuity. It is a favorite during the festive time of Carnivale.

> **Makes 1 drink**
>
> This employs a liquor called cachaca, made with sugar cane juice, and yet it's not rum! You can substitute white rum, and for a different taste, half a sweet, peeled tangerine.
>
>

Appendix A
Additional Resources

Appendix B
Find the Ingredients You Need

Additional Resources

Top Grill Manufacturers

BIG GREEN EGG LINE OF SMOKER/BARBECUES

3414 Clairmont Road
Atlanta, GA 30319
(404) 320-2066
www.biggreenegg.com

BIG JOHN GRILLS

"Country Club" series of grills
www.bigjohngrills.com

BROILMASTER

Premium gas grills
www.broilmaster.com

COLEMAN

Grills and portable cooking systems
www.coleman.com/coleman/home.asp

DUCANE GAS GRILLS

www.ducane.com

GEORGE FOREMAN

Steaks and recipes
www.georgeforeman.com

THE GREAT OUTDOORS GRILL COMPANY

Grills and smokers, smoker trailers
www.gogrills.com

JENN-AIR

Cooking systems
(800) 688-1100
www.jennair.com

TIERNAN OUTDOOR PRODUCTS

Infrared gas grills
(800) 753-1538; (806) 372-4051

KENMORE

Selling gas grills, grill covers, and accessories
www.sears.com

THERMAL ENGINEERING CORPORATION

Infrared grills
www.tecgrills.com

VIKING GRILLS

Grills, barbecues, and cooking entertainment products
(888) 470-7011
www.vikinggrillsunlimited.com

WEBER

Wide selection of gas and charcoal grills, accessories, and cooking products
24-hour grilling hotline at (800) 446-1071
Also, Grill Line and Weber certified barbecue expert: daily April 1 through Labor Day, from 6 A.M. to 10 P.M. Central Time. Grill Line: 1-800-GRILL-OUT (1-800-474-5568).
www.weber.com/bbq

Books

GRILLING
Williams-Sonoma Cooking Library
Chuck Williams, General Editor
New York: Time-Life Books, 1992

GRILLING MAESTROS: RECIPES FROM THE PUBLIC TELEVISION SERIES
Produced by Marjorie Poore Productions
San Francisco: MPP Books, 2001

JOY OF COOKING: ALL ABOUT GRILLING
Irma S. Rombauer, Marion Rombauer Becker, and Ethan Becker
New York: Scribner's, 2001

OUTDOOR COOKING
Chuck Williams, General Editor
Alexandria, Va.: Time-Life Books, 1997

WEBER'S BIG BOOK OF GRILLING
Jamie Purviance
San Francisco: Chronicle Books, 2001

Associations

NATIONAL BARBECUE ASSOCIATION
Association is committed to promoting the recognition and image of the industry, facilitating effective networking of industry resources, and fostering business opportunities.
Austin, Texas
(888) 909-2121
www.nbbqa.org

NATIONAL HOT DOG AND SAUSAGE COUNCIL
An information resource to consumers and media on questions related to quality, safety, nutrition, and preparation of hot dogs and sausages.
www.hot-dog.org

UNDERWRITERS LABORATORIES INC. AND NATIONAL SAFETY COUNCIL
Grill safety
www.ul.com

Find the Ingredients You Need

Bacon, Pork, and Ham

NIMAN RANCH
Offers good old-fashioned flavor
www.nimanranch.com

LOBEL'S OF NEW YORK
Raised by small Midwestern family farms
www.lobels.com

Beef

THE COLEMAN RANCH, ALL-NATURAL DELICIOUS FLAVOR
www.colemanmeats.com

TEXACAN BEEF & PORK CO.
Slow-cooked Texas-style barbecue meats and sauces
(703) 858-5565 or (877) 877-8766 (toll-free)

Bison/Buffalo

ARROWHEAD BUFFALO
Very lean steaks, prime ribs, burgers, and sausage
www.arrowheadbuffalo.com

Cheeses

HENRI WILLIG
www.henriwillig.com/Cheese_Shop.htm

MARS CHEESE CASTLE
Cheese, sausage, and food gifts
www.marscheese.com

Game

D'ARTAGNAN
A wide variety of hard-to-find delicacies and gourmet products
www.the-golden-egg.com

Olive Oil and Vinegars

LUCINI EXTRA VIRGIN, IMPORTED, LUCINI ITALIA CO.
Adds a refined, fruity flavor to marinades and salads.
Visit specialty and gourmet stores for extra selection. Try *www.elenas.com* or *www.greatoil.com*.

Sauces and Marinades

DEAN & DANNY'S CUSTOM FOODS
www.synergyconsultants.com/customfoods.html

SMOKIN' JOE JONES
Sauces, smokers, and glazers
www.smokinjoejones.com

Spices

BACCHUS CELLARS
Wide selection of international spices
www.bacchuscellars.com

PACIFIC FARMS
Unique selection of wasabi mustard
www.freshwasabi.com

PENZEYS
Spices online and stores around the country
www.penzeys.com

Tools

CYBERSPACE GRILL
Variety of cooking supplies and utensils
www.cyberspacegrill.com

WILLIAMS-SONOMA
Wide selection for the cook and in the kitchen
www.williamssonoma.com

Venison

BLUEBONNET FARMS
(800) EAT-LEAN

SHAFFER VENISON
www.shafferfarms.com

Index

THE EVERYTHING SERIES!

BUSINESS

Everything® Business Planning Book
Everything® Coaching and Mentoring Book
Everything® Fundraising Book
Everything® Home-Based Business Book
Everything® Landlording Book
Everything® Leadership Book
Everything® Managing People Book
Everything® Negotiating Book
Everything® Online Business Book
Everything® Project Management Book
Everything® Robert's Rules Book, $7.95
Everything® Selling Book
Everything® Start Your Own Business Book
Everything® Time Management Book

COMPUTERS

Everything® Computer Book

COOKBOOKS

Everything® Barbecue Cookbook
Everything® Bartender's Book, $9.95
Everything® Chinese Cookbook
Everything® Chocolate Cookbook
Everything® Cookbook
Everything® Dessert Cookbook
Everything® Diabetes Cookbook
Everything® Fondue Cookbook
Everything® Grilling Cookbook
Everything® Holiday Cookbook
Everything® Indian Cookbook
Everything® Low-Carb Cookbook
Everything® Low-Fat High-Flavor Cookbook
Everything® Low-Salt Cookbook
Everything® Mediterranean Cookbook
Everything® Mexican Cookbook
Everything® One-Pot Cookbook
Everything® Pasta Cookbook
Everything® Quick Meals Cookbook
Everything® Slow Cooker Cookbook
Everything® Soup Cookbook

Everything® Thai Cookbook
Everything® Vegetarian Cookbook
Everything® Wine Book

HEALTH

Everything® Alzheimer's Book
Everything® Anti-Aging Book
Everything® Diabetes Book
Everything® Dieting Book
Everything® Hypnosis Book
Everything® Low Cholesterol Book
Everything® Massage Book
Everything® Menopause Book
Everything® Nutrition Book
Everything® Reflexology Book
Everything® Reiki Book
Everything® Stress Management Book
Everything® Vitamins, Minerals, and
 Nutritional Supplements Book

HISTORY

Everything® American Government Book
Everything® American History Book
Everything® Civil War Book
Everything® Irish History & Heritage Book
Everything® Mafia Book
Everything® Middle East Book

HOBBIES & GAMES

Everything® Bridge Book
Everything® Candlemaking Book
Everything® Card Games Book
Everything® Cartooning Book
Everything® Casino Gambling Book, 2nd Ed.
Everything® Chess Basics Book
Everything® Crossword and Puzzle Book
Everything® Crossword Challenge Book
Everything® Drawing Book
Everything® Digital Photography Book
Everything® Easy Crosswords Book
Everything® Family Tree Book

Everything® Games Book
Everything® Knitting Book
Everything® Magic Book
Everything® Motorcycle Book
Everything® Online Genealogy Book
Everything® Photography Book
Everything® Poker Strategy Book
Everything® Pool & Billiards Book
Everything® Quilting Book
Everything® Scrapbooking Book
Everything® Sewing Book
Everything® Soapmaking Book

HOME IMPROVEMENT

Everything® Feng Shui Book
Everything® Feng Shui Decluttering Book, $9.95
Everything® Fix-It Book
Everything® Homebuilding Book
Everything® Home Decorating Book
Everything® Landscaping Book
Everything® Lawn Care Book
Everything® Organize Your Home Book

EVERYTHING® KIDS' BOOKS

All titles are $6.95

Everything® Kids' Baseball Book, 3rd Ed.
Everything® Kids' Bible Trivia Book
Everything® Kids' Bugs Book
Everything® Kids' Christmas Puzzle
 & Activity Book
Everything® Kids' Cookbook
Everything® Kids' Halloween Puzzle
 & Activity Book
Everything® Kids' Hidden Pictures Book
 Everything® Kids' Joke Book
Everything® Kids' Knock Knock Book
Everything® Kids' Math Puzzles Book
Everything® Kids' Mazes Book
Everything® Kids' Money Book

All Everything® books are priced at $12.95 or $14.95, unless otherwise stated. Prices subject to change without notice.

Everything® Kids' Monsters Book
Everything® Kids' Nature Book
Everything® Kids' Puzzle Book
Everything® Kids' Riddles & Brain Teasers Book
Everything® Kids' Science Experiments Book
Everything® Kids' Soccer Book
Everything® Kids' Travel Activity Book

KIDS' STORY BOOKS

Everything® Bedtime Story Book
Everything® Bible Stories Book
Everything® Fairy Tales Book

LANGUAGE

Everything® Conversational Japanese Book
    (with CD), $19.95
Everything® Inglés Book
Everything® French Phrase Book, $9.95
Everything® Learning French Book
Everything® Learning German Book
Everything® Learning Italian Book
Everything® Learning Latin Book
Everything® Learning Spanish Book
Everything® Sign Language Book
Everything® Spanish Phrase Book, $9.95
Everything® Spanish Verb Book, $9.95

MUSIC

Everything® Drums Book (with CD), $19.95
Everything® Guitar Book
Everything® Home Recording Book
Everything® Playing Piano and Keyboards Book
Everything® Rock & Blues Guitar Book
    (with CD), $19.95
Everything® Songwriting Book

NEW AGE

Everything® Astrology Book
Everything® Dreams Book
Everything® Ghost Book
Everything® Love Signs Book, $9.95
Everything® Meditation Book
Everything® Numerology Book
Everything® Paganism Book
Everything® Palmistry Book
Everything® Psychic Book
Everything® Spells & Charms Book
Everything® Tarot Book
Everything® Wicca and Witchcraft Book

PARENTING

Everything® Baby Names Book
Everything® Baby Shower Book
Everything® Baby's First Food Book
Everything® Baby's First Year Book
Everything® Birthing Book
Everything® Breastfeeding Book
Everything® Father-to-Be Book
Everything® Get Ready for Baby Book
Everything® Getting Pregnant Book
Everything® Homeschooling Book
Everything® Parent's Guide to Children
    with Asperger's Syndrome
Everything® Parent's Guide to Children
    with Autism
Everything® Parent's Guide to Children
    with Dyslexia
Everything® Parent's Guide to Positive Discipline
Everything® Parent's Guide to Raising a
    Successful Child
Everything® Parenting a Teenager Book
Everything® Potty Training Book, $9.95
Everything® Pregnancy Book, 2nd Ed.
Everything® Pregnancy Fitness Book
Everything® Pregnancy Nutrition Book
Everything® Pregnancy Organizer, $15.00
Everything® Toddler Book
Everything® Tween Book

PERSONAL FINANCE

Everything® Budgeting Book
Everything® Get Out of Debt Book
Everything® Homebuying Book, 2nd Ed.
Everything® Homeselling Book
Everything® Investing Book
Everything® Online Business Book
Everything® Personal Finance Book
Everything® Personal Finance in Your
    20s & 30s Book
Everything® Real Estate Investing Book
Everything® Wills & Estate Planning Book

PETS

Everything® Cat Book
Everything® Dog Book
Everything® Dog Training and Tricks Book
Everything® Golden Retriever Book
Everything® Horse Book
Everything® Labrador Retriever Book
Everything® Poodle Book

Everything® Puppy Book
Everything® Rottweiler Book
Everything® Tropical Fish Book

REFERENCE

Everything® Car Care Book
Everything® Classical Mythology Book
Everything® Einstein Book
Everything® Etiquette Book
Everything® Great Thinkers Book
Everything® Philosophy Book
Everything® Psychology Book
Everything® Shakespeare Book
Everything® Toasts Book

RELIGION

Everything® Angels Book
Everything® Bible Book
Everything® Buddhism Book
Everything® Catholicism Book
Everything® Christianity Book
Everything® Jewish History & Heritage Book
Everything® Judaism Book
Everything® Koran Book
Everything® Prayer Book
Everything® Saints Book
Everything® Understanding Islam Book
Everything® World's Religions Book
Everything® Zen Book

SCHOOL & CAREERS

Everything® After College Book
Everything® Alternative Careers Book
Everything® College Survival Book
Everything® Cover Letter Book
Everything® Get-a-Job Book
Everything® Job Interview Book
Everything® New Teacher Book
Everything® Online Job Search Book
Everything® Personal Finance Book
Everything® Practice Interview Book
Everything® Resume Book, 2nd Ed.
Everything® Study Book

SELF-HELP/
RELATIONSHIPS

Everything® Dating Book
Everything® Divorce Book
Everything® Great Sex Book

All Everything® books are priced at $12.95 or $14.95, unless otherwise stated. Prices subject to change without notice.

Everything® Kama Sutra Book
Everything® Self-Esteem Book

SPORTS & FITNESS

Everything® Body Shaping Book
Everything® Fishing Book
Everything® Fly-Fishing Book
Everything® Golf Book
Everything® Golf Instruction Book
Everything® Knots Book
Everything® Pilates Book
Everything® Running Book
Everything® T'ai Chi and QiGong Book
Everything® Total Fitness Book
Everything® Weight Training Book
Everything® Yoga Book

TRAVEL

Everything® Family Guide to Hawaii
Everything® Family Guide to New York City,
    2nd Ed.

Everything® Family Guide to Washington D.C.,
    2nd Ed.
Everything® Family Guide to the Walt Disney
    World Resort®, Universal Studios®,
    and Greater Orlando, 4th Ed.
Everything® Guide to Las Vegas
Everything® Guide to New England
Everything® Travel Guide to the Disneyland
    Resort®, California Adventure®,
    Universal Studios®, and the
    Anaheim Area

WEDDINGS

Everything® Bachelorette Party Book, $9.95
Everything® Bridesmaid Book, $9.95
Everything® Creative Wedding Ideas Book
Everything® Elopement Book, $9.95
Everything® Father of the Bride Book, $9.95
Everything® Groom Book, $9.95
Everything® Jewish Wedding Book
Everything® Mother of the Bride Book, $9.95
Everything® Wedding Book, 3rd Ed.

Everything® Wedding Checklist, $7.95
Everything® Wedding Etiquette Book, $7.95
Everything® Wedding Organizer, $15.00
Everything® Wedding Shower Book, $7.95
Everything® Wedding Vows Book, $7.95
Everything® Weddings on a Budget Book, $9.95

WRITING

Everything® Creative Writing Book
Everything® Get Published Book
Everything® Grammar and Style Book
Everything® Grant Writing Book
Everything® Guide to Writing a Novel
Everything® Guide to Writing Children's Books
Everything® Screenwriting Book
Everything® Writing Well Book

Introducing an exceptional new line of beginner craft books from the *Everything*® series!

EVERYTHING
C·R·A·F·T·S ®

All titles are $14.95.

Everything® Crafts—Create Your Own Greeting Cards
1-59337-226-4
Everything® Crafts—Polymer Clay for Beginners
1-59337-230-2

Everything® Crafts—Rubberstamping Made Easy
1-59337-229-9
Everything® Crafts—Wedding Decorations
and Keepsakes
1-59337-227-2

Available wherever books are sold!
To order, call 800-872-5627, or visit us at *www.everything.com*
Everything® and everything.com® are registered trademarks of F+W Publications, Inc.